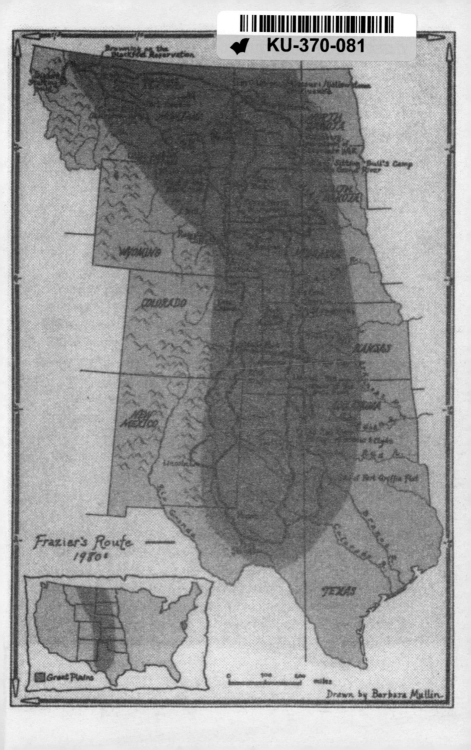

Frazier's Route ———
1980's

Great Plains

Drawn by Barbara Mullin

CLASSICS of REPORTAGE

Ian Frazier is the author of *Dating Your Mom*; *Nobody Better, Better than Nobody*; *Family*; *Coyote v. Acme*; *On the Rez*; and *The Fish's Eye*. A frequent contributor to *The New Yorker*, he lives in Montclair, New Jersey.

Ro' ...:farlane is a F... ...:...: ...llege, Cambridge, and contributes to the *Observer*, *Times Literary Supplement* and *London Review of Books*, among other publications. He is the author of *Mountains of the Mind* (published by Granta Books).

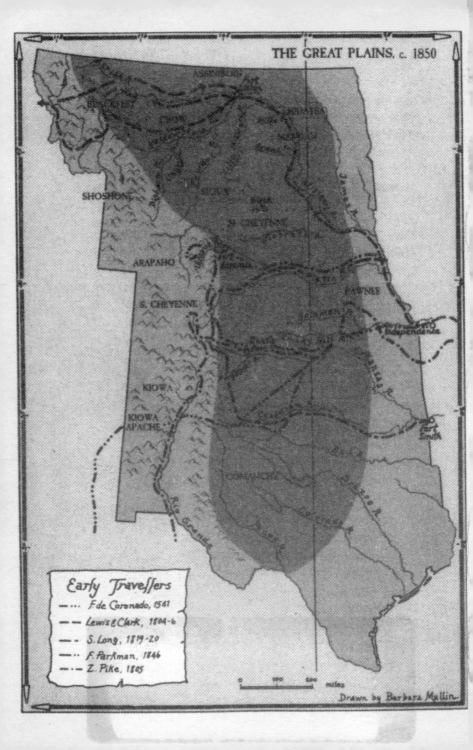

THE GREAT PLAINS, c. 1850

ASSINIBOIN

BLACKFEET

HIDATSA

MANDAN

SHOSHONE

SIOUX

N. CHEYENNE

ARAPAHO

PAWNEE

S. CHEYENNE

Independence

KIOWA

KIOWA APACHE

Fort Smith

COMANCHE

Rio Grande

Early Travellers

···· F. de Coronado, 1541
─ ─ Lewis & Clark, 1804-6
── S. Long, 1819-20
──· F. Parkman, 1846
─·─ Z. Pike, 1805

0   100   200   miles

Drawn by Barbara Mellin

CLASSICS of
REPORTAGE

GREAT PLAINS

IAN FRAZIER

Granta Books

London

To my wife, Jay

Granta Publications, 12 Addison Avenue, London W11 4QR

This edition published in Great Britain by Granta Books 2006
First published in the US by Picador 1989

Copyright © Ian Frazier 1989
Introduction © Robert Macfarlane 2006

A CIP catalogue record for this book
is available from the British Library.

ISBN-13: 978-1-86207-870-3

1 3 5 7 9 10 8 6 4 2

Printed and bound in Great Britain by
CPI Bookmarque, Croydon

MIX
Paper from
responsible sources
FSC® C020852
www.fsc.org

INTRODUCTION

Ian Frazier has been a staff writer for *The New Yorker* since 1974, but his style bears little resemblance to the manicured and evenly irrigated prose usually associated with that magazine. His writing is prairie to the New Yorker's lawn. Expansive, eccentric, colloquial, jaunty and joyful, his books—of which *Great Plains* is the finest—fuse clear-sighted reporting with a comic essayist's buoyancy and glee.

In 1982, Frazier moved from New York to Montana, with the aim of living quietly in a cedar-wood cabin, and 'trying to write a novel about high school'. Fortunately, the novel never happened. Instead, Frazier spent several summers driving his van around the Great Plains states, zigzagging from ruin to mountain to town to museum to canyon to prairie to café, covering a total of around 25,000 miles; and several winters sitting in libraries and archives, reading up on Indian tribes, homesteaders, rivers, nuclear missile technology, cattle ranching, wheat farming, bluegrass music, trapping, Billy the Kid and Crazy Horse. At the end of all that, he wrote *Great Plains*, which became a national bestseller on its publication in 1989.

The Great Plains are the core of America, its giant vertical heartland, its 'secret, sweet, semi-ruined interior', in William Kittredge's fine phrase. Thirteen states fall partly within the Plains, from Texas in the south to Montana and North Dakota in the north. Their western boundary is marked off by the

Rockies. The eastern perimeter is harder to designate, but is traditionally set at the hundredth meridian, because, as Frazier explains, 'that is the approximate limit of twenty-inch rainfall', below which level 'farmers can't grow corn, or raise dairy cattle, or do much European-style agriculture'. All told, the Plains sprawl over a land area of 1.3 million square miles. A space so vast and so various presents problems for a writer: how to do justice to its diversity without compiling an encyclopaedia? How to get under its skin?

Frazier's solution was to mesh together first-hand observation, historical research and abstract meditation, creating a hybrid form with great narrative drive. So it is that we hit the road with Frazier—rattling along in his van over potholes, or raising a rooster-tail of dust on dry highways, or wheel-sucking through mud—until he finds something that gets him talking. From there, he gyres out to grand stories of human, natural and geological history, which provoke Frazier to wonder or to anger. Then it's back in the van, and on with the road-trip.

In this respect, *Great Plains* stands alongside Barry Lopez's magnificent *Arctic Dreams* (1986)—a book about another vast and irreducible terrain—as the beginning of a new way to write about landscape. Both Lopez and Frazier make themselves into figures moving through their respective territories, adventuring, puzzling things out, peering back over the rim of time, investigating the involuted mystery of how humans and landscapes have shaped each other.

The skill in such books lies in managing the release of the narrator's ego. Too high a dose, and the narrator overwhelms both history and the reader. Too little, and history overwhelms both the narrator and the reader. Frazier and Lopez manage it brilliantly, though in drastically different ways. Where Lopez delivers his pronouncements and discoveries in hushed vatic tones, Frazier is a jaunty raconteur, a fervent anecdotalist with a baseball cap and wild hair. Opening a book by him is like pulling up a high stool at a bar, and falling naturally into conversation. He tells great stories, he knows his history, and his dry humour bowls through the book like tumbleweed.

Frazier's humour, in fact, is a clue to the other tradition out of which he emerges: the nineteenth-century American road-book, as perfected by Mark Twain and Washington Irving. Of these, Frazier is closest to Twain. He has something of Twain's egalitarian interest in everything he encounters, and something of Twain's breezy evocations of places and people. Like Twain, Frazier writes about the tedious side of long-distance travel and does a brisk trade in one-liners.

Frazier's synopses—of the difficulties of farming on the Plains, of the coming of the railroads, of the Indian wars—are thumbnail masterpieces. So too are his timeslides, the sudden moves backwards which he makes—back a decade, or a century, or a geological era. Driving over the Continental Divide and down on to the Plains, Frazier remarks to his passenger that 'when early travellers ... came through a big herd of buffalo, they could watch the human scent move through it on the wind, frightening animals eight and ten miles away'. Walking along a tree-lined riverbank, he notes that 'big cottonwoods have bark as ridged as a tractor tire, and the buffalo used to love to rub against it. In the shedding season, the river bottoms would often be ankle-deep in buffalo hair.' Other times, he just stands back and lets facts do their plain talking. Of cowboys: 'At night, on the trail, they rubbed tobacco juice in their eyes to keep awake.' Of Indian women: they used to wear 'little knives around their necks to kill their attacker or themselves if they were about to be raped.'

Then there are Frazier's lists. They are everywhere in the book—the names of the rivers, tumbling out like a psalm; the names of Indian tribes; the names of high-school baseball teams; the names of hitchhikers; the names of the homesteaders who came to the Plains to claim their 160 acres, and died for them—and their effect hovers somewhere between history on hectic fast-forward, and history as loving freeze-frame. They reach their finale in the magnificent centrepiece chapter on the Sioux, where Frazier sings out what makes Crazy Horse exceptional for him.

Great Plains is a masterpiece of haphazardness. Not knowing what will come next is part of the joy of reading it. One theme does recur, though—the ruin. Ruined missile silos, military bases, shacks, landscapes, lives. Time and again, Frazier gets drawn back to ruins. Ruins interest him because they are historical corridors: they allow us to move within time, to approach what once was. He despises the contemporary American impulse to disregard history, or to erase it. 'Nowadays,' he writes, 'the past seems almost nonexistent, even contemptible: on TV, the cop says to the criminal, "Reach for that gun and you're history."' On the Plains, though, history still lives: 'Like other arid but uninhabited parts of the world, the Plains sometimes hold pieces of the past intact and out of time, so that a romantic or curious person can walk into an abandoned house and get a whiff of June 1933, or can look at a sagebrush ridge and imagine dinosaurs wading through a marsh.'

Still, for all its drollery and haphazard charm, *Great Plains* is a book brimful of passion and sadness. From the book's extraordinary, lyrical opening page, it is clear that Frazier loves the Plains deeply: loves them despite all the appalling things that have happened on or to them—the near-genocide of the Native Americans, the extinction of the buffalo, the agricultural plundering of the prairie, the draining of the Ogallala aquifer, the emptying of the little towns.

Early in the book, Frazier notes how the identity of the Great Plains, at least as seen from the American coasts, has changed over time. It was first thought of as the Great Desert. Then it became 'the newer garden of creation', then the Breadbasket of the World, then the Dust Bowl, then Vanishing Rural America. The Great Plains, he concludes, 'are like a sheet Americans screened their dreams on for a while and then largely forgot about'. Frazier unashamedly cleaves to the belief that without understanding where we have come from, we can have no steerage over where we are going. So his book sets out to correct that amnesia—to make us care about the Plains again by restoring their particularity and variety, and to save as much of them as is still saveable from the depredations of strip mining, agribusiness and tourism.

Throughout the book, Frazier struggles to reconcile his affection for the Plains with his awareness of all that has gone so atrociously wrong with them. In the end, *Great Plains* is a jubilant, tearful, plain-speaking, celebratory elegy to the people that the landscape has destroyed, and the landscape that the people have destroyed. 'Joy,' he writes, 'seems to be a product of the geography, just as deserts can produce mystical ecstasy and English moors produce gloom.' That's tough on English moors, but I know what he means. 'Once happiness gets rolling in this open place,' he writes elsewhere, 'not much stops it.'

Robert Macfarlane
May 2005

GREAT PLAINS

1

AWAY to the Great Plains of America, to that immense Western short-grass prairie now mostly plowed under! Away to the still-empty land beyond newsstands and malls and velvet restaurant ropes! Away to the headwaters of the Missouri, now quelled by many impoundment dams, and to the headwaters of the Platte, and to the almost invisible headwaters of the slurped-up Arkansas! Away to the land where TV used to set its most popular dramas, but not anymore! Away to the land beyond the hundredth meridian of longitude, where sometimes it rains and sometimes it doesn't, where agriculture stops and does a double take! Away to the skies of sparrow hawks sitting on telephone wires, thinking of mice and flaring their tail feathers suddenly, like a card trick! Away to the air shaft of the continent, where weather fronts from two hemispheres meet, and the wind blows almost all the time! Away to the fields of wheat and milo and sudan grass and flax and alfalfa and nothing! Away to parts of Montana and North Dakota and South Dakota and Wyoming and Nebraska and Kansas and Colorado and New Mexico and Oklahoma and Texas!

Away to the high plains rolling in waves to the rising final chord of the Rocky Mountains!

A discount airplane ticket from New York City to the middle of the Great Plains—to Dodge City, Kansas, say, which once called itself Queen of the Cowtowns—costs about $420, round trip. A discount ticket over the plains— to the mountains, to Salt Lake City, to Seattle, to Los Angeles—is much cheaper. Today, most travellers who see the plains do it from thirty thousand feet. A person who wanted to go from New York to California overland in 1849, with the Gold Rush, could take a passenger ship to Baltimore, the B & O Railroad to Cumberland, Maryland, a stagecoach over the Allegheny Mountains to the Monongahela River, a steamboat to Pittsburgh, another steamboat down the Ohio to the Mississippi to St. Louis, another from St. Louis up the Missouri to Independence or St. Joseph or Council Bluffs, and an ox-drawn wagon west from there. If you left the East in early April, you might be on the plains by mid-May, and across by the Fourth of July. Today, if you leave Kennedy Airport in a 747 for Los Angeles just after breakfast, you will be over the plains by lunch. If you lean across the orthopedist from Beverly Hills who specializes in break-dancing injuries and who is in the window seat returning from his appearance on *Good Morning America*, you will see that the regular squares of cropland below you have begun to falter, that the country is for great distances bare and puckered by dry watercourses, that big green circles have begun to appear, and that often long, narrow rectangles of green alternate with equal rectangles of brown.

Chances are, nothing in the seat pocket in front of you will mention that those green circles are fields watered by central-pivot irrigation, where a wheeled span of irrigation pipe as much as a quarter mile long makes a slow circuit, like the hand of a clock. If you ask the flight attendant about those green and brown rectangles, chances are he or she will not say that in the spring of 1885 a wheat farmer on the Canadian plains named Angus Mackay was unable to plant a field which had already been plowed when his hands left to help suppress a rebellion of frontiersmen of French and Indian ancestry against the Dominion of Canada, and so he left the field fallow, cultivating it occasionally to kill the weeds; that when he planted it the following year, it weathered a drought to produce thirty-five bushels of wheat per acre, thirty-three bushels more than continuously cropped land; that the practice he had initiated, called summer fallow, was an effective way to conserve moisture in the soil in a semi-arid climate, and many other farmers adopted it; that the one problem with summer fallow was the tendency of fields with no crop cover sometimes to dry up and blow away; that in 1918 two other Canadian farmers, Leonard and Arie Koole, experimented successfully with crops planted in narrow sections at right angles to the prevailing winds, to protect sections of fallow ground in between; and that this refinement, called strip farming, turned out to be the best way to raise wheat on the northern plains.

Crossing high and fast above the plains, headed elsewhere, you are doing what rain clouds tend to do. You are in a sky which farmers have cursed and blasted with dynamite barrages and prodded with hydrogen balloons and seeded with silver-iodide crystals and prayed to in churches every day for months at a time, for rain. Usually the clouds wait to rain until they are farther west or east—over the Rockies, or the Midwest. Probably, as you look out the airplane window, you will see the sun. On the plains, sunshine is dependable. Most of the buildings on the plains have roofs of galvanized metal. As dawn comes up, and the line of sunlight crosses the land, the roofs of barns and equipment sheds and grain silos and Department of Agriculture extension stations and grain elevators and Air Force barracks and house trailers and pipe warehouses and cafes and roadside-table shelters start to tick and pop in scattered unison, all the way from Canada to Texas.

The Great Plains are about 2,500 miles long, and about 600 miles across at their widest point. The area they cover roughly parallels the Rocky Mountains, which make their western boundary. Although they extend from the Southwestern United States well into Canada, no single state or province lies entirely within them. North to south, the states of the Great Plains are:

Montana	North Dakota
Wyoming	South Dakota
Colorado	Nebraska
New Mexico	Kansas
	Oklahoma
Texas	

The Great Plains include the eastern part of the first column, the western part of the second column, some of west Texas, and all of the Texas panhandle. In Canada, they include southern Alberta, Saskatchewan, and Manitoba. They are five hundred to a thousand miles inland from the Pacific Ocean, and over a thousand miles inland from the Atlantic. The Texas plains are about five hundred miles from the Gulf of Mexico.

Just where the Great Plains begin and end is not always certain. To the west, they sometimes continue past the Rocky Mountain front through gentle foothills all the way to the Continental Divide. To the north, flatlands stretch past the Arctic Circle, but the open prairie has given way to boreal pine forests long before that. In the Southwest, a change from semi-arid grassland to true desert is sudden in some places, slow in others. Of all the Great Plains boundaries, the eastern one is the hardest to fix. Many geographers and botanists have said that the Great Plains begin at the hundredth meridian, because that is the approximate limit of twenty-inch annual rainfall. Before Europeans came, it was more or less where the tall grasses of the East stopped and the Western short grasses started. (The hundredth meridian is the eastern line of the Texas panhandle; a map of the lower forty-eight states folds in half a little bit to the right of it.) Since the same amount of rain never falls two years in a row, this eastern boundary always changes. Sometimes it happens to coincide at certain points with the Missouri River; the eastern side of the river will be green and lush, and the western side will be a tan and dusty cowboy-movie set. Farmers can't grow corn, or raise dairy cattle, or do much European-style agriculture at all on sub-twenty-inch rainfall, and when they first moved out onto the Great Plains, they sometimes had difficulty borrowing money. Many banks and insurance companies had a policy of not lending money for the purposes of agriculture west of the hundredth meridian. So, whether or not the rain stopped exactly at the hundredth meridian, at one time lots of Eastern loan officers did. If you were beyond their help, you knew you were on the Great Plains.

It makes sense that traditional finance would balk there, because the Great Plains don't exactly qualify as real estate. In fact, the Great Plains are probably better described in terms of the many things they aren't. They aren't woodlands; their subsoil doesn't have enough moisture for tree roots. You can go a long way out there without seeing a single tree. They aren't mountains (although they contain the Black Hills in South Dakota and the Bearpaw Mountains in Montana and the Cypress Hills in Canada), and they aren't Land of a Thousand Lakes (although they used to have many sweetwater springs, and hundreds of rivers and streams, and an underground aquifer the volume of Lake Huron), and they aren't standard farmland (although they export two-thirds of the world's wheat, and could export more). And although they have suffered droughts about every twenty years since white people first settled there, and millions of acres have gone to blowing sand, and although Zebulon Pike, who happened to pick a route that led through the sandhills region when he explored for the government in 1806–7, compared the Great Plains to the deserts of Africa, and although the members of a later expedition, in 1819–20, agreed with Pike, and published a map with the words "Great Desert" across the southern plains, and although a popular atlas of 1822 extended the label over more territory and in another edition changed it to "Great American Desert," and although that appeared in the middle of North America on maps and globes for fifty years afterwards, and generations of geography students wondered about it and dreamed of going there, the Great Plains are not a desert.

White people did not consider moving onto the Great Plains in any numbers until after the Civil War. When they did, railroad promoters, governors of empty Western states, syndicates with land to sell, emigration societies, scientists, pretend scientists, politicians in crowded Eastern states, U.S. Geological Survey officials, Walt Whitman, *The New*

York Times, The New York Tribune, all loudly advertised the Great Plains as a garden spot. The idea of the Great American Desert came in for much scoffing and debunking. Strangely, the Great Plains greened up with good rains several times just as another wave of homeseekers was about to go there. People thought they'd harvest a couple of good crops and pay off their starting costs and be in business. In the 1870s and '90s, and in 1918–24, and, most spectacularly, in the 1930s, drought knocked parts of these waves back. Since their days as a Great Desert, the Great Plains have also been the Frontier (supposedly of such importance in the formation of the American character), the "newer garden of creation" (Whitman's phrase), the Breadbasket of the World, the Dust Bowl, Vanishing Rural America. The Great Plains are like a sheet Americans screened their dreams on for a while and then largely forgot about. Since 1930, two-thirds of the counties on the Great Plains have lost population. About fifteen years ago, the Great Plains reappeared, briefly, as part of the New Energy Frontier. The Great Plains contain more than fifty percent of America's coal reserves. When we finally do run out of oil, somebody will probably think up yet another name for the Great Plains.

In the fall of 1982, I moved from New York to Montana. I sublet my apartment to my sister, packed my van, and headed west. On the way, I stopped in Cleveland to usher at my other sister's wedding. At the reception, to entertain the bridesmaids, I ate a black cricket the size of my thumb. Later, I was driving around the city's west side by myself singing "Jerusalem" with the windows open, tears streaming down my face. The next morning I wanted to call the hangover ambulance and go to the hangover hospital. The singing, and the feel of the cricket's toothpicky legs between my teeth, replayed in my mind on a tight tape loop. I took my van to Mike's Sohio Service Center for a tune-up, and when they were done I drove to Chicago. I stayed with friends there for one night, and then I drove on through Wisconsin, Minnesota, South Dakota, and didn't really stop until I crossed the Montana state line. At the edge of a little town, I pulled off the road, took off my shoes, moved some stuff from the mattress, and fell asleep, the gasoline still sloshing back and forth gently in the tank.

America is like a wave of higher and higher frequency toward each end, and lowest frequency in the middle. When the ticking of the car roof in the sun woke me, I looked out the windshield and saw nothing. A Hefty trash bag against a barbed-wire fence, maybe, torn to pennants by the wind; a metal prefab building in the distance; bunch grass blowing; a road as straight as a string. I started the car and went on. I didn't pass a single place that looked as if it was in any way expecting me: no landscaped residential communities, no specialty sporting-goods stores, no gourmet delis offering many kinds of imported beers. Just grain silos, and flat brown fields with one cow on them, and wheat fields, and telephone poles, and towns with four or six buildings and a "No U-Turn" sign at each end. In the larger town of Shelby, Montana, I went to a cafe called Ma's, and people looked at me. I bought a newspaper to see about houses for rent, and from a picture at the top of a column recognized the columnist, a man with a large waxed mustache, sitting one table away. I continued west, across the Blackfeet Indian Reservation, into the foothills of the Rocky Mountains, and then up through the mountain canyons. All at once a low-slung '67 Pontiac full of long-haired Indians passed me, going about ninety. Then a Montana state highway cop, with no sirens going. Then several more cars of Indians, then another highway cop, then more Indians. Just across the Flathead River and inside the boundary of Glacier National Park, I came upon the cars again. They were now pulled every which way off the road; policemen and Indians, both, were just standing there, hands in pockets. Some were looking off into the brush. Nobody's mouth was moving.

On the other side of the mountains, in the city of Kalispell, Montana, I finally saw a few people who looked kind of like me. I parked my van and took a $15-a-week room in the Kalispell Hotel. The bathroom was down the hall; the walls were thin. I spent several hours listening to a man in the next room trying to persuade another man to trade him five dollars for five dollars' worth of food stamps. Daily, I looked at houses to rent—shotgun cottages by the rail yards, ski chalets with circular fireplaces, and a house that was built under a small hill, for energy reasons. Finally I found one I liked, a cedar A-frame cabin with a wood stove and a sleeping loft and a flower box with marigolds. The house was on a long road that went from pavement to dirt and back to pavement. Beyond the road were foothills, clear-cut of timber in patches, like heads shaved for surgery, and beyond the hills were mountains. At the rental agency, I overheard a secretary giving someone else directions to the house. I mentioned to the agent that I could pay a two- or three-month security deposit in cash. The next morning, the agent left a message for me at the Kalispell Hotel and I called her back and she said I had the house.

I did not know one person in Montana. I sat in the house and tried to write a novel about high school; I went for walks, drank quarts of Coors beer, listened to the radio. At night, a neighbor's horse shifted his weight from hoof to hoof out in the trees, and sometimes cropped grass so near I could hear him chew. The first snowstorm blew in from the north, and crows crossed the sky before it like thrown black socks. For years in New York I had dreamed of Montana. Actually, I had also dreamed of joining the Army, going to truck-driving school in New Jersey, building a wooden sailboat, playing the great golf courses of the world, and moving to Fiji. I had examined all those ideas and then rejected them. Montana made the most sense to me. I saw the movie *Rancho Deluxe* (filmed in Livingston, Montana) eight or nine times. At parties, I told people, "Well, I'm going to be moving to Montana soon." Now here I was. Suddenly I no longer had any place to dream about.

So I started to dream about the Great Plains. For fantasies, the Great Plains are in many respects the perfect place. They're so big that you could never know all there is to know about them—your fantasies could never wear them out. Even the plural in their name seems to make them extend farther into a distant romantic haze. Also, they are a place where I will probably never live. This is important, because anyplace I move, I ruin. Look at the north side of Chicago. Look at SoHo. I move in, the rents go up, coffee shops become French restaurants, useful stores close. Don't ask me how I do it—it's just a talent I have. A hundred years ago, it was not unusual to hear of single men and women and young couples with families moving out to start farms on the Great Plains. Today you hear of people my age being urban pioneers in some neglected neighborhood, or moving to the suburbs, or moving to Northern California or Washington or northwest Montana, like me. You never hear of us moving to the Great Plains.

Whenever money and the weather allowed, I would cross the mountains and drive around on the plains. A friend came to visit in the spring, and the first thing I did was take her there. My friend is from the West Indies; she had never seen the American West, except for California. We followed U.S. Highway 2 to Glacier National Park, and then we went up the Going-to-the-Sun Highway, past the standing dead trees burned in the lightning fire of 1967, through tunnels in the rock, past precipitous drops on the passenger side, past cliffs dripping water, past old snow-drifts with graffiti scratched on them, past our own chilled breath blowing out the car windows, past mountains with white, sharp tops, and then across Logan Pass, on the Continental Divide. I kept telling my friend I wanted her to see the Great Plains. The road began to descend, and at the turn of each switchback another mountain range would disappear, like scenery withdrawn into the wings, while the sky that replaced it grew larger and larger. We left the park and turned onto U.S. Highway 89. A driver coming down this road gets the most dramatic first glimpse of the Great Plains I've ever seen. For some miles, pine trees and foothills are all around; then, suddenly, there is nothing across the road but sky, and a sign says HILL TRUCKS GEAR DOWN, and you come over a little rise, and the horizon jumps a hundred miles away in an instant. My friend's jaw—her whole face, really—fell, and she said, "I had no idea!"

We came through the lower foothills, with vertebrae of rock sticking through their brown backs, and soon we were driving on a straight dirt road through unfenced wheat fields. We stopped the car and got out. The wheat—of a short-stemmed variety bred to mature at a height convenient for harvesting machinery—stretched in rows for half a mile in either direction. Through the million bearded spikes the wind made an "s" sound bigger than we could hear. We drove on, and birds with long, curved bills (Hudsonian godwits, the bird book said) flew just above us, like gulls following a ship. The sky was 360 degrees of clouds, a gift assortment of mares' tails and cumulus and cirrus, with an occasional dark storm cloud resting on a silvery-gray pedestal of rain. We could see the shadows of the clouds sliding along beneath them far into the distance. I said that when early travellers on the plains came through a big herd of buffalo, they could watch the human scent move through it on the wind, frightening animals eight and ten miles away. Suddenly we crossed the path of one of the rainclouds, and the hard dirt road turned to glue. Mud began to thump in the wheel wells, and the car skidded sideways, went off the road, and stuck. We got out in cement-colored mud over our ankles. Two pieces of harvesting machinery sat in a field nearby; other than that, there was no sign of people anywhere. I tried to drive while my friend pushed, then she drove while I pushed, then I left it in gear and we both pushed. We whipped the mud to peaks. It clotted on the wheels until they became useless mudballs. Finally I took a flat rock and got down on all fours and scraped the mud off each wheel. Then my friend drove carefully in reverse for one wheel turn until the wheels were covered again. Then I scraped the mud off again, and we drove another revolution. We kept doing this over and over until we made it back to dry ground. It took about two hours. Another event early travellers mentioned in their diaries was miring their wagons in the gumbo mud of the Great Plains. Now I knew what they meant. When I got back in the car, I was all-over mud and my fingernails were broken. From her purse, my friend produced a freshly laundered white cotton handkerchief.

For hours we drove on roads which Rand McNally & Company considers unworthy of notice. A moth glanced off the edge of the windshield, and in the sunset the dust its wings left sparkled like mascara. That night, my friend said on a gas-station pay phone, "I'm on the Great Plains! It's amazing here! The sky is like a person yawned and never stopped!"

Eventually, over several summers, I drove maybe 25,000 miles on the plains—from Montana to Texas and back twice, as well as many shorter distances. I went to every Great Plains state, dozens of museums, scores of historic sites, numerous cafes. When I couldn't travel, I borrowed books about the plains from the Kalispell Public Library—*Curse Not His Curls*, by Robert J. Ege (a ringing defense of General Custer), and *Crow Killer: The Saga of Liver-Eating Johnson*. I also watched the local newspapers for items about the plains, and finally I learned why the Indians and policemen I had seen by the road the day I first arrived were standing that way. They were at the place where the bodies of two missing Blackfeet Indians, Thomas Running Rabbit and Harvey Mad Man, had been found earlier in the afternoon.

Police in Eureka, California, had arrested two Canadians for robbing a convenience store, and had discovered that the Canadians' car was the same one the young Blackfeet men were driving when they disappeared. In custody, one of the Canadians, a nineteen-year-old named André Fontaine, said that they and another man had hitchhiked down from Red Deer, Alberta, to West Glacier, Montana; that there the three met two Indians in a bar; that they drove west with them in the Indians' car; that the Indians stopped the car; that his companions took the Indians into the woods; that he heard two shots; that his companions came running from the woods; that the three then drove away. Aided by this information, police soon caught the third man, a Canadian named Ronald Smith, in Wyoming. All three were returned to Montana and held in the Flathead County Jail. At first, they pleaded not guilty, but then Ronald Smith confessed to shooting both the young men. Smith was twenty-four, and he said he had always wanted to see what it felt like to kill somebody. He said that it felt like nothing. While awaiting trial as an accomplice, André Fontaine was asked to appear as a guest on F. Lee Bailey's television show, *Lie Detector*. The Flathead County Attorney, a county sheriff's detective, a local police detective, and a court-appointed defense attorney accompanied André Fontaine back to California for the taping. The show put them up in North Hollywood at the Beverly Garland Hotel, except for the prisoner, who stayed in the Los Angeles County Jail. When Ronald Smith confessed, he had requested the death penalty. He had said that he felt he was beyond rehabilitation, and that the Indians in the Montana prisons would probably kill him anyway. Shortly before his execution date, he changed his mind. Lawyers took his appeal through the county and state courts, which denied it, and to the U.S. Supreme Court, which refused to hear it. Then they filed another appeal in the federal courts challenging the constitutionality of the death penalty. Three years after the crime, while the appeal was still at the state level, I moved from Montana back to New York.

2

AMONG the rivers of the Great Plains are the Cimarron, the Red, the Brazos, the Purgatoire, the Trinity, the Big Sandy, the Canadian, the Smoky Hill, the Solomon, the Republican, the Arikaree, the Frenchman, the Little Blue, the Big Blue, the South Platte, the North Platte, the Laramie, the Loup, the Niobrara, the White Earth, the Cheyenne, the Owl, the Grand, the Cannonball, the Heart, the Knife, the Little Missouri, the Yellowstone, the Powder, the Tongue, the Bighorn, the Musselshell, the Judith, the Marias, the Milk, the Missouri. Some of these rivers have several forks, like the Clear, Salt, and Double Mountain Forks of the Brazos, or the Clear and Crazy Woman Forks of the Powder. All of them have had at least one other name; the Spanish, who were the first Europeans to explore the southern plains, called the Purgatoire the River of the Souls in Purgatory. Before the Lewis and Clark expedition discovered and named the Marias, the Indians called it the River That Scolds at All the Others. The bigger rivers on the plains run roughly west to east. Carrying alluvial sands from the Rocky Mountains, they helped make the plains. Some, like the Brazos, flow to the Gulf of Mexico. Some run into the Red or the Arkansas, which both continue east to the Mississippi. The others end up in the Missouri, which follows a 2,500-mile course from the northwest until it finally joins the Mississippi at St. Louis.

The rivers of the southern plains are dry much of their length, much of the year. All-terrain-vehicle tracks cross the white sand in the bed of the North Fork of the Red. As you go north, the rivers are more likely to have water. Descending from the flat benchland into their valleys can be like walking off a hot sidewalk into a spa. Cottonwood trees grow in all the valleys; suddenly there is something between you and the sun. The trees lean at odd angles, like flowers in a vase. In the summers, windrows of cottonwood-seed down cover the ground. Big cottonwoods have bark as ridged as a tractor tire, and the buffalo used to love to rub against it. In the shedding season, the river bottoms would often be ankle-deep in buffalo hair. At sunset, the shadows of the cottonwoods fall across the river and flutter on the riffles. Carp sometimes rise up and suck insects off the surface with the same noise the last of the bathwater makes going down the drain. Sandbar willows grow as straight as dowels in the gray-black mud along the banks. Game trails six inches wide wind through the willows. For a while, the air is smarting with mosquitoes, and weird little bugs that don't bite but just dive right for your eyes. Later there are stars, and silence. At dawn, birds pipe the light through the trees.

Nineteenth-century travellers who wanted to see the interior of the Great Plains when it was still a wilderness used to ascend the Missouri the way people do the Amazon or the Nile today. The Indians who lived along the river grew maize and beans, dried them, and traded them to tribes who followed the buffalo herds. The river Indians usually built their villages near where the Missouri and another river joined, and the white traders who came later followed this example. Between 1805 and 1860, traders built posts at every major confluence along the river. In 1828, the American Fur Company began to build the biggest trading post on the Great Plains, on the northern bank of the Missouri a few miles upstream from where it joins the Yellowstone. At first, they called the post Fort Floyd; later, in hope of the trade that would converge here, they called it Fort Union.

Until it was abandoned in 1867, Fort Union was like the Times Square of the plains. Indians from all over the upper Missouri watershed and beyond came to trade their furs—beaver skins and buffalo robes, mainly—for alcohol, and also muskets from London or Liège, scalping knives from Sheffield, blankets from the Cotswolds, steel traps from Manchester, powder and shot and dried corn from St. Louis, clothes from New York, clay pipes from Cologne, falcon bells and hand mirrors from Leipzig, glass beads from Milan, sugar and coffee from New Orleans, calicoes from Marseilles, and hardtack from Milton, Massachusetts. The buffalo robes were good for keeping warm in carriages in northern cities. Beaver fur was usually made into felt, which was made into top hats, which appeared on the heads of rich men almost everywhere. Prime beaver fur has two kinds of hair: the longer guard hairs, on the outside, and a matted coat of finer hairs, called "beaver wool," underneath. Furriers combed this beaver wool from the pelt, and then the wool was mashed together, soaked, stiffened with adhesive and shellac, and pressed into felt. Because beaver hairs are barbed, they stick together well, and the felt they make is sturdy, easily molded, weather-resistant, and fine-grained. Its color is warm and lustrous. Men today seldom wear any garment as elegant as high-crowned hats of beaver felt used to be. Some countries had sumptuary laws which forbade the poor from wearing beaver; usually, a beaver hat signified a doctor or lawyer or above. The decline of Fort Union began at about that point in the nineteenth century when fashionable men discovered high top hats made of silk from the Orient.

Furs, and beaver furs in particular, were a main temptation of empire in North America. Animals in cold lands grow the best fur, so the countries which first explored the northern part of the continent—England, France, and the Netherlands—were the leading rivals for the trade. The Dutch trade came down the Hudson River to the posts of the Dutch West India Company at Manhattan and Fort Orange (Albany). The French trade came through French Canada, to independent traders at Quebec and Montreal. After a century and a half of wars and treaties, the English finally had Canada and New England to themselves, and their Hudson's Bay Company, with exclusive rights to trade in millions of square miles of northern Canada, became the biggest fur-trading company in the world. The next rival to the English appeared after the American Revolution, when a German immigrant to New York named John Jacob Astor started the American Fur Company. For many years, the Hudson's Bay Company and the American Fur Company were the Exxon and Mobil of the fur trade. As John Jacob Astor expanded his company west through the American territories, he destroyed and bought out and merged with many smaller companies. Fort Union was built by men from the former Columbia Fur Company, which once had posts from the Great Lakes to the Missouri.

At its height, Fort Union ate six hundred to eight hundred buffalo a year, and the boss of the fort (called the bourgeois) had his private stock of brandy, gin, smoked hams, plums, herrings, almonds, ketchup, and half-pint bottles of capers by the dozen. At his table, one had to wear a jacket to dinner. Frenchmen, Spaniards, Russians, lapsed English noblemen, Swiss, Italians, Indians, half-breeds, escaped slaves, and Yankees worked at the fort. Naturalists, Indian agents, missionaries, sportsmen on hunting trips, Army officers, river pilots, surveyors, territorial governors, writers, and rival traders visited. George Catlin arrived on the steamboat *Yellowstone* in 1832, and painted portraits of Indians while sitting on a twelve-pound cannon in one of the bastions. The Swiss painter Karl Bodmer came with Prince Alexander Philipp Maximilian, of the German principality of Wied-Neuwied, in 1833, and held the attention of an Indian named Nothing But Gunpowder with the help of a musical snuffbox. Some of the Indians thought the box must have a little white man hidden inside.

By the time they meet, the Yellowstone and the Missouri are both big rivers. When they're low, they expose acres of mud dried to jigsaw cracks. Full, they're both hundreds of yards across, and flow smoothly at the lip of their banks, suddenly boiling up with a sucking sound, then flowing smoothly again. The Great Plains usually give few hints about the uses people should make of them, but the expanse of flat tableland surrounding the confluence of these rivers strongly suggests a city site. It's like the junction of the Schuylkill and the Delaware, minus Philadelphia, or the confluence of the Allegheny and the Monongahela into the Ohio, minus Pittsburgh. The reason no city grew at the confluence of the Missouri and the Yellowstone is that in 1866 the Army built a post called Fort Buford a few miles east of Fort Union, and in 1868 created a thirty-mile-square military reservation with the post at the center. Since the reservation was closed to all settlement, the city which people eventually built was farther down the Missouri, at the junction of the Little Muddy River. Today this city is called Williston, North Dakota, and it gets much of its income from oil, and its long commercial highway strips wax and wane. Fort Buford was abandoned in 1895, and farms and ranches have since taken up the military reservation lands. All of which means that the confluence of the Yellowstone and the Missouri, the surrounding landscape for as far as you can see, looks about the same in life as it does in the painting Karl Bodmer made from sketches drawn on a bluff north of Fort Union 156 years ago.

The land Fort Union stood on was declared a National Historic Site in 1967. I have been there three times since. I liked to stand by the visitor center, which was a converted double-wide house trailer, and look up the driveway, past the barbed-wire fence, past the county road, past the railroad tracks, and across the mile of open plain to the bluff where Bodmer sketched. Owen McKenzie, half-Indian son of Kenneth McKenzie, the fort's most famous bourgeois, used to run wolves on his fast buffalo horse on this plain. An Assiniboin Indian wife of another bourgeois used to put on her best clothes and race her pony here, her "magnificent black hair floating like a banner behind her," according to one account. Here, also, Prince Maximilian watched a tribe of Assiniboin approach the fort; they wore eagle feathers, prairie-chicken feathers, wolf skins, antelope horns with yellow horsehair at the points, green leaves. Their faces were painted with white clay and vermillion and black paint. Crooked dogs with backbones showing pulled packs lashed to dragging travois poles. The warriors advanced in a group of two or three hundred, and sang a song which reminded the prince of one he heard the Russian soldiers sing during the Napoleonic Wars. On this plain, or near it, John James Audubon, who spent about nine weeks at the fort in 1843, once timed a lark to see how long it stayed aloft at a stretch (thirty-six minutes). Nobody rides or sings or walks or even drives very much on this plain today.

People don't drink as much here as they used to, either. In some ways, the history of the confluence area since white men first came is the history of a binge. Lewis and Clark, when they camped across the river in 1805, were so pleased at their arrival that they issued whiskey to all the party, and somebody got out a fiddle, and "they spent the evening with much hilarity," Lewis says. The main trade item at Fort Union was always alcohol. Many Indians would give or do anything for it. Traders made "Indian Whiskey" from straight alcohol boiled with ingredients like river water, ginger, molasses, red peppers, gunpowder, chewing to-bacco, and (occasionally) strychnine. Whiskey with strychnine was said to produce an exceptionally crazy drunk. A man who was chief clerk at the fort for many years said that he sometimes stayed up all night dragging drunken Indians out by the arms and legs. He said that Indians sometimes snatched burning logs from the fire and rubbed them on their heads. Of course, Indians who were drunk also killed themselves and each other and froze to death and drowned and burned up and fell from their horses and died of withdrawal. John Jacob Astor, who owned the American Fur Company until 1834, once met in New York with George Simpson, of the Hudson's Bay Company, and suggested that both companies stop trading in alcohol. But finally Simpson and Astor agreed that if they did, the smaller whiskey traders would ruin them. Astor said that Simpson's company would hold the head of the cow, and his own would hold the tail, and all the others would get the milk. Astor never went West himself. He lived most of his life on Manhattan Island, and built his first fortune on the fur trade. His son, William B. Astor, reported in 1831 that the American Fur Company brought them returns of half a million dollars a year.

For miles around the confluence in every direction, whiskey bottles littered the prairie. When the Army moved in, the first commander of Fort Buford, Captain William G. Rankin, spent much of his time under arrest for drunkenness. Drink often confined his successor, Colonel Andrew Bowman, to bed. The post surgeon recorded interments in the cemetery of soldiers like Bartholomew Noon, a private who apparently drank himself to death on a night when there was "much drunkenness in the garrison." Whiskey killed laundresses, scouts, teamsters, and more Indians. In 1889, the first North Dakota legislature voted to make their state dry, and in 1903 several men, including a German immigrant who was also an agent for Blatz Beer, founded a town three miles west of the confluence. The town was called Mondak, because it straddled the Montana–North Dakota state line, and the half of the town in Montana (which was wet) had nine saloons. Train crews from the Great Northern Railroad often stopped in Mondak to drink, and sometimes men would pass out on the tracks. It is said that the Great Northern ran over more people in Mondak than at any other place along the line. Except for some foundations, a small structure covered in red pressed tin, and a couple of rows of concrete cells which used to be part of its jail, Mondak has disappeared. As I watch the purple clouds building to the north, the cottonwood leaves showing their pale undersides in the wind, the whitecaps rising on the river, the veils of dust blowing from a butte, I wonder if maybe this scenery has somehow been permanently altered by the thousands of drunken eyes which have looked at it before.

Employees of the Park Service have done enough minor excavation of the grassy eminence where the fort used to stand that they can indicate the different parts with markers. For years, their caretaking left undisturbed a ghost population as dense as any on all the ghosty plains. (More recently, the Park Service has decided to rebuild much of the fort; now archaeologists are digging up and photographing the site, to record what construction will destroy.) The walls of the fort were squared-off cottonwood logs about seventeen feet high set in a rectangle 220 by 240 feet. Against the inside of one of the walls for much of its length was a one-story building called the Dwelling Range, where some of the fort's employees lived with Indian wives and children. These employees had names like Michel Bellehumeur and Michel Carrière and Joseph Joyaille and Bonaventure LeBrun. Overlooking the walls were two whitewashed stone bastions. At the center of the fort was a 63-foot-tall flagstaff, surrounded by a fenced plot of lettuce, radishes, and cress. Near it, a man who had just shot a clerk named Isidoro Sandoval through the head with a pistol in the retail store announced to the fort: "I, Alexander Harvey, have killed the Spaniard. If there are any of his friends who want to take it up, let them come on." None did. At one end of the fort was the bourgeois's house, which had glass windows, green shutters, and a red-shingled roof. Kenneth McKenzie once caught his squaw in the bedroom there with a young blond-haired trapper named Bourbonnais, and chased him from the fort with a club. Bourbonnais started walking around outside the fort yelling death threats, McKenzie got all the clerks to sign a paper agreeing Bourbonnais could be killed if necessary, somebody warned Bourbonnais, he didn't stop, and McKenzie paid a mulatto named John Brazo to shoot him from the bastions. Badly wounded, Bourbonnais left for downriver some months later.

In a bed in the interpreter's room in the Dwelling Range, a young artist named Rudolph Friedrich Kurz once lay on buffalo robes, dreaming of milk. Like Karl Bodmer, Kurz was Swiss. The two had met in Paris in 1839, several years after Bodmer's return from Fort Union, and Bodmer had advised him to develop his technical skills further before heading for the wilderness. Kurz's study of painting and drawing had already consumed five years; he went back to Switzerland, studied and travelled for another seven years, and finally sailed for America in 1846. Kurz had elaborate theories about art, all of which seemed to revolve around the beauty of the nude figure. In St. Louis, he had to decide whether to go farther up the Mississippi or turn west up the Missouri. The Mississippi lost out, partly because (as he wrote in his journal) the Indians along that river "wore too many clothes." He wanted "Nude Indians, with their beautifully proportioned figures, their slender yet well-formed limbs, their expressive eyes, their natural, easy bearing . . ."

Since he didn't have enough money for an extended stay upriver, he continued his journey as an employee in the fur trade. From the deck of the steamboat *St. Ange*, he watched through a telescope given him by his brothers Louis and Gustave as a group of Indian women and girls bathed in the Missouri: "As they thought themselves well concealed they were sportive and animated in a natural way. There were several dainty figures among them—so slender yet so round, so supple yet firm. How they splashed and romped behind the partially submerged tree that they thought screened them from observation. Others dreamily dried themselves in the sun, in postures and movements so natural and unrestrained, and yet such grace!"

He clerked for a while at Fort Berthold, near the mouth of the Little Missouri. Then he went on to Fort Union, where he cut tongues out of buffalo heads and packed the tongues in brine, issued meat and lard from the storehouse, painted a portrait of the bourgeois with his hand in his waistcoat, rowed customers back and forth across the river, refused to paint a nude female figure for the bourgeois, and recaptured a fox, an eagle, and a bear when they escaped from their cages. He wore spectacles, and the Assiniboin called him Ista Topa (Four-Eyes). The bourgeois's sidekick, a man named Jim Hawthorne whose duties included cutting his boss's tobacco, once got mad at Kurz and said he was ready to fight him with any weapon "from rifle down to needle." (Kurz did not take up the challenge; his family motto was *Fier mais sensible*.") Often he had to share his bedroom with visitors to the fort, like the Assiniboin chief L'Ours Fou, who woke him up throughout the night to teach him Indian words and do imitations of animals. L'Ours Fou's imitation of a hog made Kurz laugh until tears ran down his cheeks.

In his spare time, he did pencil sketches of the fort, a

beaver dam, a snowshoe, saddles, moose horns, himself, the fox, a meeting in the reception room, an ox yoke, a dogsled, tattoos, and Indians—all disappointingly clothed at this latitude, though he was always careful to indicate the forms underneath. Supplies ran low toward the end of winter, and the bourgeois sent him and a young Scotsman on a hunting trip so the fort wouldn't have to feed them for a while. Their camp was flooded twice by the swollen Missouri, their dogs ate up most of the meat, they found almost no game, storms blew their tent down, and Kurz spent days wrapped in a buffalo robe, keeping the fire alive. When he got back to the fort, he decided that since he was almost out of drawing paper, he might as well go home. He worked his way back down the river by rowing in a company keelboat. By the time he reached St. Louis, he was suffering from ague and dropsy. A man who owed him $140 had disappeared, so he sold some of the collection of Indian artifacts which he was intending to use to accompany exhibits of his planned masterworks of the Far West. On his way east he passed Niagara Falls, which he did not feel like looking at. In New York, he sold two watercolors and another part of his artifact collection. He bought a steerage ticket to Europe, was too sick to eat solid food the entire thirty-day voyage, and went straight home to Berne as soon as he landed. Reflecting later on his trip, he wished he "had taken more of an interest in things, such as studying the different species of ducks, etc." His journal ends, "To earn my livelihood as artist in Berne. Alas! What a prospect."

The first time I visited Fort Union was on an afternoon in early fall when the only other vehicle in the parking lot was a dark-green Park Service pickup. I had been driving for several days, talking only to order in cafes, and sleeping in my van at night. I walked around the fort site for a while, and then I went in the visitor center. The ranger who was there heard the door open, came out of his office, introduced himself, took me on a tour, showed me the elk-skin winter moccasins he was sewing, led me inside a canvas tipi he had set up on the grounds, showed me some decorative porcupine quillwork he had done, took out a pipe of red pipestone, filled it with kinnikinnick (a mixture of tobacco and the dried inner bark of the red willow, which Indians used to smoke), lit it, and passed it to me. He was six feet five inches tall, barrel-chested, with one black braid falling across the National Park Ranger badge on his left breast pocket, and another falling across a name tag which read "Gerard Baker" on his right. I asked, and he said he was a Mandan-Hidatsa Indian.

Gerard Baker told me that the Mandan and Hidatsa have been neighbors and allied tribes for generatons; that the Hidatsa were also called the Minnetaree or the Gros Ventre; that today many Mandan and Hidatsa live on the Fort Berthold Reservation in North Dakota; that when the Hidatsa were first sent there, some of them didn't like it, and moved to the Yellowstone–Missouri confluence area; that his own grandfather told him he remembered camping near here, and also remembered the soldiers who eventually marched them back; that one band of Hidatsa came originally from the sky, another from underneath the earth, and another from the big water; that, before white men, the Hidatsa lived by the mouth of the Heart River in villages of round earth-lodges; that they made many objects of the sandbar willow, and were called the "people of the willows"; that their war parties went on raids hundreds of miles from home; that some people say it was the Hidatsa who gave history a nudge when they captured a Shoshone girl named Sacajawea and brought her back with them from the Rocky Mountains to the Missouri, where she later met Lewis and Clark; that he and other Hidatsa believe Sacajawea was in fact a Hidatsa who had been captured by the Shoshone and who escaped from the Rocky Mountains back to the Missouri with the aid of wolves; that the Hidatsa were skilled plant breeders who developed a strain of maize still in use today; and that there were about twelve hundred Hidatsa before the smallpox epidemic of 1837 killed more than half of them.

Later, I learned that the smallpox epidemic of 1837 came up the river on the American Fur Company steamboat the *St. Peter's.* One of the carriers was Jacob Halsey, who was going upriver to take over as bourgeois at Fort Union, and who came down with the disease on board. He had been vaccinated and soon recovered. The traders at the posts along the Missouri made efforts to keep the Indians away from the boat, efforts which unfortunately did not include turning the boat around and sending it back downriver. The disease spread quickly. In early July, it broke out among the Mandan. They rolled in fires, took sweat baths, gave all their possessions to medicine men, jumped in the river, threatened the traders' lives, killed their own families, killed their horses, killed themselves by pushing arrows down their throats. Their unburied corpses turned black and swelled to three times normal size. One observer said that 1,569 of 1,600 Mandan died.

No tribes were camped near Fort Union when the *St. Peter's* arrived there, and the traders attempted to contain the disease before the summer's trading began. They locked up the fort and inoculated all the Indian residents and a few white men with the smallpox itself, following a practice outlined in a popular home-doctoring manual. Most of the thirty Indian women in the fort died. With the gates locked, the traders could not remove the bodies, and you could smell the fort from three hundred yards away. The Assiniboin came in to trade and hung around outside the walls and soon caught the disease. The bourgeois later estimated that ten out of every twelve Assiniboin died.

After the steamboat's arrival, the traders had sent a keelboat loaded with supplies farther upriver to the post among the Blackfeet. On the way, the crew came down with smallpox. Perhaps fifty-five hundred Blackfeet were camped by the post. The epidemic of 1837 eventually killed a total of about six thousand Blackfeet, and marked a sudden decline in their power on the plains. Indians fleeing the disease carried it to tribes far from the Missouri, and the epidemic did not slow down to the north until it reached the neighborhood of the Hudson's Bay Company posts in the Canadian territories. By 1837, most doctors knew that the English doctor Edward Jenner had demonstrated forty-one years earlier that injections of the virus of the milder cowpox could immunize people against smallpox. With almost two hundred years' experience in Indian trade behind it, the Hudson's Bay Company had sent supplies of smallpox vaccine to its traders. Not many used it at first, but when they saw the epidemic approaching, they were able to vaccinate and save many Indians.

In fact, about half of the Assiniboin in the neighborhood of Fort Union who survived were ones the Hudson's Bay Company had persuaded to be vaccinated. Although anyone familiar with recent history along the Missouri River could have recalled several other times when smallpox brought by whites had killed Indians by the thousands, the American Fur Company never felt obliged to vaccinate its customers. Apparently, when the epidemic came in 1837 none of the American Fur Company posts even had any vaccine on hand. Here in the wilderness they had falcon bells from Leipzig, French fabrics, gin from Holland, capers, almonds, ketchup by the quart—but no smallpox vaccine. Jacob Halsey, one of those who brought the disease, later wrote to his superiors in St. Louis, "The loss to the company by the introduction of this malady will be immense in fact incalculable as our most profitable Indians have died." At Fort Union, trade stayed about average; those Indians not yet dead wanted to trade more, and have a good time before the end.

Afterwards, the company increased its small trade in Indian skulls, always one of the favorite curios of the plains. Other tribes occupied the empty villages of the Mandan and Hidatsa, and then moved on. The earth lodges fell down and eventually disappeared, except for shallow round depressions in the ground, where the floors used to be. Today, empty fields where the villages once stood are still faintly marked with clusters of these depressions; from a distance, the fields look like a smallpox survivor's face. At Fort Union, the cemetery where some of the Assiniboin smallpox victims were buried was partially dug up in the early 1950s, before the state and then the Park Service took over the fort site. Highway contractors, needing fill, took away truckloads, and the bones of Assiniboin smallpox victims mixed with the gravel used to pave the county roads.

Gerard Baker had a double-bladed throwing ax, and he and I spent an hour or so fooling around with it. On the grounds near the fort site he had set up a forked cottonwood log as big as a man, and had worn a path to it from marks at ten, fifteen, and twenty-odd paces. At each mark, he knew just how to hold the ax when he threw so that its end-over-end flight would conclude with one of the blades deep in the wood and the handle quivering. The first time I saw him hit from the farthest mark, I cheered. When I threw, the ax glanced off with a clatter. Sometimes he would run up to retrieve the ax, sometimes I would. He kept showing me the right way to hold it. Sometimes I missed the tree entirely. Finally I got the ax to stick from ten paces. We threw again and again.

I was talking a blue streak. I don't remember what I said. Then Gerard Baker suggested we take a sweat bath. This ceremony was and is an important part of many Indian religions. It involves going naked into a small hut made of blankets or hides draped on a willow-branch frame, pouring cold water onto white-hot rocks inside, breathing steam as hot as you can stand, burning bunches of sweet grass, smoking and passing a sacred pipe, talking, praying, pursuing visions, and then coming out, rubbing yourself with sage, dousing yourself with cold water or a river plunge, and dressing again. I said I would like to, but I really should get going. Gerard Baker picked up his ranger hat from the ground where he had set it and walked me to my car. We stood for a moment looking across the plain to the north, and I told him I had imagined the tribe of Assiniboin Prince Maximilian described crossing it a century and a half ago. Gerard Baker sighted along his arm to a small break in the bluffs beyond. "I bet that's the place they came through," he said. "I've found the trail of travois poles in the rock there. You can see the marks on each side where the poles dragged. There's all kinds of trails in those bluffs, and on top of a couple I've found eagle pits, where they used to wait with a rabbit or something for bait and grab eagles. I found buffalo jumps up there, too—places where they used to chase buffalo off cliffs to kill them. And my grandfather told me that when the Hidatsa were camping here after they left the reservation, they sometimes buried people way back in those bluffs, using the old way of burying, with the bodies wrapped in hides and tied to platforms."

"Really? Could you maybe go up there and find those burials and find beads and pipes and stuff?" I asked.

Behind his brown eye, a shutter dropped. ". . . Well," Gerard Baker said, "I suppose you *could* . . ."

3

HITCHHIKERS:

Someplace in Wyoming, I picked up a guy who said his name was Darryl. He told me that he was an irrigator, and that he had just been fired from the ranch he worked for because he fell asleep and neglected to close a dam and flooded out half a mile of highway. He told me he was hungry, and that if I were to run over a jackrabbit we could build a fire and roast it. Whenever a jackrabbit would pop up along the road, he would yell, "*Hit* the son of a bitch!"

Someplace in North Dakota, I picked up a guy from Black River Falls, Wisconsin, who said he was a truck driver in the process of moving to California. An axle had snapped on his rented trailer, or something, so he was hitchhiking. He said he had to leave Wisconsin because after his sixth drunk-driving conviction the state had taken away his driver's license. He said that once he established residence in California, he would get a new license.

Someplace in Kansas, I picked up a guy from Stuttgart, West Germany, who said he was a graduate student in anthropology spending a term at Wichita State University. He had a suitcase, a backpack, a beard going blond at the ends, khaki shorts, tanned, blond-haired legs, and eyes so blue they looked white. He looked at the landscape and said, "Ach! Zo vlat." Then he said he was going to South Dakota to see Bear Butte, a landmark important to the religions of several plains tribes. "Za vite people in America haff done zuch terrible sings to za Indians," he said. "Za vite people haff destroyed zo many uff za Indians' zacred blaces."

I looked at him. "What is your name?" I asked.

"Gerhard Stadler," he said.

I asked him to spell it. He did, and then shut up.

At a convenience store–gas station in Sheridan, Wyoming, a guy with a green baseball hat and long, dark hair asked me if I would give him and his wife and baby a ride back to their car, which had a flat tire thirty miles east. He said that his spare was flat, too, so they had hitched here with it to get it filled, and had been asking for a ride back since eight that evening. It was now about midnight. I said okay. He told me his name was Lydell White Plume and his wife's name was Anna. They were on their way back from a powwow at the Crow Reservation in Montana and had stopped by his brother's house in Busby, on the Northern Cheyenne Reservation, to pick up a television. The baby was completely quiet. Anna sat on the bed in the back of the van snapping gum. Lydell White Plume said that they lived in Riverton, Wyoming, on the Wind River Indian Reservation, and had to be there tomorrow for the funeral of his brother's sixteen-year-old stepson, who had hanged himself two days before. The stepson was one of nine young men who killed themselves on the reservation that year. Lydell White Plume said he thought the problem was lack of communication.

There were no cars or lights most of the way. Occasionally we would pass a big orange flame at a well site, throwing spokes of shadow across the prairie. When we reached the car, I held a flashlight while Lydell White Plume changed the tire. He told me that he was a Fancy Dancer, who entered dance competitions at reservations all over the West and in Mexico. He opened the hatchback of his car and carefully lifted out parts of his dance costume to show me. From the darkness, the two of us leaned into the glow from the car's rear overhead light while he pointed out the detail in his dance bustle—the turkey feathers, the white, yellow, and ginger-colored plumes, the beaded center. Then he set the bustle back into the car, saw that no parts were going to get crushed, and pushed the hatchback shut.

South of the town of McLaughlin, South Dakota, on a gravel road on the Standing Rock Indian Reservation, I picked up a guy who was walking in the other direction. He was short, in his fifties, wearing a white shirt with a brown paisley pattern. He got in and looked at me and said, "I remember you. You passed me by on the highway." I said I didn't remember seeing him. He said, "Yep. You passed me right by." In his hand was a brown terry-cloth washrag. He mopped his face with it. The afternoon was cloudless, maybe ninety-five degrees.

I told him I was trying to find the site of Sitting Bull's cabin. An exhibit in a museum in Mobridge, S.D., said that it was on the Grand River on a marked road off U.S. Highway 12. I had been driving around for hours and couldn't find any marked road. I couldn't even find the Grand River. "I'll take you right to him," he said. "I'm Sioux Indian. I own all this land. This is all tribal land.

I've walked or drove every damn inch of it." We shook hands. His name was Jim Yellow Earring.

I knew the actual cabin wasn't there. The one-room log house where the famous Hunkpapa Sioux chief spent his final reservation years was disassembled some time after his death and hauled away in wagons so that it could be displayed at the Chicago World's Fair of 1893, and I had read that it eventually ended up in the Chicago city dump. But I wanted to see the place Sitting Bull liked enough to live there. Places Indians liked are different from what you see while driving the grid of roads stencilled over the Great Plains. Sometimes when you find such a place it makes that grid seem to disappear.

Jim Yellow Earring directed me from the gravel road to a one-lane dirt road. Soon a strip of grass growing between the wheels brushed under the car. Then we were on no road at all, just prairie with faint wheel tracks across it. Then we bounced into a road with deep ruts, and red dust came up through the holes in the floor. Nowhere up ahead did I see anything that looked like a river valley. Jim Yellow Earring said to keep going.

Sitting Bull may have picked such a remote site for his cabin because he wanted to put plenty of distance between himself and Major James McLaughlin, Indian agent at Standing Rock. The two did not like each other. On McLaughlin's part, the feeling was closer to abhorrence. By the time Sitting Bull lived here, he was a celebrity. He had travelled America and Canada with Buffalo Bill's Wild West Show, had met President Cleveland and former President Grant, had spoken through an interpreter to large crowds on a fifteen-city lecture tour, had carried the flag at the head of a procession celebrating the opening of the

Northern Pacific Railroad. He received fan letters in English, French, and German, hate mail, and letters from lunatics. He not only had an Indian agent, he had a booking agent. He sold his autograph for a dollar each. Fame made him a lot of money, but his colleague Annie Oakley remembered that he gave all the money away to ragged little boys. McLaughlin maneuvered to undercut his influence on the reservation, and favored other chiefs over Sitting Bull and tried to humiliate him, and Sitting Bull was ornery right back. Sitting Bull was on the way to becoming one of the best-known Americans in history; the process would probably have been difficult even for someone who had not hated and fought white people most of his life.

Jim Yellow Earring pointed to a speck across the prairie. "That's my brother-in-law's house," he said. "He's got a well with the best damn water, makes the best damn coffee in the world. I'm pretty dry. I been walking all day. Do you have anything to drink?"

"There might be a couple of beers somewhere, but they're hot."

On the floor, he spotted a plastic bottle of amber liquid with the brand name Mix-I-Go. "Hey!" he said, "what's this? Whiskey?"

"God, no! That's gasoline additive! For the car!"

He looked at the bottle for a moment, reading the small print. Then, reluctantly, he set it back on the floor.

Another reason Sitting Bull chose to locate his cabin on the banks of the Grand River was that he was born there. In fact, one biography says that he was born in March of 1831 at a spot within a few miles of where his cabin later stood. The Grand River was called the Ree then, and the place was called Many-Caches. Sitting Bull was a quiet and deliberate child, and one of his names was Slow. Like many Westerners, he spent so much time on horseback when he was little that he grew up bowlegged. He had a good singing voice, and women always loved him. As a young man, he was in many battles with other tribes and white people. A Crow shot him in his left foot in a fight on Porcupine Creek, near the Yellowstone River. Sitting Bull killed the Crow, and limped for the rest of his life. At a skirmish near White Butte, on the Little Missouri River, a soldier shot him in the left hip with a pistol. At a battle with some Flatheads near the Musselshell River, he was shot through the bones of the left forearm with an arrow. In a standoff fight with the Army escort of a railroad surveying party in the Yellowstone valley, he sat down within range of the soldiers' rifles and smoked a pipe while bullets hit around him. Several other Indians joined him, and when the pipe was finished, they got up and ran; Sitting Bull walked. Before the Battle of the Little Bighorn, Sitting Bull made a spiritual offering of one hundred pieces of his flesh, and sang while his adopted brother, Jumping Bull, cut fifty, each the size of a matchhead, from each arm. After that battle he eventually fled with other Sioux north to Canada, and returned to surrender at Fort Buford in 1881. The Army promised him amnesty, held him for two years at another fort, and sent him to the Standing Rock Agency in 1883.

This is not the kind of history that breeds immediate warmth and trust between peoples. In the rearview mirror I looked at my eyes, marked by worry and second-guessing with little lines like the calibrations on a camera lens. Then I looked at Jim Yellow Earring's eyes—calm, bloodshot, brown as a deer's. "Keep going, I'll take you right to him," he said. The road had now become so deeply rutted that the trick was finding the exact moment to steer from one set of ruts into a new set to the right or left. Just as we were about to high-center, Jim Yellow Earring would yell, "My side! Come over to this side! . . . Okay, okay, now your side!"

Sitting Bull naturally attracted to him the wildest and most unreconstructed Indians on the reservation, and they pitched canvas tipis and built cabins close to his, and the place became known as Sitting Bull's camp. When the Ghost Dance religion swept the Indian reservations of the West in 1889–90, Sitting Bull's camp was where all the reservation's Ghost Dancers gathered. The Ghost Dance religion was one of the saddest religions of all time. It was the invention of a Paiute Indian called Wovoka, who may have been inspired by the doctrines of an earlier Paiute holy man called Tävibo. Wovoka had lived with a white family, who knew him as Jack Wilson. Part of his education had consisted of Christian religious training, and he sometimes said he was the Messiah returned, and his followers called him the Christ. It may be impossible for any white person ever to explain Ghost Dancing, but evidently the idea came to Wovoka in a vision during an eclipse of the sun on January 1, 1889. He said that he went to heaven and saw God, who told him that if the Indians did a dance which He would teach him, and danced long enough and hard enough, all white people would be submerged under a layer of new earth five times the height of a man, and the buffalo would return, and all the Indians who had ever lived would come back to life, and the land would become a paradise. Certainly, this would be an attractive philosophy for any American Indian at the end of that century, who was likely to have more friends and close relations among the dead than among the living. News of Wovoka's vision spread among the Western tribes, and many sent delegates to meet and talk with him. One of the Sioux delegates reported later that he "saw the whole world" when he looked into Wovoka's hat.

The road now led down a gully so steep that Jim Yellow Earring was thrown forward. His handprints were still in the red dust on the dashboard months later. I said I wasn't going any farther. I put the car in reverse and tried to back up. Nothing happened. So we headed on down, with bushes now scraping the side. A branch came through the open window and caught me on the side of the head. Jim identified it as a branch of the wild plum tree. He said that wild plums were delicious. The high grass bent down under the front bumper and then sprang up when we passed. In the river bottom, where we finally stopped, the grass was above the door handles.

Ghost Dancers danced past exhaustion, and often lay on the ground in a trance, their skin shivering, for days at a time. When they regained consciousness, they told of the distant stars they had visited, and of the long-dead friends and relatives they had talked to. Sometimes they brought back white, grayish earth—a piece of the morning star—as proof. Desperate as it was, the Ghost Dance did not originally have violent implications, but among certain tribes (the Sioux in particular) it soon acquired them. Indians often painted symbols of the dance on muslin shirts, and some began to say that these paintings made the shirts bulletproof.

"This is the place," Jim Yellow Earring said. "It was plentiful with deer in the old days. Back then, it was all flat ground and them cottonwoods growin' like weeds.

In 1949—that's when the river really came. That was the big flood. That's why these banks are here. This used to be a big prairie-dog village, but the government poisoned 'em all. From here it's about twelve miles to the town of Bullhead, *ichipasisi*. That means walking along a river crossing back and forth, you know, like sewing."

The Ghost Dance frightened white people on and near the reservations, and the Indian agents jailed its leaders and called for military support. One agent, R. F. Royer, of the Pine Ridge Reservation, whom the Indians nicknamed Young Man Afraid of the Sioux, sent so many telegrams to Washington that the Army soon responded with thousands of troops. Agent McLaughlin, as a matter of pride, preferred to handle problems at his reservation with his own Indian police, and he ordered them to arrest a fierce warrior named Kicking Bear, leader of the Ghost Dancers there. Somehow Kicking Bear caused the police to return, dazed, without him. At Sitting Bull's camp was a wealthy widow from Brooklyn named Catherine Weldon, who was a representative of the National Indian Defense Association, and who was serving Sitting Bull as secretary. She thought the Ghost Dance was a Mormon plot, and she challenged Kicking Bear to an open debate. Apparently, Kicking Bear declined.

The spot where Sitting Bull's cabin stood is surrounded by a woven-wire fence with a swinging gate. Inside the fence is a stone obelisk, and a metal plaque erected by the South Dakota State Historical Society. The plaque's inscription begins: "Sitting Bull, best known American Indian, leader of the 'hostile groups' for a generation, a powerful orator, a clever prophet . . ." A grove of bur oaks grows above the fence, and the grass is high all around. I walked over to look at the Grand River, and suddenly a three-foot-long rattlesnake reared out of the grass, rattling. I saw the white of his belly as he flopped over on his back trying to get away. Jim Yellow Earring went for him like a man chasing a bus. "I'll snap his tongue out of his bone head for you," he said. I asked him please not to.

McLaughlin eventually induced Kicking Bear to leave the reservation. McLaughlin hoped that with the coming of cold weather the dance would die out. Sitting Bull told the people that this year the weather would stay fair, and they could dance all winter, and he was right. McLaughlin sent a telegram to the Commissioner of Indian Affairs in Washington recommending that rations be suspended for all Ghost Dancing Indians at Standing Rock. The Commissioner sent a telegram back asking for the names of Indian "leaders of excitement or fomenters of disturbance" who should be arrested. McLaughlin told the Indian police that they might have to arrest Sitting Bull, and they resigned. McLaughlin appointed new police, under the command of a Yankton Sioux named Henry Bullhead. Catherine Weldon could not get the Indians to listen to her, was outraged when Sitting Bull proposed marriage, and finally left Sitting Bull's camp in disgust. Sitting Bull drove her in his wagon to the town of Cannonball. In Chicago, Buffalo Bill Cody found out that Sitting Bull was to be arrested, persuaded an Army general to give him the arrest order, took a train to Standing Rock, and was on his way to Sitting Bull's camp with a wagonload of candy and presents, drunk, when McLaughlin delayed him long enough to get the order rescinded. McLaughlin heard that Sitting Bull planned to leave the reservation, so on the morning of Monday, December 15, he sent forty-three members of the Indian police to Sitting Bull's camp to arrest him. About a hundred U.S. Cavalry, with a Gatling gun and a gun that shot explosive shells, waited in reserve three miles away.

One of the Indian police said later, "Sitting Bull was not afraid; *we* were afraid." In Sitting Bull's camp were men who had killed a lot of people in the past, men who had recently decided that they were bulletproof. The police rode into the camp before dawn and found Sitting Bull in bed. The camp woke up right away and backed the police up against the cabin when they tried to put Sitting Bull on his horse. One policeman had Sitting Bull around the waist, two others had his arms. Somebody yelled something; Sitting Bull yelled something; a man named Catch the Bear shot Bullhead; Bullhead, falling, shot Sitting Bull; then, thousands of shots were fired. Sitting Bull, punctured so often in the past, was hit seven times. He, his son Crowfoot, Jumping Bull, his son Chase-Wounded, Catch the Bear, Blackbird, Spotted Horn Bull, and Brave Thunder died. The police lost Little Eagle, Hawk Man, Arm Strong, Middle, Afraid of Soldier, Bullhead, and Shavehead. Throughout the fight, no English was spoken.

"Someone went to quite a bit to write that down," Jim Yellow Earring said, leaning on the fence to read the plaque. "Ol' Sittin' Bull—he didn't give a damn if he was comin' or goin'." I copied the inscriptions on the plaque and the obelisk in my notebook. Then I asked Jim Yellow Earring to write for me the Sioux words for rattlesnake, for walking-along-a-river-crossing-back-and-forth, and for yellow earring (*Zewiy*—"I wisht I'd'a' used that name in the service"). The Sioux script taught at Indian schools looks as pretty as spoken Sioux sounds. The sun was now shoulder high. It made the tassels of the grass look red, and it caught the white spot under the wings of nighthawks that flew above us as erratically as the insects they were chasing.

I made sure I had a place to turn around, and then we started out. I was afraid I'd never get up the steep gully, but I did, my rear wheels tiptoeing along the edges of the ruts. It seemed longer this way than it had coming in. Jim Yellow Earring told me about an argument he had had with the Farmers Home Administration when he asked for a loan; about his days in the Army in Fort Benning, Georgia; about his mother, who was dead; about a man named Straight Pine, a short, stocky fella who used to run the best damn Hereford cattle in the area; about how the Crow Indians in Montana drink Lysol, also known as "Montana gin," which will sure get you drunk, but which can collapse your lungs if you don't mix it right; about how much he loved to dance; about how his mother used to take him and his brothers down to the Grand River to play; about how he owned all the land I was looking at, and so what if they wouldn't let him run cattle in here he'd take and run cattle in here anyway; about what a tough guy Bullhead (he pronounced it "Bull'id") was; about how Sitting Bull pulled a good shot on Custer; about all the white people who dig ruts in this road on their way to see Sitting Bull's camp. He kept telling me, "My side! Your side! My side!" He did imitations of different accents—Navaho, black, New York. He sang a song about being a thousand miles away from home, waitin' for a train. He asked me, "Do you ever get lonesome? My mom died nine years ago, and we used to live—well, did you see that old washing machine we passed back there? Well, that's where our house was."

"That was your washing machine?"

"It was *my mother's* washing machine."

4

IN former times, Indians thought the white men's custom of shaking hands was comical. Sometimes two Indians would approach each other, shake hands, and then fall on the ground laughing. Indians swam differently than white people, built smaller campfires, sharpened knives only on one side, and did not use the stars to guide themselves. White butchers saw through bones and cut meat across the grain, but Indians usually cut with the grain and rarely sawed bones. Some Indians would not eat meat cut across the grain. Indians usually did not (and do not) grow a lot of hair on their faces or arms or legs, and some found the hairy bodies of white men disgusting. Indians were shocked by the way white parents grabbed their children by the ears to discipline them; because of this custom, some Indians called white people "Flop Ears." Almost all Indians, at one time or another, composed verses about events in their lives or visions they had seen, but they did not use rhyme. For many Indians, swearwords or "Whiskey!" were the first English they learned. In front of white people, Indians did not like to refer to each other by name.

Indian children played with toy bows and arrows, and

often put each other's eyes out. There were many one-eyed Indians. Indian children did not have to be in bed by a certain hour, and often stayed up through the night. The historian Francis Parkman, when he lived in a Sioux camp in 1846, kept a short stick for punching the heads of kids who climbed on him in his sleep. An Indian camp in no danger of attack was likely to be noisy all night long. People chanted, dogs howled, women mourned, gamblers shouted. Many Indians loved to gamble, and played guessing games with objects hidden in one hand or the other. Many also knew card games like monte, poker, and seven-up. In winter camps, gambling was sometimes about all the men did.

Most Indians did not know how old they were. They measured time in days, moons, and winters, but they had no weeks, hours, or minutes. On the eve of an important event, when they were afraid they might oversleep in the morning—for example, when a war party discovered an enemy camp and wanted to make sure to wake up and attack it at first light—Indians would drink a lot of water before going to bed.

Indians loved crowbars. They used them for digging prairie turnips, bitterroot, tobacco root, and holes for tipi poles. When freshly pitched, tipis were nice inside, with the grass still green and fresh. It took twelve to fourteen tanned buffalo hides to make an average-sized tipi, and as many as fifty to make a big one. As the hides aged, they became like parchment, and let more light through. At night, a tipi with a cooking fire inside was a cone of light. A fully equipped tipi had almost as many ropes, lines, pegs, and parts as an old-time sailing vessel. Women were in charge of putting up and taking down tipis; Kit Carson, the famous frontier scout, lived for years in a tipi with no idea how to pitch one. Tipi poles were made of the slender trunks of young lodgepole pines, and were rare items on the treeless plains. Tribes made special trips to the Rockies or the Black Hills to get them. Since the poles dragged on the ground behind horses during moves, they quickly wore down. All plains tribes constructed tipis with poles set one after the other in a central framework of three or four poles. If you lay on your back and looked out the smoke hole in the top of the tipi, the poles made a spiral going up into the sky.

In the barter system of the plains, five tipi poles might equal one horse. Price in this system varied with circumstance, but the horse served as a loose standard. One good horse might be worth a panther skin, an eagle tail of twelve feathers, eight or ten peyote beans, two gallons of shucked corn, or six tanned buffalo robes. Mules were hardier and rarer than horses, so one mule was worth at least two horses. Indian women liked to decorate their dresses with the smooth lower incisors of the elk; one horse was worth 100 to 150 elk teeth. Two knives, a pair of leggings, a blanket, a gun, a horse, and a tipi might be the price of one wife. A wife, if she worked hard, could prepare ten buffalo robes for trade in a season. At the traders', one buffalo robe was worth from seven to nine cups of sugar. A white mackinaw blanket with a black stripe—Indians preferred that style, so it was more expensive—cost two or three robes. Indian men learned that the more wives they had, the more robes they had to trade. A dressed deer skin equalled from fifteen to twenty rifle balls and powder, an elk skin from twenty to twenty-five. All the meat of one buffalo cow was worth from twenty to forty balls and powder, depending on how far away the herds were. A prime beaver pelt was worth $6 to $8 a pound. For ten months of work, setting traps in cold water, dodging Indians, starving, freezing, getting attacked by bears, a trapper made about $150. The boatmen who brought trade goods up the Missouri as far as the Yellowstone made $220 for the round trip. Prices at the trading posts averaged nine times higher than back East. There were no pennies on the Great Plains—west of St. Louis, the nickel was the smallest coin. Indians used gold and silver coins for buttons on their shirts. When a band of Indians plundered a Missouri River keelboat carrying $25,000 worth of gold dust in buckskin sacks, they poured the gold dust onto the sand and kept the buckskin sacks.

All kinds of Indians lived on the plains. In fact, after the coming of the horse, iron, and colored beads, but before smallpox, alcohol, and the Army, Indians generally prospered and multiplied on the plains. The Sioux, who moved there from the lake region of present-day Minnesota in the mid-eighteenth century, were also called the western or the Teton Sioux, to distinguish them from the Yankton and the Santee Sioux, who remained in the East. On the plains, the Teton Sioux soon numbered seven bands: the Hunkpapa, the Oglala, the Miniconjou, the Oohenonpa, the Sihasapa, the Sicanju, and the Itazipcho. The Sioux's favorite enemy, the Crows, were originally Hidatsa who had moved west from the Missouri River in the 1700s after an argument between two chiefs. The Crows were also called the Absaroka, and they hunted in the Yellowstone valley. Later, other bands of Crows moved even farther west, to the Rockies, so then there were River Crows and Mountain Crows. To the north of the Crows were the Blackfeet, a tribe which killed white trappers by the score, and which ranged into the Canadian plains. The Blackfeet divided themselves into the Bloods, the Piegans, and the Northern Blackfeet. To the northeast of the Blackfeet were the Atsinas, who did not trap beaver, and the Crees, who did. Traders liked the Crees better than the Atsinas, which made the Atsinas hate the Crees. There were Plains Crees, Woodland Crees, and Swampy Crees.

The Cheyenne, who also once lived in Minnesota, hunted the region of the Black Hills and the central plains. In the early nineteenth century, many Cheyenne moved south, to the present-day Oklahoma and Kansas, so the tribe became the Northern Cheyenne and the Southern Cheyenne. To the west of the Cheyenne were their allies the Arapahos, also divided into Northern and Southern branches, and to the west of the Arapahos, roughly speaking, were the Shoshone, sometimes called the Snakes. In the southwest were the Kiowa, the Kiowa Apache, and the Comanche. The Comanche lived mainly in present-day Texas, and raided as far south as Central America. There were five major bands of Comanche, with names that meant Honey Eaters, Those Who Turn Back, Antelope, Buffalo Eaters, and Root Eaters. Lots of other tribes, like the Pawnee, the Miami, the Otoes, the Osages, the Arikara, the Delawares, the Tonkawas, the Kansas, sometimes came to the plains to hunt or fight from the south and east, as the Flatheads and the Nez Percé and the Utes and the Apaches came from the west. I pass over which several of the plains tribes were also known at one time or another as the Gros Ventre (Big Bellies). Often, bands within the tribes were further divided into sub-groups along kinship lines. Most of the tribes would steal horses from or fight most of the others. The fact that their culture tended to fragment itself into so many different tribes and bands was probably a disadvantage to the Indians in the long run. But it certainly was a big help to early pioneers trying to come up with colorful place-names.

The Sioux disinfected the navels of newborn babies with the powder from a puffball. The Hidatsa, when travelling in winter, packed babies in cattail down. Sioux (and other Indian) children nursed until they were as old as four or five. White observers of Indian encampments were surprised to see children standing on the ground and nursing at women going about their chores. The Crows thought long hair was fashionable, and sometimes gummed horse-tails into it to increase its length. In the 1830s, the Crows had a chief called Long Hair whose hair (all his own) was eleven feet six inches long. Measuring Long Hair's hair was a favorite pastime of white travellers. The Crows were skilled horse thieves, and stole from everybody, including each other. They claimed never to have killed a white man except in self-defense. They explained to one trader that if they killed white men there would be fewer to rob.

When the Crows killed a buffalo cow, they sometimes raped it. Crow men and women sometimes made love in public, in broad daylight. The Cheyenne were famous for their chastity. Many Cheyenne women belonged to a housewives' guild, which taught domestic arts and decoration. Cheyenne women got together and bragged of their tanning or decorating feats the way the men bragged of feats of war. Many pieces of Cheyenne hide decoration and beadwork survive in modern museums. The Plains Cree never washed their clothes, just bought new ones at the trader's twice a year. The Blackfeet, when their leather shirts got dirty, repainted them. The Blackfeet let each thumbnail grow long, until it crooked like a claw. They often made presents of their relatives' corpses to whites. Cheyenne men, as an exercise in spiritual devotion, sometimes stood on a hill from sunrise to sunset without moving except to keep their faces turned to the sun, or stood in water up to their necks all day. The Crows chopped joints off their fingers in mourning so often that they hardly had a whole hand among them. The men generally saved their thumbs and one or two trigger fingers.

Sioux medicine men collected tiny, glistening pebbles from anthills and used them in medicine rattles. The Hidatsa rushed eagerly into hailstorms and gathered hailstones to cool their tepid Missouri River drinking water. The Mandan and others loved European toys. The Cheyenne at one time painted their arrows blue, in reference to the waters of a sacred lake in the Black Hills. Cheyenne warriors put on their best clothes and painted themselves and rebraided their hair before going into battle; if they didn't have time to, they ran away. Whenever the Assiniboin sent each other presents of food, they also sent along a little boy to bring back the dish. The Assiniboin cleaned their pipes with pointed sticks decorated with porcupine quills, which they carried stuck in their hair. The Sioux might eat a dead horse, but would never kill one for food. The Kiowa, when moving from a campground they especially liked, would leave strings of beads or little pouches behind, as a "gift to the place." The Osages were said to be the best-looking of the plains tribes; Maria Tallchief, the ballerina who became the third wife of Russian-born choreographer George Balanchine, is half Osage. Balanchine once said that by marrying her he had at last become truly American.

The Arikara, also called the Rees, lived on the Missouri River in earth lodges, like the Mandan and the Hidatsa. According to reports of traders, the Arikara stuck their hair together with gum, clay, grease, and paint, had many large lice which they picked off each other and crushed between their teeth, practiced incest, communicated venereal diseases to their children, filled the spaces between their lodges with garbage, killed lone white men indiscriminately, were poor warriors and horse thieves, shot you with one hand while shaking hands with the other, gambled and smoked all winter, spent the summers sleeping, catching catfish, and chasing each other's wives, and caused neighboring tribes on the Missouri to move away from them. Among the traders, the Arikara were known as the "Horrid Tribe." What the Arikara called the traders is not recorded. Many nineteenth-century white observers liked to list Indian vices, sometimes switching to Latin when the subject was sex. That the Indians who were easiest to observe tended to be the ones most affected by white trade apparently never occurred to them.

The Comanche, who probably killed more settlers than did any other American Indians, made a distinction among whites between ·Texans and all others. Then, as now, it was possible to tell the difference. Texans rode big Kentucky horses, did not parley or give presents, wore homespun clothes dyed butternut, and were trigger-happy. The Comanche hated Texans the most of all. The Comanche were a whirlwind on horseback, but awkward on foot. They were small and bandy-legged, the jockeys of the plains. Comanche raids against Spanish towns in Mexico kept the plains supplied with horses, and discouraged Spain from expanding her empire north. The Comanche had a lot to do, indirectly, with the development of the handgun. The first time the Texas Rangers used Samuel Colt's new revolving pistol in a fight with Comanche was the first time they whipped them. The revolver was the perfect horseback weapon against an enemy who could shoot twenty arrows and ride three hundred yards in a minute. It amazed the Comanche, who remembered that encounter for generations. The rangers made suggestions to help Colt improve his gun, and gave him his first fame. The Comanche prided themselves on their stealth. They had a story about a tribesman who stole a sleeping woman from her husband's side so quietly that neither woke. They often took captives during their raids, and sometimes raised them in the tribe. Women captives had an especially miserable time; even if they were rescued, they usually did not live long. The Comanche enjoyed torturing prisoners. After a day of torture, when they wanted to get some sleep, they would cut the prisoners' tongues out. The Comanche thought the roadrunner was a good-luck charm, and hung its skin in their tipis. They also made fans of the tail feathers of the scissor-tail flycatcher, which they wore at the shoulder like epaulets. After the Army sent troops after them in the winter of 1874, and the Comanche lost many women and children, they surrendered their horses and guns and moved to reservations.

Indians ate young, fat dogs (killed, singed, scraped of hair, gutted, beheaded, boiled, served unaccompanied—a delicacy), ants (scooped from anthills in the cool of the morning, washed, crushed to paste, made into soup), grasshoppers (taken in drives, then dried, boiled, or roasted), beaver tails (cut into small slices, boiled with prairie turnips until very tender—another delicacy), wild peas (robbed from the caches of field mice, boiled with fat meat), chokecherries (stones and all, with a noise "fully as loud as horses eating corn," according to one observer), rose pods (pounded, mixed with bone grease), buffalo berries, wild plums, turtle eggs, serviceberries, wild artichokes, morning-glory roots, cottonwood bark, wild onions, juneberries. They would eat a wild turkey only when they were near starvation. They did not eat many trout, although the soldiers who fought them caught and ate thousands. Indians thought eating pork was disgusting; some believed that the federal inspection stamp was in fact a tattoo, and the meat was white man.

Of course, Indians mainly ate buffalo. There were maybe seventy million buffalo on the plains before white men came. Before the horse, Indians hunted buffalo by chasing them over blind cliffs (called buffalo jumps), up box canyons, or into steep-sided sand dunes where the animals' cloven hoofs would flounder. Horses made hunting buffalo much easier. An Indian who chased a buffalo and killed it with a lance or an arrow might, if he was hungry, cut it open on the spot and eat the warm liver seasoned with bile from the gallbladder. The women followed to do the butchering, and could slice the meat as thin as paper. When it was hung on racks, the plains wind and sun dried it, and then it would last for months. The Comanche liked to kill young buffalo calves and eat the curdled, partially digested milk from the stomach. The Assiniboin made a dish of buffalo blood boiled with brains, rosebuds, and hide scrapings. The Arikara retrieved from the Missouri drowned buffalo so putrefied they could be eaten with a spoon. With stone mallets, Indians cracked buffalo bones to get at the marrow. There were cuts of buffalo just as there are of beef; the Hidatsa had names for twenty-seven different cuts. The Sioux boiled buffalo meat with heated rocks in a buffalo paunch, then ate the paunch, too. Roasted fat hump ribs, boiled tongue, and coffee was a meal Indians dreamed about. Buffalo meat did not make you feel full. Some Indians could eat fifteen pounds of buffalo meat at a sitting.

Among the Indians, no part of the buffalo was ever wasted—except sometimes, when a tribe might kill a herd of fourteen hundred and cut out the tongues to take to the traders for whiskey, or when a war party on enemy hunting grounds would shoot animals and leave them on the ground to rot. White people were likely to kill buffalo for pleasure. Noblemen from the British Isles took long safari-like hunting expeditions on the plains and killed thousands. Early travellers on the Oregon Trail hunted when they got a chance, and the buffalo split into two herds, the northern and the southern, to avoid them. Nobody in history, however, consumed buffalo the way the railroads did. Between 1867 and 1880, the Union Pacific, the Kansas Pacific, the Northern Pacific, and the Santa Fe all reached the Great Plains. The remaining buffalo—maybe thirty or forty million—disappeared up the tracks like water up a straw.

Not that any industry was crying out for buffalo products at the time. Fresh buffalo meat was hard to ship, because it would not travel except in the cold months. Buffalo hams and tongues were complicated to smoke or salt. The easiest part of the buffalo to move was the hide. All you had to do was shoot the buffalo, skin it, scrape the flesh from the hide, and peg the hide out on the ground to dry. You were left with a hard, flat thing with hair on one side, a thing which could be stacked and bailed and loaded in freight cars. When these hides (called flint hides) arrived in the East, they proved more difficult than cowhide to tan commercially. But since the hides were cheap, tanners soon solved the problem. Tanned buffalo leather is too soft and pliant to use for shoes or belts or harnesses, but it makes excellent buffing rags. Tanneries eventually bought hides by the millions. In New York, the price of a buffalo hide went from $1.25 to $3.50 in just a few years. From the railheads, professional buffalo hunters fanned out across the plains.

These hunters preferred to be called "buffalo runners," but they did not chase buffalo and shoot them from horseback. Once they found a herd, they sneaked up to within rifle range on foot. Some wore kneepads to help them crawl. Then they set their sixteen-pound guns on a rest of crossed hardwood sticks and shot buffalo one after another with bullets an inch long and half an inch across. Many buffalo hunters used the fifty-caliber Sharps buffalo rifle, which could kill a buffalo bull at six hundred yards and a man at up to a mile. The hunters tried to kill as many animals as possible in one spot, for the convenience of their partners who did the skinning. Buffalo hunters usually worked in parties of four, with one shooter, two skinners, and one hide stretcher and cook. Everybody wanted to be the shooter. On a busy day, the guns heated up quickly. If the hunter had no water to pour on the barrel, he might urinate on it. Many skinners used mules to pull the hides off. At night, the men sometimes got out a fiddle and pegged down a dry buffalo hide and danced on it. They wore heavy clothes which they seldom changed. Dried blood caked in their beards. When a group of them walked up to a bar, they would reach into their clothes, and the last one to catch a louse had to buy. The prostitutes who catered to them were a special type.

The years when railroads first crossed the plains are when most Western novels and movies and TV shows take place. Those years are what people mean when they talk about the Wild West. The Army was fighting the Indians winter and summer, trying to force them onto reservations, and eventually it more or less succeeded. The buffalo were disappearing, and buffalo hunters had millions of dollars to spend. General Phil Sheridan, commander of the Army's Department of the Southwest, applauded the hunters for "destroying the Indians' commissary." He said, "Let them kill, skin and sell until the buffalo are exterminated. Then your prairies can be covered with speckled cattle and the festive cowboy." Newspaper editors in the new towns along the cattle trails got a kick out of the phrase "the festive cowboy," and used it often in their accounts of shootings and brawls. Even before the buffalo were gone, cowboys were driving thousands of cattle north from Texas to railroad shipping points, or to summer ranges, or to Indian agencies. By 1880, the thousands had become hundreds of thousands. Most of the cattle were Texas longhorns, a breed descended from cattle brought to the New World by the Spanish in the sixteenth century. The longhorns' ancestors were runaways who grew up wild in the brushy bottoms of south Texas. In just a few centuries they evolved horns up to four feet long and an uncowlike fierceness. Texans and Indians hunted them like game, sometimes getting killed in the process, because longhorns were skilled at ambushing people in the brush. When the railroads provided a market for beef, suddenly the six million longhorns running loose in Texas were worth something. Cowboys drove them from the brush and herded them north. Steers which were wild and unwilling sometimes had their eyes sewn shut with linen thread. By the time the thread rotted, the animal was usually tame. Although longhorns were dangerous to cowboys and horses and each other, and so skittish that a man striking a match at night could put them into a stampede, they were also strong travellers, with long legs and an ability to cover miles without water. Each steer had a travelling partner which it walked with every day. Longhorns were skinny and dusty, of many dun colors—mulberry blue, cream, red, yellow, ring-streaked—and their meat was stringy. Sometimes, after months on the trail, they would keep on walking around and around in the freight-yard pens for a week or so after they arrived.

Meanwhile, in the nearby saloons, the cowboys who had brought them drank and acted crazy. Cowboys were often kids who had grown up hungry in Texas during the Civil War. They had names like Bump Miskimmins and Real Hamlet (first name Real, last name Hamlet). At night, on the trail, they used the rotation of the Big Dipper around the North Star to tell when their watch was over, and rubbed tobacco juice in their eyes to keep awake. They sang a song about the trail, and every river they crossed—the Nueces, the Colorado, the Red, the Washita, and on up—had its own verse. They liked canned food, a new convenience at the time. Fads swept them; one day a cowboy named Charlie Colcord appeared on the streets of Medicine Lodge, Kansas, carrying a toothbrush, and soon every cowboy had one sticking from his vest pocket. Just as the cowboys were often from the South, so the saloonkeepers and marshals and livery-store owners and railroad brakemen and small farmers they met along the way were often former Yankees. Fights tended to be at distances where the flame from one man's pistol would set the wadding of the other man's coat on fire.

People with money back East and in Europe quickly realized that the Great Plains cleared of Indians and buffalo meant endless acres of free grass. English lords, Irish dukes, Scottish linen manufacturers, Boston bank presidents, Edinburgh lawyers, St. Louis shoe manufacturers, the Cunard family, actors from New York and Chicago invested in cattle ranches bigger than Eastern states. The Earl of Aberdeen and Baron Tweedmouth founded a ranch called the Rocking Chair Ranche, which took up much of the Texas panhandle. Its offices were at 25 Piccadilly, London. The English-owned XIT Ranch had an English foreman whose name was Walter de S. Maud. By 1884, foreign interests controlled more than twenty million acres of Great Plains ranchlands. Many rich people came West to oversee their ranches themselves: East Coast Biddles and Aldriches and Sturgises, Winston Churchill's Aunt Clara (wife of English-born cattleman Moreton Frewen), Baron Walter von Richthofen (grandfather of the World War I ace), Teddy Roosevelt (recovering from the death of his wife; he told friends he would never be happy again), and a Frenchman named Antoine Amédée Marie Vincent Amat Manca de Vallombrosa, Marquis de Morès. "I am weary of civilization; I long for wilderness; I want an absolute contrast to the old life," the marquis said. He bought ranchland in the valley of the Little Missouri River in North Dakota and built a big house on a bluff. His wife, Medora von Hoffman, of New York, brought along silver hairbrushes in sets of two, for either a right-handed or a left-handed lady's maid.

In general, the rich people had a lot of fun on the plains. They drove around in fancy traps and four-in-hands, raised polo ponies, experimented with new breeds of cattle, rode to the hounds after coyotes, fly-fished for trout, and imported oysters, fresh flowers, and opera companies. The opening of the Cheyenne, Wyoming, Opera House featured an opera titled *Olivette*, with programs printed in blue on perfumed white satin. Teddy Roosevelt knocked down a man who was mean to him in a bar, and caught three other men who stole a boat from him, and cheered up. Refrigerated steamships opened Europe to American beef, and people in England especially began to eat more of it, and some investors made a lot of money. A book called *The Beef Bonanza; or, How to Get Rich on the Plains*, by General James S. Brisbin, explained, with many pages of figures, how an investment in the cattle business would double in five years and pay an annual dividend of ten percent all the while. More money went into cattle, more cattle came to the plains. A De Kalb, Illinois, farmer named Joseph Glidden invented a kind of barbed wire which was easy to manufacture, and suddenly farmers had a way to build cheap fences on treeless land. The line of towns and smaller farms moved farther west.

Other ranchers on the plains were not rich. These men—former soldiers, miners, storekeepers, freighters, cowboys—were concerned about the big increase in rustling which came with the cattle boom. In Montana, they got together and formed a Vigilance Committee. Its members gave themselves new names, like X or No. 84. The railroads had killed off the steamboat trade, and all along the Missouri River the woodlots that had supplied the boats were now deserted. Men with a lot of time on their hands took to living in the woodlots and thinking up ways to steal horses and cattle. Often these men were buffalo hunters, newly unemployed after killing off their profession. Members of the Vigilance Committee rode all over the state and into North Dakota looking for men they thought were rustlers. When they found them, they hanged them from barn beams, hay frames, pine trees, auction-corral gateposts, unfinished buildings, butcher's hoists, and balm of Gilead trees.

By 1886, cattle were overcrowding the range. That summer was dry; the winter that followed was so bad that accounts of it tend to be hour-by-hour: at about ten o'clock in the evening of January 9 the temperature began to drop, it dropped forty degrees in two hours, the wind picked up from the north, snow started to fall, it fell all night, when dawn came you couldn't see any but the faintest light, etc. One snowstorm followed another. In bad weather, buffalo usually faced into the wind until they found a hollow or a valley for shelter; cattle, with thinner coats, tend to travel with the wind. In the winter of '86–87, storms took cattle hundreds of miles. Some ranchers never found their herds at all. Most found them far to the south, piled up five and six deep in ravines, buried in drifts, drowned in rivers. Sixty percent of the cattle in Montana died. Throughout the rest of the plains, the winter killed hundreds of thousands more. Ranchers sent their cowboys out to skin and bring back the hides.

Investors who had been making millions before now lost millions. Ranches folded right and left. The rich people on the plains usually went elsewhere for the winters; after '86, few returned. Winston Churchill's uncle went back to England. Teddy Roosevelt counted the dead cattle on his land in the spring, and never had much to do with ranching after that. The Marquis de Morès, who had wanted to build a transcontinental meat-packing empire, eventually lost about a million and a half dollars and went back to France. Later he became involved in the French anti-Semitic movement, wounded a Jewish newspaper editor in a duel, killed a Jewish Army officer in another duel, and was himself robbed and killed by Tuareg tribesmen in North Africa while on a personal mission to forge a Franco–Islamic alliance against England and the Jews.

When the buffalo were slaughtered, they lay so thick on the ground that you could walk for miles on the bodies. After time passed, only the bones were left, and the railroads took those, too. Hundreds of trainloads were shipped from places like Dodge City, Kansas, and Miles City, Montana, to factories in the East, where the bones were used to make fertilizer and china. Ranchers who had not been upset to see dead buffalo everywhere were sickened by what the winter of '86 did to their cattle. Some gave up ranching entirely; some could never own a cow again. Those who stayed in business reduced their herd to numbers which they could more easily feed and take care of year round. The winter of '86 was the end of all but a few of the giant investor-owned ranches. It was also the end of people coming to the Great Plains in any numbers from far away just for the sake of adventure or fun.

5

I dropped Jim Yellow Earring off in the town of Bullhead, South Dakota. He asked me if I had a couple bucks I could lend him. I gave him a five. He started to ask for more, and I told him to look at the bill. He said, "*Oh!* You done better than I thought!" A station wagon loaded down to the road with Indians came by. The driver, a woman with a face so broad it seemed to fill the whole side window, gave me a dark look. Jim Yellow Earring asked me where I was going next. I told him Strasburg, North Dakota, the birthplace of bandleader Lawrence Welk. He said, "Goddam! All right!" I asked him if he knew that Lawrence Welk was from Strasburg. He said everybody knew that. He said Lawrence Welk was one of the greatest people ever to come from around there.

I drove on for a while and then pulled off the road and slept in my van. The next morning was Sunday. In the cafe where I had breakfast, everybody was still dressed up for church. I heard a young waitress say to an older one, "I think I'm really gonna like these new hours I've got." I drove on through fields with nobody working in them. Gusts of wind crossed the wheat like messages across a Fan-

O-Gram. The leaves of the cottonwoods along the road were dark green, or khaki with dust. I turned off at the town of Hague, North Dakota. It had a Catholic church breathing cool church smell through its open doors, a red firehouse, a grocery store, a grain elevator, a big Behlen Quonset hut near the railroad tracks, a Knights of Columbus hall, a bar called Lit'l Gillys, a Coke machine on the sidewalk, one-story houses with octagon clotheslines and eight or ten rows of corn in the back yards, a lawn sprinkler shaped like a little tractor in one front yard, a few cars angle-parked on the main street, and three blond kids bouncing on a mattress in the back of a pickup truck outside the cafe.

Hard to believe that one night more than sixty years ago, during a dance that had turned rowdy, someone hit Lawrence Welk over the head with a brick in Hague, North Dakota.

Strasburg, North Dakota, is fourteen miles away. Although both are small towns, everything about Strasburg seems to be one size bigger. Strasburg could be Hague's older brother. Like a number of benign towns on the northern plains, Strasburg has a public campground with a restroom and a free shower. I used it and shaved and changed my shirt. Then I found a shady place to park on Main Street and watched people walking by. Strasburg, a town of 623, also has a municipal swimming pool. Kids in bathing suits were walking along the sidewalk in that shivery way you walk after getting out of a swimming pool. Kids on their way to the pool clutched coins in one hand. Kids coming back left wet footprints on the sidewalk. A girl going said to a boy coming back, "Mom wants you home right now." In the distance were kids' swimming-pool shrieks, and the clink of somebody throwing horseshoes, and the

Rolling Stones singing "Faraway Eyes" from speakers set out on a lawn.

Lawrence Welk's family did not live in town, but on a farm three miles away. He was born there on March 11, 1903, the seventh of eight children, to Ludwig and Christina Welk. As a child, Lawrence was fascinated by his father's accordion, an heirloom which had come with the family from Europe. In the summer after fourth grade, Lawrence suffered a ruptured appendix, was driven to the hospital seventy miles away in Bismarck, and nearly died. He spent seven weeks there and another three months at home in bed with a drain in his side. As in the lives of many artists, illness revealed his vocation. During the year of his convalescence, his parents let him play his father's accordion as much as he wanted. He taught himself many tunes, and also went around discovering the sounds he could get from pitchforks, rain barrels, and anvils. After missing a year of school, he did not want to go back and be older than everybody in his class, so his parents let him stay home and work on the farm.

One winter, between chores, Lawrence ran a trapline, and with the earnings from his furs bought a $15 mail-order accordion. Unequal to his enthusiasm, it soon broke. Lawrence was a big fifteen-year-old, and sometimes made money playing for dances in the Strasburg pool hall. He told his father that in return for the $400 he needed to buy a good accordion he would work on the farm until he was twenty-one and give his father all the money he earned playing. His father agreed. The new accordion made him feel like a professional musician for the first time. He played many weddings, birthdays, and dances in and around Strasburg. He drove to jobs in a buggy, often returning home just in time to begin the morning's chores. When he was hit with the brick, he never told his parents.

The day after his twenty-first birthday, Lawrence left home to be a musician. His father said he would fail. He went to Aberdeen, South Dakota, because he had heard there was work for musicians there. He could not read music, and had trouble getting jobs. The worst moment of his life occurred after a dance in Oldham, South Dakota, when he overheard one of the other band members say, "Did you get a load of that accordionist? If I had to play every night with him, I'd go back to jerking sodas." After that, Lawrence practiced playing more softly, and tried to blend in better with the other instruments. After touring with several bands, he finally got a job playing every weekday morning on WNAX radio in Yankton, South Dakota. It was the only radio station for miles, and Lawrence's band soon drew a following. One of the fans who often came by the studio to listen was a young woman named Fern Renner, a nurse at Sacred Heart Hospital. Lawrence asked her to go out with him many times, but she always refused. Finally he decided to enter the hospital for minor surgery, in the hope of seeing more of her there. The tactic worked, and they were married in April 1930.

In the thirties, Lawrence travelled all over with his band—to Tom Archer's Rigadoon Ballrooms in Sioux City, Iowa, to O. K. Farr's Rainbow Ballroom, in Denver, to the Mirador Ballroom in Phoenix, Arizona. When hiring band members, Lawrence always preferred less talented musicians of good character over brilliant musicians of unstable character. Once, he discouraged a band member from fooling around with a local girl by arranging for a policeman to pretend to arrest him on a paternity charge. The Depression had hurt the ballroom business, and Lawrence briefly owned a hotel in Dallas, an appliance store in Yankton, and a restaurant in Mason City, Iowa. The restaurant sold hot dogs and hamburgers in accordion-pleated boxes with pictures of band members on the side.

In 1936, the Welks moved to Omaha, where their second daughter was born. In 1938, the band got a job at the ballroom of the William Penn Hotel, in Pittsburgh. Many of the big hotels broadcast their Saturday-night shows over the radio, and someone at the local station suggested the band bill itself as "Lawrence Welk and His Champagne Music." From then on, the band (now grown to an orchestra) played many big hotel ballrooms—the Edgewater Beach and the Agora, in Chicago; the Roosevelt, in New York; the St. Francis, in San Francisco. For ten years, their semi-permanent home was the Hotel Trianon ballroom, in Chicago. When they played the Aragon Ballroom, in Ocean Park, California, in 1951, the first TV station in Los Angeles, KTLA, began to broadcast their show, and it was such a hit that ABC decided to broadcast it nationally. The Welks, who had moved to River Forest, Illinois, moved to Brentwood, California. "The Lawrence Welk Show," sponsored by Dodge, premiered on ABC on July 16, 1955. Soon forty million people were watching it every Saturday night. Six thousand people a week sent letters and postcards. In 1957, the Lawrence Welk Orchestra played at Eisenhower's Inaugural Ball. *Life* magazine called Lawrence Welk "the most popular musician in U.S. history." Lawrence invested in real estate and golfed with Bob Hope. Comedians did impressions of him. On the subject of his music's appeal, he said, "We play not to please ourselves, but the listeners. I simply have no use for those smart alecks who perform only for one another and ignore the public."

* * *

The doors of the Sts. Peter and Paul Catholic Church in Strasburg were open; the parking lot was empty. The town had worshipped, now it swam. Inside, the silence teemed. There was a smell of polished wood, hymnals, and rubber floor mats. The empty air was still vibrating slightly with the suppressed fidgets of children. Except for the pews and the floors, almost every interior surface was covered with statues or paintings. Two girl-sized statues of angels holding fonts of holy water stood by the main door. The tall, narrow windows each had a saint in stained glass. Angels and biblical scenes covered the ceiling. The altar had a crucified Christ in the center, statues of the Virgin Mary, St. Anne, St. Peter, St. Paul, the Last Supper, candles, scrolls, filigrees, more angels—a scene as colorful and crowded as the finale of the Radio City Easter Show. All the vents at the bottoms of the windows were open. At the front of the church, Emerson Seabreeze electric fans on wheeled stands faced the congregation.

Lawrence Welk's family sometimes battled snowdrifts to get to this church. In fact, if his parents had been less serious about their religion, Lawrence Welk probably would not have been an American. Both of his parents were born on farms near the city of Strasbourg in what was then called the Alsace–Lorraine region of France. After the Franco-Prussian War in 1870, Prussia annexed Alsace–Lorraine and outlawed Catholicism. With other Catholics, the Welks moved to southern Russia, where they helped found a town called Strasburg. Their Catholicism was so different from the local Russian kind that the congregation was accused of heresy and had to move again. This time they came to America, to Strasburg, Pennsylvania, where people they knew from home had settled. But land was scarce in Pennsylvania, so they went on to the Dakotas and founded this Strasburg—the fourth one they had lived in.

Tens of thousands of other German-speaking people came to the Great Plains to farm. This was partly because Americans encouraged them to. According to many nineteenth-century speechmakers, the settling of the West was just another chapter in the triumphal march of the indomitable Anglo-Saxon race. Germans were right for the job. The railroads, with tracks crossing hundreds of miles of empty prairie, had perhaps the most to gain from settlement. Railroad executives agreed with the popular notion that Germans made the best farmers in the world. All the Western roads sent promoters to Europe to convince people to emigrate. (Most Western states did, too.) The Burlington Railroad thought so highly of Germans, and so little of French and Italians, that it printed advertising brochures in the first language and did not bother with the other two. Promoters were always watching for political changes that might produce refugees; in 1871 the Burlington directed a special pamphlet at the people of Alsace–Lorraine, suggesting the state of Nebraska as the perfect place to escape their oppressors.

All the promoters were at some pains to explain that land in the American West was free. Which it was, more or less. The Homestead Act of 1862 said that on surveyed but unclaimed public land any citizen or intended citizen could claim a quarter section—160 acres—and own it outright after living on it and improving it for a period of five years. The homesteader needed a small filing fee, and a much larger amount of cash to survive until the farm got going. Of course, most of the land available for homesteading was far from the railroad lines, because the government had given the railroads large grants of land along their rights-of-way to finance construction. And because the railroads often followed river valleys, not many homestead acres lay in well-watered bottomlands.

The idea behind the Homestead Act was that a nation of small, independent farmers would make the best foundation for democracy. It was an idea as old as the United States. In the years just before the Civil War, politicians from the North wanted to fill the West with farmers on 160-acre homesteads to stop the spread of slavery. The Homestead Act finally passed during the war, when the South could no longer object. Unfortunately, the 160-acre homestead, as well as the larger ones provided for in later legislation, turned out to be wrong for the Great Plains. To expect a person to make a living on a little square of this vast region where animals and Indians used to travel hundreds of miles looking for food, where clouds slide all over before the winds, where you have to import many necessities—it was like expecting a fisherman to survive on just a little square of ocean.

The central plains were where the first railroads crossed, so they were the first to be settled. The northern plains between the Missouri River and the Canadian border had no railroad until 1889, and people were still filing first-time homestead claims in northern Montana through the 1920s. Homesteading the plains might not have been possible at all without the invention of barbed wire for fencing, and of a windmill which reduced its blade surface in high winds to keep from blowing apart. As ingenious as either of these was a public-relations device which some scientists, college professors, U.S. Geological Survey officials, and railroad promoters came up with. This device was the meteorological theory that "rain follows the plow." According to this theory, cultivation of the soil, human activity, steam from railroad engines—all the developments that accompany settlement—produced increased rainfall. The Santa Fe Railroad went so far as to identify the "rainline," the front edge of this advancing rainfall, which supposedly moved at a rate of about eighteen miles a year, staying just ahead of the new settlements.

Another theory favored by the railroads and their experts taught that deep cultivation of the soil conserved moisture, so the homesteaders broke up virgin sod undisturbed since the last Ice Age and plowed furrows twelve and eighteen inches deep. As it turned out, rain did not follow the plow any more than it followed anything else. Some farmers made enough money to buy more land and survive drought years and stay in business. Many thousands of homesteaders ended up owning farms on the Great Plains. But an even larger number went broke, lost their crops to grasshoppers, saw their fields dry up and blow away, went into debt, went crazy with loneliness, sold out, left, and never came back. Homesteads in particularly unpromising parts of the plains often saw dozens and dozens of would-be owners over the years before the message finally got through. Farmers and ranchers are still going out of business on the plains today.

The early homesteaders used dried buffalo droppings for fuel, carted buffalo bones to the railroads for cash, and cleaned the buffalo off the plains so thoroughly that today a buffalo bone is a rare find. Abandoned farmhouses, on the other hand, are everywhere. From Canada to Texas, they are a constant of the landscape. Sometimes when I would drive by one in the middle of blank prairie,

I would make myself stop and take a look. About five miles from Winifred, Montana, I climbed a barbed-wire gate with a "No Hunting" sign on it and walked up to a cabin made of eight-inch cottonwood logs. It had two intact stone chimneys, green shingles, a boarded-up door, window frames with no windows. My heart sped up; as I got close enough to see how tight the hand-hewn carpentry was, I felt more and more like a trespasser. I stuck my head through the window, and instantly several swallows dive-bombed out past me. I hit the dirt and lay there panting. Finally I stepped through the window. The hard-wood floor was spotted with droppings, but still in fine shape. Someone had laid it as tight as the floor of a gym. I could see the blue sky through a small hole in the roof. The walls were plastered, and in the front room the white wallpaper had a red geometric pattern in a faded Art Deco design.

Whenever you see an abandoned house, you wonder. Usually, I was too shy to stop the car and go closer. The way a man in Texas looked at me when he drove up the driveway of an abandoned house as I was peering through the window and writing in my notebook ("busted air conditioner / empty Field Trial high-protein dog food bags / electric-fence transformer / pair of white water skis in corner") gave me an idea of the way the ghosts in these houses might look at me if they existed and could take shape for a moment. Behind the wheel of his pickup truck, the man was one big question mark: Why in the world did I want to nose around the house where (as it turned out) he had grown up? We talked for a few minutes, and the mild, complete puzzlement never left his face. As my van pulled out of the driveway, it slunk.

Most of the abandoned farms—the driveways lined with double rows of cottonwoods sometimes leading to nothing, the spavined barns, bladeless windmills, crumpled stock tanks, tree-sheltered homeplaces with the home missing, fallen-down corrals, splintered stock chutes, rusting farm machinery—I saw from the road, at sixty miles an hour. A friend of mine in Montana who had grown up on the plains loaned me a centennial history of his county, *The Wonder of Williams: A History of Williams County, North Dakota*. (Williams happens to be the county that includes the Fort Union site, and much of the Yellowstone–Missouri confluence area.) This book, published by the Williams County Historical Society, has a chapter on every township in the county, with a list of the families who live there. Many chapters end with a section titled "Others Who Were Here." Sometimes in the evenings in a motel room, after a day of passing abandoned farms, I would read from "Others Who Were Here":

ELLA SPAWN proved up on her homestead in fourteen months and then sold it. Her parents owned a cafe in Williston. She married Rush Blankenship.

THORSTIEN ODDEN homesteaded 80 acres in Section 33. A single man who came from Norway, he loved to play his Hardanger violin. He refused to help with the threshing because he thought the fork handle would stiffen his fingers . . .

GULLICK GULLIKSON came from Numesdal, Norway, about 1910. He homesteaded in Barr Butte, stayed for a short time, then went back to Norway where he operated a trucking business.

CHARLEY BURKE was a coal miner. He was smothered in Billy Kirk's mine when a prairie fire ignited the straw at the entry to the mine. All efforts to save him failed. His faithful dog was with him and also smothered.

WILLYS IRVING was the town boxer . . .

E. J. BURNS came from Missouri and homesteaded. He was an attorney and wrote poetry. A poem he wrote during World War I was entitled "Wave Flag, Wave." He wrote many others.

MARTIN LARSON homesteaded, then moved to Washington. He was said to have money but lived like a hermit.

OLE OLSON HALLING homesteaded in Section 1. When he left the homestead he rode his pony to Cooperstown. He died there . . .

C. D. HELMS homesteaded in 1904 or '05. They lived here until 1925. There is no record of what happened to the family.

ANDREW EDWARDSON BOLI homesteaded in 1909. He lived on the homestead only a short time, then went back east.

GILBERT FUNKHOUSER came from Virginia in 1907. He was never married and passed away in 1921.

MARTIN ROSSING homesteaded in Bonetraill in 1909 but he stayed there only a couple years. He used to play the violin.

JIM KENNEDY, who homesteaded, was a veteran of the Spanish-American War. He later moved to Toledo, Ohio.

BEECHER LEACH came to North Dakota with his parents in 1906 from Missouri. He remained unmarried his entire life . . .

STELLA SWAB homesteaded in East Fork sometime before 1914. She married a druggist and later they moved to Red Lodge, Montana . . .

CONRAD WESTKEMPER—His son became a priest. Reports are they went to Florida.

ENOC SAMUELSON—Sold out and went to Minot to work on the railroad.

JULIUS SMITH—Sold his land to Oliver Haugen and went back to Sweden.

ROBERT A. SMITH—A negro who worked out for others digging rocks. He is remembered by some for his fried bread doughs, called 'Bob Smiths' . . .

HENRY BOGSTI—Had $10 and a saddle horse when he came here. He sold out, went to Wildrose, and worked in an elevator. His son was killed in a flax bin.

JOHN SONNENS—Conrad Westkemper got his homestead. Some remember how Mrs. Sonnens shocked all the grain, topping each shock with two bundles.

HANS BREKTO—Came from Wisconsin. Remembered by having no damper in his stove pipe . . .

OLOUS P. LINDSTEDT—Olous and his son, Albert, came to this area from Hillsboro or Caledonia. One day Olous rode a mule over to Ed Haugen's and when Marie asked him to have dinner with them, he said, "You don't have to ask me twice."

HENRY AND SARAH WINDEL both homesteaded. Sarah must have been a sister or wife of Henry. His land belonged to her for many years.

OLIVER FEDGE was a bachelor. He left by 1916.

HANSENA OLSON was single when she homesteaded. Somebody came along and married her and she ended up in Canada.

OLE HEEN (no relation to Lars) was called "Goliath." He choked to death on meat in a cafe in Ray some years ago . . .

EMIL PERSON was tall and lean. He had so many pictures of women on the walls of his claim shack they overlapped . . .

A. B. SMITH, known as "Saleratus," lived quietly to himself and always carried a pistol. Why? Nobody knew. He got his name from his menu: Saleratus bread, boiled potatoes, bacon, and bacon grease for butter and gravy.

PETER KARLSRUD put in the minimum time to prove up his claim. He was a grain buyer and bought grain for some years in Scobey, Montana.

MARTHA FORGAARD, an excellent dressmaker, later moved to Canada.

OLE INGLADSON died in the flu epidemic in 1918.

VICTOR BERQUIST, a bachelor, came in 1905. One evening in the spring of 1923, after visiting a neighbor's home, he walked away and disappeared. His homestead shack showed no signs of his having prepared to leave. Everything was left exactly the way it had been. A group of neighbors searched for him, but no sign of him was ever found.

Sometimes an abandoned house has enough minor fame that it is mentioned on a historical marker near it on the highway. Just before a bridge on U.S. Highway 83 north of Wellington, Texas, I pulled over to read this marker:

THE RED RIVER PLUNGE
OF BONNIE AND CLYDE

On June 10, 1933, Mr. and Mrs. Sam Pritchard and family saw from their home on the bluff (west) the plunge of an auto into Red River. Rescuing the victims, unrecognized as Bonnie Parker and Clyde and Buck Barrow, they sent for help. Upon their arrival, the local sheriff and police chief were disarmed by Bonnie Parker. Buck Barrow shot Pritchard's daughter while crippling the family car to halt pursuit. Kidnapping the officers, the gangsters fled. Bonnie and Clyde were fated to meet death in 1934. In this quiet region, the escape is now legend.

In the town of Lutie, a few miles up the road, I found out that the house was not "on the bluff (west)," but on a little rise just above the marker. I went back and pulled into the weedy drive. The house, long abandoned, still had walls and a roof. I crossed the back stoop, a slab of concrete with small dog footprints in it. The kitchen floor was floral print linoleum now cracked like old oil paint, covered with wrecked-house mast of junk plaster, broken crockery, a rusted Mohawk canned-ham can. Long strips of ceiling lath sheared down into the rooms. The kitchen wallpaper was a design of flowers and leaves in vases; in the living room, the wallpaper had red and white blossoms, light-green leaves with dark-brown stems, a silver background. Even the pantry had flowered wallpaper. I imagined this place on a summer night, with June bugs against the window screens, lamplight, a man reading the paper, a woman doing the dishes, music on the radio; then—Bonnie and Clyde.

Bonnie Parker was tiny—4′10″, 85 pounds. Clyde Barrow was 5′7″, 127 pounds. The night they were here, she was twenty-two, he was twenty-four. (Buck Barrow, Clyde's brother, was twenty-eight.) Clyde always drove fast, which was probably why they missed a detour sign and crashed into the river. They also liked to drive far. Frank Hamer, the Special Investigator for the Texas prison system and former Texas Ranger who followed Bonnie and Clyde for 102 days before setting up the ambush in which they were killed, said that Clyde "thought nothing of driving a thousand miles at a stretch." He said he once traced them as far east as North Carolina, where all they did was visit a cigarette factory and turn around. The officers they kidnapped at this house were Sheriff Dick Corry and Marshal Paul Hardy, who were taken into Oklahoma, handcuffed together, and tied to trees with barbed wire cut from a fence. In a crime spree of over two years, Bonnie and Clyde kidnapped many other people, robbed many small-town businesses, and killed nine law officers, two grocers, and one lumber salesman.

Clyde had on his right arm the tattoo of a girl and the name "Grace." Bonnie had on the inside of her right thigh a tattoo of two hearts joined by an arrow, with "Bonnie" in one heart and "Roy" in the other. They kept a white rabbit, and took it with them on their travels. Clyde also brought along his saxophone and sheet music. Bonnie read true-romance magazines, painted her toenails pink, and dyed her hair red to match her hats, dresses, and shoes. When Frank Hamer and other Texas and Louisiana lawmen shot them to pieces on a road near Plain Dealing, Louisiana, Bonnie was wearing two diamond rings, one gold wedding ring, a small wristwatch, a three-acorn brooch, and a chain with a cross around her neck. Congress passed a resolution thanking Frank Hamer for his part in ending Bonnie and Clyde's career. He was also awarded their guns. Collectors offered a lot of money for the guns. Both Bonnie's mother and Clyde's mother wrote indignant letters to Frank Hamer, demanding that he turn over their children's guns to them.

In front of the house was an old slippery-elm tree—once a friendly tree in a yard, now just a tree—with big roots knuckling up through the ground. The roots were skinned and smooth from people sitting on them, and on the bare dirt in between I spotted a silver-and-purple tube of Wet 'n Wild lipstick. The tube was fresh, the stick still a little ice-cream-coned at the edges, of a shade of reddish-pink which its manufacturer calls Fuchsia Pearl. I thought about the kids who dropped it. They probably come here sometimes to park and make out. Bonnie Parker would have been happy to find this lipstick. She would have opened it and sniffed it and tried the color on the back of her hand. As I examined it, my own hand seemed for a moment as ghostly as hers. I made a mark on a page of my notebook with the lipstick, recapped the tube, and put it back on the ground.

You can find all kinds of ruins on the Great Plains; in dry regions, things last a long time. When an enterprise fails on the plains, people usually just walk away and leave it. With empty land all around, there is not much reason to tear down and rebuild on the same site. In the rest of America, you are usually within range of the sound of hammers. A building comes down, another goes up, and soon it is hard to remember what used to be there. Nowadays, the past seems almost nonexistent, even contemptible: on TV, the cop says to the criminal, "Reach for that gun and you're history." But, for many places on the Great Plains, the past is much more colorful and exciting and populous than the present. Historical markers are everywhere. In many towns I stopped in, the public buildings were a store, a gas station, and a museum.

The Great Plains have plenty of room for the past. Often, as I drove around, I felt as if I were in an enormous time park. Near Medicine Bow, Wyoming, I visited a rock shop made entirely of fossilized dinosaur bones. Just north of the shop is Como Bluff, a low ridge about six miles long which was the site of one of the world's classic discoveries of dinosaur and early-mammal fossils. During the Jurassic period, from 190 to 136 million years ago, when seas advanced and retreated over much of the Great Plains, the rocks of Como Bluff were sediments at the edge of a coastal plain. Animals that died in rivers upstream tended to wash down there. By the end of the Jurassic, many bones had become fossils in deposits of clay and sandstone. Fossils are harder to remove intact from sandstone than from clay. As it happened, a number of geologic circumstances combined at Como Bluff to preserve thousands of fossils in clay deposits at or near the surface. Fossil bones were just lying around in the open. In 1877, some years after the railroad came through, a station agent for the Union Pacific and his section foreman wrote to Professor O. C. Marsh, of Yale University, about the bones they had found. Professor Marsh sent one of his collectors out, and later identified the odd, multi-pronged object which someone at the station had tied to a rope to keep a horse from wandering as the fossilized tail weapon of a stegosaurus. Professor Marsh eventually took almost five hundred ton-sized wooden boxes of bones from the Como Bluff quarries. The brontosaurus in New Haven's Peabody Museum is from there. Discoveries on the Great Plains were the basis for much of our modern knowledge of dinosaurs. More than half the specimens in the dinosaur rooms at the American Museum of Natural History come from the American or Canadian plains.

On a dirt road on a cattle ranch, also in Wyoming, a

rancher reached over and opened the glove compartment of his pickup and showed me dozens of worked pieces of stone which were rattling around with fence pliers, staples, binoculars, and candy wrappers. Some of the stones were oval, some were thumb-shaped, some appeared to be fragments of projectile points. The rancher said, "A guy came up here from Denver a while ago and said he wanted to look for artifacts on our land, and I asked what kind of artifacts, and he said, 'Early-man tools.' We all thought that was pretty funny—whenever we'd need a rock for something, we'd say, 'Hey, hand me one o' them early-man tools.' Then one day the guy comes down off the ridge and he's got this beautiful spearpoint about six inches long. Ever since, I've been keeping my eye on the ground, and picking up chippings and points and hide scrapers all over the place. Some of these rocks I don't even know what they were, but I know they were something."

The oldest human remains found so far on the Great Plains date from the end of the last Ice Age—about twelve thousand years ago. Archaeologists divide the early inhabitants into elephant hunters and bison hunters. Elephant hunters came first, and used a distinctive type of stone point, called the Clovis point, to kill Ice Age animals like mammoths, which were larger than modern elephants and had curved tusks fourteen feet long. After the mammoths disappeared, hunters used a smaller point, called the Folsom point, to kill prehistoric bison. Folsom points are believed to be between eight thousand and nine thousand years old. More recent points are, in general, harder to date and classify. The ones in the rancher's glove compartment come from a three-thousand-year-long pre-Christian period called the Early Plains Archaic.

On a dirt road above the valley of Horse Creek, also in

Wyoming, another rancher pointed to a federal construction site on the bluff opposite, where archaeologists working for the government had just discovered evidence of a prehistoric camp. "They found a couple of round grinding slabs and a metate—a grinding stone. They told me the camp was maybe three thousand years old," he said. "What I can't get over was that the grinding slabs and the metate were made of sandstone. I keep thinking about those grains of sand in the food."

The big game animals disappeared from the plains about six thousand years ago, and archaeologists have as yet found little evidence of any game at all there for maybe two thousand years after that. Experts in the subject of paleoclimates believe that during these years—from about 4000 B.C. or 4500 B.C. to 2000 B.C.—the Great Plains went through a period of heat and drought which turned the land to near-desert. This period is sometimes called the Altithermal. As the climate gradually became cooler and more moist, humans again moved in, usually following river valleys. Stone grinding tools are often found at village sites dating from the last years of the Altithermal; in that environment, apparently, people were grinding up and eating just about anything organic they could find.

On the banks of the Sun River, in western Montana, I sat at the center of a wheel made of rocks, with spokes stretching across the prairie. I had read about the wheel in an astronomy column in a local newspaper; many people believe that these prehistoric stone alignments, called "medicine wheels," found at a number of sites on the plains, were astronomical timepieces. The day of my visit was the summer solstice, June 21. I wanted to see if the sun would set exactly at the end of one of the spokes. The wheel once was whole, but the river eats away more of the bank every year, and now less than half remains. The hooves of cattle going down to the water have trampled out most of the wheel's center. As I watched, the sun got lower, the blossoms on the little prickly-pear cactus caught the light, the shadows of the grass slid along the ground, the bluffs on the near riverbank turned dusky, the bluffs on the far bank turned pink. Then, beyond the low peaks of the Rocky Mountain front, the sun went down at a point indicated by none of the spokes of the wheel. I had with me a diagram of the wheel when it was less damaged, which showed a small double row of rocks on the approximate line of the sunset. The medicine wheel is on private land, and a trail used by ranch vehicles has scattered those rocks. Astronomers say that many of the medicine wheels on the Great Plains are aligned to the summer solstice. A well-preserved wheel in the Bighorn Mountains in Wyoming indicates with spokes ending in rock cairns the points on the horizon where the sun rises and sets at the solstice; others of its cairns may be intended to show where the stars Aldebaran, Rigel, and Sirius appear at dawn in the summer sky. For most tribes of plains Indians, the summer solstice was the time of the Sun Dance, their most important religious ritual. In the years since white men came, none of the Indians has been much help in explaining who built the medicine wheels, or why.

In the valley of the Madison River, also in western Montana, I stopped at the Madison Buffalo Jump State Monument. A display in a kiosk near the parking lot indicated a nearby bluff off which Indians used to chase buffalo in the days before the horse. I climbed to the top of the bluff and walked away from it across the rolling prairie; when I looked back, I could find no hint that the land beneath my feet was about to end abruptly. It looked like just another rise. It would have fooled me, let alone a buffalo. The bluff is the end of a narrowing tongue of land which would have funnelled the herd to a point. The drop from the bluff—sixty or seventy feet—then turned the animals into a rain of meat. On the spot where so many buffalo would have landed and died, almost no grass grows, maybe out of tact. Indian hunters used this perfect natural trap over and over for thousands of years before the horse put it out of business. From the interstate highway which runs nearby, nothing about this bluff looks any different from thousands of others.

At Fort Griffin State Historical Park, in north-central Texas, I walked the edges of a plowed field where much of the town of Fort Griffin Flat once stood. In the 1870s, the equation that turned buffalo hides into buffing rags brought a lot of money here. Today, only the ruin of a Masonic Lodge remains. Among the many people who came here to profit from the buffalo hunters' earnings was the famous gambler Dr. John Henry Holliday, known as Doc. Doc Holliday had been to dental school in Baltimore, and he had good hands. He also had tuberculosis. He was one of a long list of people who came to the dry plains for their health. After a career which involved him in countless knife- and gun-fights, including the shootout at the O.K. Corral, the most famous Western gunfight of all, he finally died of his disease in bed in a hotel in Glenwood Springs, Colorado. His last words were, "This is funny."

Here at Fort Griffin Flat, according to the later recollections of his friend Wyatt Earp, Doc Holliday reprimanded a man during a card game for looking through the discard pile. The man, named Ed Bailey, pulled a gun, and Doc

Holliday killed him with a knife he carried in his breast pocket. Doc Holliday was jailed, and when some of Bailey's friends decided to lynch him, a woman named Big Nose Kate set the livery stable on fire, sprung Doc Holliday in the confusion, and rode with him six hundred miles north to Dodge City. No grave in the old cemetery near the town site has a headstone with the name of Ed Bailey. In fact, none of the graves has any marker at all, and the graveyard itself is unmarked and untended. In this part of Texas, the ground is mostly limestone rock, so a lot of graves in this cemetery were the classic heap-of-stones type familiar from Western movies. With the years, the centers of such graves sag back to the ground.

Just outside the town of Holcomb, in western Kansas, I pulled into the driveway of the house where the Herb Clutter family was murdered one night in 1959, and where, later, the writer Truman Capote came to research his book *In Cold Blood*. Wind-bent trees line both sides of the driveway, and cross their branches above. I drove past a "Keep Out" sign; since the murders, the house has been mostly untenanted. The murderers parked in the shadows of a tree. The ambulances drove up to the front door. The history of this house makes everything here look different; it makes warm afternoon sunshine into the flash of a police photographer's camera. The shots that stopped four lives in this house also seem to have stopped time. From my car, I could see that the lawn was recently mowed, that the beige frame-and-brick exterior did not need new paint, that a bruise-colored curtain was drawn in a downstairs window. A detail that transported the whole scene back to 1959 was the elaborate television antenna on the roof; anybody as interested in television today would have a satellite dish.

On the open prairie in west-central Montana, near no town, I came across perhaps my favorite ruin on the Great Plains. This ruin is an unfinished structure about twenty feet high which covers more than an acre. The outside of the structure angles inward, like the base of a pyramid; the walls are nine feet thick, mostly sheathed in bulldozer-yellow steel plate. On the concrete floor inside are tire tracks, and skid marks where kids have done wheelies or donuts. Swallows fly around inside and chirp. The ping of dripping water echoes. Pages of a water-stained Bible rustle in the wind. Through the main entry, you could drive a small house. On the exterior, someone has written in spray paint, "172 Million Dollar Monument to America's Stupidity."

From a local person (it took about an hour of driving to find one), I learned that this structure was originally intended to be a command center for the Safeguard Anti-Ballistic Missile system. Later, from a public-information officer at Malmstrom Air Force Base, in Great Falls, Montana, I learned that the Army had been in charge of Safeguard and that construction of the center was suspended in 1974 when the United States got rid of parts of the ABM system in compliance with the SALT I Treaty. The command center was built to withstand nuclear attack; now, tearing it down would be too expensive to be worthwhile. Even damaging it at all seriously would require patience, cutting torches, and heavy equipment. Usually, ruins refer to the past, but what I like about this one is that it probably will still be here a thousand years from now. Inadvertently, it has become timeless, like the pyramids or the Great Wall. If the Army were using it for its original purpose, barbed wire and security forces would keep me far away; abandoned, viewed from up close, this monument of cold-war architecture has begun to look a little like a frame from an old James Bond movie. Paleontologists sometimes infer from a fragment of mandible whole skulls, species, cultures. Maybe in thousands of years this ruin will be evidence from which people infer nuclear weapons, the internal-combustion engine, automated banking, Phil Collins albums, and diet pancake syrup. As my van rocks gently on its springs in the wind, and as the wind whistles through the grama grass, I feel as if the car and the grass and I are all flesh to this ruin's bone.

In or near the towns of Colstrip, Montana; Rock Springs, Wyoming; Zap, North Dakota; Stanton, North Dakota; and Beulah, North Dakota, there is a different kind of ruin. At those places, and many others on the Great Plains, enormous power shovels strip away the land to dig out coal. From a distance, their posture on a ridge is that of a crow on carrion. Near Zap, you can see two or three of them on the horizon at one time, their booms swinging back and forth like feelers. At Colstrip, Rock Springs, Stanton, and other places, on-site power plants, also called mine-mouth plants, turn the coal into electricity. In Stanton, the strip mine and power plant are within sight of the location of a Mandan village which was emptied by the smallpox epidemic of 1837. That 95-acre expanse is now a National Historic Site, with posted signs saying "Digging Prohibited by Law." Railroad tracks lead away from all the strip mines. From the mine-mouth plants, tall two- and four-armed pylons file across the prairie east and west, to places where more people live.

Obviously, I don't like strip mines. The only not horrible

aspect of strip-mining I can think of is that the machines it requires are a real spectacle. Especially if you come upon one at night, all lit up, eating away under banks of lights miles from anywhere. Basically, a strip-mining machine is a steam shovel, exponentially enlarged. The cab section can be the size of a multi-story apartment block, with windows, ladders, catwalks, lunchrooms, and (for all I know) bowling alleys. The bucket has teeth the size of a man, and room to park three stretch limos. The biggest of these machines can strip an area of several city blocks without moving. In their wake, they leave not ruins but ruin. The coal companies sometimes attempt "reclamation" by planting grass or trees in the ruin and calling it a recreation area or a game preserve. Land that has been strip-mined, "reclaimed" or not, demonstrates that the rest of the Great Plains is a palimpsest: unstripped ground looks the way geology, wind, water, buffalo, cattle, the railroads have made it look. Like other arid but inhabited parts of the world, the plains sometimes hold pieces of the past intact and out of time, so that a romantic or curious person can walk into an abandoned house and get a whiff of June 1933, or can look at a sagebrush ridge and imagine dinosaurs wading through a marsh. In the presence of strip-mined land, these humble flights fall to the ground. Scrambled in the waste heaps, the dinosaur vertebrae drift in chaos with the sandstone metate, the .45-70 rifle cartridge, the Styrofoam cup. It is impossible to imagine a Cheyenne war party coming out of the canyon, because the canyon is gone.

Among the many booms that have occurred on the Great Plains have been several booms in archaeology. One began in the late forties, when the Army Corps of Engineers was getting ready to dam the Missouri River and submerge forever hundreds of miles of riverbed and thousands of square miles of bank and valley. Teams of archaeologists working for the government went along the river examining sites and recording data. Another boom followed the Arab oil embargo of 1974, when energy companies were considering mining more coal and building bigger mine-mouth plants to burn it. By law, anyone who plans to dig up public land must first hire an archaeologist to report on the land's historical significance. Archaeologists who do that kind of work are called contract archaeologists. In a booklet called *Early Peoples of North Dakota*, written for schoolchildren, C. L. Dill, an archaeologist with the State Historical Society of North Dakota, explains: "If a site is dug up before it is investigated, the information in the site will be lost forever, just like tearing a page from a book. Archaeologists excavate sites carefully and record everything they see and find. That's like reading the page before it is thrown away."

Strip-mined land is land thrown away. Usually, trash exists in a larger landscape; after strip-mining, the larger landscape *is* trash. Instead of adding a new layer to the palimpsest of the Great Plains, strip-mining destroys the palimpsest itself. Of a place where the imagination could move at will backward and even forward through time, strip-mining creates a kind of time prison. Even after "reclamation," land that has been stripped gives you no year to think about but the year when the stripping happened.

I fear for the Great Plains because many people think they are boring. Money and power in this country concentrate elsewhere. The view of the Great Plains from an airplane window is hardly more detailed than the view from a car on the interstate highways, which seem designed to get across in the least time possible, as if this were an awkward point in a conversation. In the minds of many, natural beauty means something that looks like Switzerland. The ecology movement often works best in behalf of winsome landscapes and wildlife. The Great Plains do not ingratiate. They seldom photograph well—or rather, they are seldom photographed. Images of the plains are not a popular feature of postcards or scenic calendars. And, in truth, parts of the plains are a little on the monotonous side. Convincing someone not to destroy a place that, to him, seems as unvaried as a TV test pattern is a challenge. The beauty of the plains is not just in themselves but in the sky, in what you think when you look at them, and in what they are not. A strip-mining machine could eat the Madison Buffalo Jump—a one-in-a-million piece of ground which fooled buffalo for thousands of years—for breakfast. By leaving nothing behind but a landscape of trash, strip-mining insults the future. By destroying the physical record, and by making the history of white people on the Great Plains look like nothing more than the progress of appetite, strip-mining also insults the past. Land that has been strip-mined reduces the whole story of the Great Plains to: chewed up, spit out.

6

ONE day, on the street in front of my apartment in New York (this was before I moved to Montana), I met a Sioux Indian named Le War Lance. I had just been reading a study of recent economic conditions on Sioux reservations. The authors seemed puzzled that so few Sioux were interested in raising sugar beets or working in a house-trailer factory. As I waited for the light to change, I noticed that the man standing next to me resembled many pictures of Sioux that I had seen. I said, "Are you a Sioux?" He smiled and said, "I'm an Oglala Sioux Indian from Oglala, South Dakota." He said his name and asked for mine. He had to lean over to hear me. He was more than six feet tall. He was wearing the kind of down coat that is stuffed with something other than down—knee-length, belted around the waist, in a light rescue orange polished with dirt on the creases—blue jeans lengthened with patches of denim of a different shade from knee to cuff, cowboy boots, a beaded leather ponytail holder. His hair was straight and black with streaks of gray, and it hung to his waist in back. After I saw him, I never cut my hair again. In one hand he was holding a sixteen-ounce can of beer.

"Your name is Lou?" I asked. "*Lou* War Lance?"

"*Le!*" he said. He pronounced it kind of like "Leh" and kind of like "Lay." He said it meant "this" in Sioux. I had never before met anyone whose first name was a pronoun. Next to him was a compact woman with straight auburn hair. I had not thought they were together. "Do you know each other?" Le asked. She recoiled just perceptibly. "Oh," he said. "Noelle, this is—" I said my name.

He and I talked through several changes of the "Walk" signal. I gave them directions to Astor Place. Back in my apartment, I took out my Lakota–English dictionary and paced up and down. It had never occurred to me that there might be a Sioux within twenty yards of my front door. I called several friends and told them about the encounter. I paced around some more. Then I went up to the store and bought lamb chops for dinner. On the way back, at the triangle made by the intersection of Greenwich Avenue, Christopher Street, and Sixth Avenue, I saw Le again. He was just standing there, like a man waiting in line at a bank. He was still holding a sixteen-ounce can of beer. I went up and said Hi. "The girl went home," he said. "She had to go back to New Jersey."

For a moment, we considered this. Then I said, "Le, would you mind telling me if I'm pronouncing this right: *Hehaka Sapa*."

Le's eyes saw me for the first time. "What?" he said. "You mean *Hehaka Sapa*—Black Elk? Black Elk was a great holy man. He was Oglala, like me. *Sapa* means black. *Hehaka*—elk." He said the second *h* back in his throat. The word even sounded like an elk.

"How about *Tasunke Witco*?"

"*Hoka hey!*" he said. "*Tasunke Witco*—Crazy Horse!" He took my right hand in the "power" handshake. Nobody had stood this close to me in weeks. "I can see that we were meant to run into each other again today," he said. "Crazy Horse was my gran*'father*!"

"Really?"

He smiled and nodded in my face. Then I started asking him questions about Crazy Horse: Before battle, did Crazy Horse streak his pony with dirt thrown up by a burrowing mole, and touch a little of the dirt to his hair, so that the mole's blindness would make him and his horse harder to see? Did he wear a medicine bag around his neck containing the dried heart and brain of an eagle mixed with dried wild-aster seeds? Did he wear a round, flat rock on a buckskin thong, always keeping the rock between his heart and the enemy? Did he always dismount to shoot, so as to improve his aim? Did he always give his captured ponies to the needy boys of the camp? Was he always by himself? Did he have a wild coyote that followed him around like a dog? Did bullets and arrows vanish before they reached him? Did he never wear white man's clothing? Did he say that after his death his bones would turn to rock and his joints to flint? Was his bay war pony the fastest on the plains? Le War Lance smiled and nodded. Occasionally he exclaimed *"Hoka hey!"* or *"Crazy Horse was my gran'father!"* When I asked where Crazy Horse's name came from, he said, " 'Twas a vision!" A drizzle started to fall. I cradled the bottom of the paper bag containing my lamb chops. Taxicabs were screaming at each other. People streamed past us on all sides. I asked if it was true that Crazy Horse never painted his face for battle. "Crazy Horse painted his face blue with white hailstones," Le War Lance said.

Unlike most Indians who had won names for themselves during wars with white men on the Great Plains, Crazy

Horse never visited New York. In fact, of all the famous plainsmen in history, Crazy Horse was the only one who neither came to the plains from somewhere else nor ever left. As a teenager, he once went along on a raid against a village of Omaha Indians in what is now eastern Nebraska; other than that, as far as anybody knows, he lived his entire life between the hundredth meridian and the Rocky Mountains. Crazy Horse was probably born in 1840 at the foot of Bear Butte, near where Sturgis, South Dakota, is now. He had sandy-brown hair, and his parents called him Curly. During his boyhood, bands of his tribe often camped near Fort Laramie, which was on the Oregon Trail in present southeast Wyoming. In August of 1854, he saw thirty soldiers kill a chief named Conquering Bear and several other peaceful Sioux with a cannon in a dispute which had begun over a lost or stolen cow belonging to a Mormon emigrant. He also saw the Indians respond by killing all the soldiers but one. When he went on the raid against the Omahas, he killed an Omaha woman, and authorities at her agency wanted him arrested. From his late teens on, he fought many battles against the Crows, the Shoshones, and the Army. After a fight with the Arapahos where he charged the enemy alone, took two scalps, and came back wounded, his father gave him his own name, Crazy Horse. In 1866, he was one of the hundreds of Sioux and Cheyenne who besieged Fort Phil Kearny, in present north-central Wyoming, and so enraged the defenders that an officer named William Fetterman, who had bragged that with eighty men he could whip every Indian on the plains, rashly chased a few decoy warriors into an ambush where his entire party— about eighty men, as it happened—was killed. Crazy Horse was one of the decoys.

"I will tell you about one of the war stunts that Crazy Horse pulled off that I thought was great," a Sioux named Short Buffalo said to an interviewer years later. "It was in a fight with the Shoshones in which the Shoshones outnumbered the Oglalas. Crazy Horse and his younger brother were guarding the rear of their war party. After a lot of fighting, Crazy Horse's pony gave out. Crazy Horse turned it loose and the younger brother, who did not want to leave him, turned his own pony loose. Two of the enemy, mounted, appeared before them for single combat. Crazy Horse said to his brother, 'Take care of yourself—I'll do the fancy stunt.' Crazy Horse got the best of the first Shoshone; the other one ran away. He got the horses of the two Shoshones and [he and his brother] caught up with their party. They had saved themselves and their party and got the two horses and the scalp of the Shoshone who was killed."

At the Battle of the Rosebud River, in June of 1876, Crazy Horse led a thousand or so warriors against a force of eleven hundred soldiers commanded by General George Crook, and inflicted on that distinguished Civil War veteran the most galling defeat of his career. Eight days later, at the Battle of the Little Bighorn, Crazy Horse was at the head of the attack which pinned and later wiped out Custer on the ridge of the famous Last Stand. In the intense military campaigns which followed Custer's defeat, Crazy Horse managed to stay ahead of the Army until January 8, 1877, when General Nelson Miles attacked his camp on the Tongue River. Crazy Horse and most of his band managed to escape. In the spring, relatives and friends who were already living at Indian agencies came to his camp and urged him to stop fighting and return with them. They said there would be presents and rations and no trouble. Crazy Horse was at first so opposed to the idea that he killed the ponies of those who decided to go. But finally he gave in. The Army would certainly come after him again. Staying out would mean leaving his home territory and going to Canada, as Sitting Bull had done. Crazy Horse said he would go into the agency if that was what everybody else wanted to do. On May 6, 1877, he led 899 people, including 217 warriors, with a two-mile-long train of camp equipage, to Fort Robinson, Nebraska, where they surrendered their guns and their herd of two thousand ponies to the Army.

Le War Lance and I stood talking about Crazy Horse for a long time. My grocery bag started to fall apart, so I held it under my coat. Le War Lance also told me about himself: that he once took part in a march for Indian rights which began in Alcatraz, California, and ended in Washington, D.C., and he wore out many pairs of boots on the way; that he was born June 14, 1942; that he rode a horse to school for first and second grades; that he and a woman named Joni were the only ones of twenty-two in his grade-school class still alive; that he served time in prison for a theft involving a lard bucket full of coins, which turned out to be a coin collection, which theft he did not commit; that his father's name was Asa Walks Out. He said, "I'm getting hungry. Come and eat with me. I'll make us some beans and ham hocks." I said I had to get home. We exchanged telephone numbers. He wrote only his first name, in script—a big loop connected to a smaller loop. I told him that I hoped someday to learn how to speak Sioux. He took my right wrist and pressed his thumb tightly against my pulse and then spoke a sentence. The sound of Sioux is soft and rippling, like something you might hear through a bead curtain. I asked him what he had said. "I said, 'If your pulse speeds up, then I will know that you are lying, and then I will have the right to kill and scalp you.' " Then he smiled a sunny smile which turned his mouth and eyes to crescents. A few minutes later I started to leave, and he stopped me to sing me a song. He closed his eyes and chanted in a high, wavering voice. He finished one song and then started another. Then he opened his eyes and looked at the Sixth Avenue masses hurrying past with shopping bags. "Immigrants!" he shouted. He shook his head, and said, "Pasta!" Did I hear that right? Yes; in tones of exasperation, as if this was really the last straw: *"Pasta!"*

So thoroughly did Crazy Horse avoid contact with white people away from the battlefield that history records the name of the first white man ever to shake his hand. Lieutenant J. Wesley Rosencrans was among the party of soldiers and Indians from Fort Robinson and the Red Cloud Indian Agency who met the Crazy Horse Indians about a day's journey from the fort, with ten wagons full of presents and a hundred head of beef cattle. Apparently, Lieutenant Rosencrans's party wanted to make sure that Crazy Horse came in to Fort Robinson and did not decide to go to the Spotted Tail Agency, which was about forty miles northeast of Fort Robinson. General Crook (late of the Battle of the Rosebud) had promised, through emissaries, that Crazy Horse and his band could go on a buffalo hunt in the fall. This gave some of the Crazy Horse Indians the impression that they would only have to stay at an agency for a short while, and then would be allowed to return to their campgrounds on the northern plains. When they were a few miles from the fort, more soldiers came out to hold council with them, and that was when the Indians realized that they were expected to surrender. *The New-York Times* (it had a hyphen then) reported, "The surrender was made as impressive as possible. As the Indians entered the broad valley of White River, near the point selected for the camp, the warriors formed in five bands, 40 in each band, and filed across the stream, chanting songs suited to the occasion." Several observers remarked that the band looked more like a victorious army than like one laying down its arms. Crazy Horse himself surrendered three good Winchester rifles. The surrendered ponies were given to Indians from the Red Cloud Agency "as a reward for their cooperation in subduing the hostile bands," the *Times* said. There was no formal written surrender agreement. Crazy Horse never signed anything. He was never officially enrolled at any agency. In one of his first meetings with the soldiers, Crazy Horse was promised that he would soon be able to choose a place for his own agency. He said he would like his agency to be on Beaver Creek, west of the Black Hills (now eastern Wyoming). For the time being, he was to stay at the Red Cloud Agency. Like every other Indian at that agency, he was now forbidden to travel farther than three miles away and stay overnight without special permission. He moved more than the three miles he was allowed, and pitched camp at the junction of Little Cottonwood Creek and White River.

At that time, Indian agencies had Army posts nearby. The Red Cloud Agency was three-quarters of a mile from Fort Robinson. The Spotted Tail Agency was near Camp Sheridan. Indian agencies were under the supervision of the Bureau of Indian Affairs, which was (and is) part of the Department of the Interior. The agencies were to distribute goods and promote the Indians' welfare. The Army posts were to keep the Indians in line. The Indian agent in charge of the Red Cloud Agency was James Irwin. The Indian agent at the Spotted Tail Agency was Lieutenant Jesse M. Lee. Red Cloud, the Oglala chief who got credit for driving the Army from the northern plains in a series of engagements (including the Fetterman fight) later known as the Red Cloud War, was the most important chief at the Red Cloud Agency. At the Spotted Tail Agency, his counterpart was Spotted Tail, a Brulé Sioux chief famous as an orator and diplomat. Spotted Tail was the most persuasive of the emissaries sent by General Crook to get the Crazy Horse band to surrender. Both Spotted Tail and Red Cloud had signed peace treaties and moved to their agencies some years before, and neither took part in the Custer fight or the other last battles between the Sioux and the Army.

Because thousands of agency Indians did take part, Congress had recently given the Army final authority in running the agencies. The officer at Fort Robinson who superintended the Crazy Horse Indians' surrender was Lieutenant William Philo Clark; the Indians called him White Hat. Keeping an eye on Crazy Horse was Clark's special responsibility, and he often visited the Crazy Horse camp. The commanding officer at Fort Robinson was General Luther P. Bradley. His immediate superior was General George C. Crook, commander of the Department of the Platte, with headquarters in Omaha. Crook's superior was General Philip Sheridan, commander of the Department of the Missouri, with headquarters in Chicago. Sheridan's superior was General William T. Sherman, General-in-Chief of the Army. Soon after Crazy Horse surrendered, Sherman wrote to Sheridan, "If some of the worst Indians could be executed I doubt not the result would be good—but that is impossible after surrender under conditions . . . Rather remove all to a safe place and then reduce them to a helpless condition."

The first thing Crazy Horse did after arriving at Red Cloud was to request that a doctor from Fort Robinson treat his wife, Black Shawl. Assistant Surgeon Dr. Valentine T. McGillycuddy went to the Crazy Horse camp on horseback and discovered that Black Shawl had tuberculosis. Dr. McGillycuddy returned often to bring her medicines and note her progress. Eventually, he got to know Crazy Horse perhaps better than any other white man did. He thought Crazy Horse was "the greatest leader of his people in modern times." He asked several times to take his photograph, but Crazy Horse always refused. Crazy Horse told him, "My friend, why should you wish to shorten my life by taking from me my shadow?" D. F. Barry, a well-known photographer of Indian life, said he often tried to bribe Crazy Horse to sit for a photograph, without success. Crazy Horse's name was magic all over the plains and beyond. The *Times* referred to him simply as Crazy Horse; no further identification was needed. Red Feather, the brother of Black Shawl, told an interviewer in 1930, "All the white people came to see Crazy Horse and gave him presents and money. The other Indians at the agency got very jealous." Not long after Crazy Horse came to Red Cloud, he took a second wife. Her name was Nellie Larrabee, and she was the eighteen-year-old part-Indian daughter of an Army scout at Fort Robinson. She may have been a present herself, engineered for Crazy Horse by Lieutenant Clark.

In June of 1877, at the solstice, the Indians from the Red Cloud Agency and the Spotted Tail Agency held the biggest

Sun Dance in history at Sun Dance Creek, about halfway in between the two. Twenty thousand Indians were there. On July 1, Agent Irwin at Red Cloud informed his superiors that he did not have enough flour to make the week's issue, even at half rations. At the time, most of the annuities and supplies owed the Sioux by treaty were being sent not to Red Cloud Agency but to a new agency on the Missouri River, where Congress and the Army had long wanted them to move. None of the western Sioux had lived on the Missouri for generations, and they had no desire to now. They protested the planned move in councils with Indian agents and the Army. For many hundreds of Indians confined at Red Cloud, this was the first time they could remember being hungry in the summer. In August, the Indians met with General Crook and Agent Irwin, who renewed the promise that everyone who wanted could leave the agency for forty nights to hunt buffalo. After the council, followers of Red Cloud told Irwin that if the Crazy Horse band went to hunt buffalo they would never come back, and would use the guns and ammunition to kill whites.

That same summer, the Nez Percé, a Rocky Mountain tribe who had never before killed a white man, resisted being sent from their hunting grounds to a small reservation in Idaho, killed some settlers, lost thirty-four people in one battle with the Army and about eighty-nine in another, killed two vacationers in the newly created Yellowstone National Park, and by the end of August escaped onto the northern plains. Perhaps because this put them in the vicinity of the Sioux buffalo grounds, perhaps because of Red Cloud's warning, Agents Irwin and Lee withdrew permission for the hunt. The Sioux were disappointed. But right away Lieutenant Clark got the idea of taking Crazy Horse and sixty other Sioux north to fight the Nez Percé. Some of the Sioux, who were still getting used to the idea of never going to war again, found Clark's offer confusing. Touch the Clouds, a seven-foot Miniconjou Sioux from Spotted Tail Agency and a friend to Crazy Horse, told Clark that he felt like a horse with a bit in its mouth being turned first one direction and then another. Crazy Horse said that he had come in to the agency for peace, that he had promised not to go out on the warpath anymore, but that if the Great Father wanted him to fight the Nez Percé, he would go north and fight until not a Nez Percé was left.

Clark's interpreter at this council was a man named Frank Grouard, one of the strange characters of the plains. No one knew for sure whether he really was a Sandwich Islander brought to America by Mormons, as he often claimed. His half sister said that he was the son of an American Fur Company employee named John Brazeau. (John Brazo, you may remember, was the man hired by Kenneth McKenzie, bourgeois at Fort Union, to shoot a Frenchman who had threatened his life.) Grouard had lived with the Sioux. Apparently, Sitting Bull had once saved his life. To his biographer, Grouard made many bizarre claims; he said that he once owned a piece of buckskin which he got from Crazy Horse's father which detailed the history of the Sioux nation for the past eight hundred years, and that he also once owned a huge "scalp cape" made from the scalps of the white victims of Sitting Bull, but that both these objects had been destroyed in a fire. He also said that he and Crazy Horse were closer than brothers. ("I never had any use for Gruard," Dr. McGillycuddy said.) For some reason, Grouard mistranslated the end of Crazy Horse's speech to Clark, to the effect that Crazy Horse would go north and fight until not a *white man* was left. At this, Clark became angry, the interpreters began arguing, Grouard walked out, Crazy Horse got fed up, and the council finally fell apart. Crazy Horse did not try to learn what the trouble had been about; even before he came to the agency, he was not much for councils. The rumor that Crazy Horse was going on the warpath caused great excitement at both agencies, and Agent Lee, who managed to get the story straight after talking to Touch the Clouds and others, rode from the Spotted Tail Agency to Fort Robinson to explain to Clark. As Lee later wrote, Clark "seemed POSITIVE that there was no mistake."

In the midst of these events, General Crook arrived at Fort Robinson. Clark had conveyed his fears to General Bradley, who had telegraphed General Sheridan, who ordered Crook to look into the situation. All the Indians at the Red Cloud Agency were told to move their camps to a central spot for a big council. Crazy Horse did not want to go to the council. He was afraid that there would be trouble there. General Bradley and another man had that afternoon given him presents of a knife and two cigars in a way that made him nervous. All the Indians at the Crazy Horse camp who wanted to go to the council were told to move from one side of Little Cottonwood Creek to the other. He Dog, a childhood friend of Crazy Horse who lived to be a hundred years old, told the other Crazy Horse Indians, "All who love their wife and children, let them come across the creek with me. All who want their wife and children to be killed by the soldiers, let them stay where they are." Later, in Crazy Horse's tipi, He Dog asked if moving across the creek would make him Crazy Horse's enemy. Crazy Horse laughed in his face and said, "I am no white man! They are the only people that make rules for other people, that say, 'If you stay on one side of this line it is peace, but if you go on the other side I will kill you all.' I don't hold with deadlines. There is plenty of room; camp where you please."

Soon after, as General Crook and Lieutenant Clark were on their way to the council, a Sioux named Woman Dress came up to their interpreters and said that Crazy Horse planned to kill Crook at the council. Woman Dress told the interpreters that a man named Lone Bear had said that a man named Little Wolf had said that Crazy Horse was going to grab Crook when he shook his hand, and that sixty of his followers would then kill Crook and all the people with him. Crook asked the interpreters, William Garnett and Baptiste Pourier, if Woman Dress was reliable, and Pourier, whose wife was Woman Dress's wife's first cousin, said he was. Crook said, "I never start any place but what I like to get there." Clark said the Army had already lost one irreplaceable man in General Custer. Crook said what excuse could he make. Clark said he'd take care of it.

Crook turned back, and Clark sent William Garnett to the council to tell the Indians that a message had come for Crook and he had to leave. Neither Crazy Horse nor his followers were at the council. Clark also gave Garnett a list of Indians to summon to the fort. Then, in General Bradley's apartments at the fort (Bradley himself being absent), Crook, Clark, Grouard, Pourier, Garnett, and thirteen Sioux, including chiefs Red Cloud and American Horse, plotted to kill Crazy Horse that night in his camp. Clark offered $300 and his fast sorrel horse as a reward to the man who did it.

In the conductive atmosphere around the fort, General

Bradley immediately found out about the plot. He said that he would not countenance such an attack, and ordered Clark to call it off. Crook outranked Bradley, but since Crook's participation in the plot—and the plot itself—was unofficial, Clark obeyed. Crazy Horse found out almost as quickly as Bradley did. He had given his gun and gun case to Red Feather, and so awaited the attack in his camp armed only with a knife.

Sometime the same day, Crook gave Bradley orders to capture Crazy Horse, jail him, and send him east under guard on the railroad. Crook then left. Before sunup the next morning, eight companies of cavalry and 250 Indian scouts—about 850 men in all—assembled at the fort and then rode in two columns to Crazy Horse's camp to make the arrest. When they got there, they found that Crazy Horse, his wife Black Shawl, and others of his band had left for the Spotted Tail Agency. (Crazy Horse's second wife, the eighteen-year-old Nellie Larrabee, stayed behind.) Clark offered a reward of $200 to the man who caught Crazy Horse, and fifteen or twenty Indian scouts rode fast in the direction of Spotted Tail. Crazy Horse and Black Shawl arrived at Spotted Tail in the afternoon, just ahead of their pursuers. The scouts finally caught up and asked Crazy Horse to return with them, and he said, "I am Crazy Horse! Don't touch me! I'm not running away!"

Agent Lee had warned Clark not to let Crazy Horse get away from the Red Cloud Agency, and Clark, who had many spies among the Indians, had said that Crazy Horse couldn't make a move without his knowing. The sudden arrival of Crazy Horse at Spotted Tail struck Agent Lee "like a clap of thunder." It also caused near-panic among Crazy Horse's many friends there. In the camp of the Miniconjou—most of whom, like Crazy Horse, had only recently come into the agency—all three hundred tipis came down in an instant as the people prepared for flight. If more experienced agency Indians hadn't talked them out of it, they and Crazy Horse might have taken off across the prairie, with a new Indian war the likely result.

Instead, a force of three hundred armed Miniconjou then rode with Crazy Horse to the office of the post commander. Crazy Horse had come to the Spotted Tail Agency to get away from the danger and intrigue at Red Cloud, and he wanted permission to stay. At the post's parade ground, they were met by an equal number of armed Brulé Sioux loyal to their chief, Spotted Tail. Before this multitude, an Indian named Buffalo Chips called Crazy Horse a coward and demanded that the authorities hang him in his place. The commanding officer laughed and said, "We don't want to hang you; we don't want to hang anybody." Then Spotted Tail made a speech to Crazy Horse about how peaceful this place was and how great the power of Spotted Tail. He concluded, "If you stay here, you must listen to me! That is all!" Crazy Horse then went in the office and met with Agent Lee. "He seemed like a frightened, trembling wild animal brought to bay," Lee said later.

By messenger, Clark had asked Lee to have Crazy Horse arrested when he arrived. Saying nothing about the arrest order, Lee told Crazy Horse that he must return to Fort Robinson to talk with General Bradley. Crazy Horse was ready to agree to anything at that point. Lee told Crazy Horse to come back at nine the next morning to leave for Fort Robinson, and the post commander made Touch the Clouds responsible for his safekeeping during the night.

Black Shawl was sick with a swollen arm, and Crazy

Horse left her in the care of her mother, who was camped with Spotted Tail's band. When he met Lee the next morning at nine, he said he had changed his mind about going back. He said he "was afraid something would happen." Lee said that no one would hurt him, that he owed it to his band at Red Cloud, and that he should return peaceably. Crazy Horse finally agreed to go if Lee accompanied him on the journey. He also asked that neither of them take arms, that he be allowed to explain the interpreter's mistake to Bradley, and that he be transferred to Spotted Tail. Lee promised everything except the transfer, and they and an interpreter set out with an escort of Indians—some friends to Crazy Horse, some not. Lee asked him to ride in the ambulance (a closed wagon for carrying troops), but Crazy Horse said he preferred to ride horseback. He said riding in the ambulance made him sick. By the time they were about halfway, over forty Indian scouts from Spotted Tail had joined them. Crazy Horse may have realized then that he was a prisoner. At one point he suddenly galloped away over a ridge, and in the next valley met an Indian family. He stopped and talked with them, and they may have given him a knife. The Spotted Tail scouts quickly overtook him. Lee then told him to stay behind the ambulance. The rest of the way, Crazy Horse was closely watched, and seemed "nervous and bewildered," Lee said.

When they reached Fort Robinson, Lee left Crazy Horse in the adjutant's office and went to ask General Bradley that Crazy Horse be allowed to speak to him. Lee and his interpreter were afraid that when Crazy Horse was jailed, the Crazy Horse Indians would kill them for bringing Crazy Horse here. On the parade ground, Lee met Dr. Mc-Gillycuddy, and said, "I'm not going to be made a goat of in this affair." But General Bradley told Lee that Crazy Horse must be locked up, and that not even General Crook himself could change the order. Bradley knew, because he had wired Crook asking to have the order revoked before Crazy Horse arrived. Crazy Horse's fate had been decided by someone further up. According to the *Times*, "It was the intention of General Sheridan to send him to the Dry Tortugas and keep him there." The Dry Tortugas are a small atoll in the Gulf of Mexico, about seventy miles due west of Key West, Florida. The Army had a fort and a prison there, with cells which were holes dug in the coral with bars across the top.

Agent Lee came back and told Crazy Horse that it was too late in the day for General Bradley to talk to him. He said that he would have a chance to talk tomorrow. Then he repeated the only order that Bradley had given: Crazy Horse was to go with the officer of the day, and "not a hair of his head should be harmed." Crazy Horse's face lighted up at this, and he warmly shook the hand of the officer of the day, Captain Kennington. Little Big Man, an old friend who had ridden next to Crazy Horse at the surrender, walked by his side. Agent Lee then went to join his wife, who was staying with friends at the post.

Frank Grouard, the interpreter who had helped create this mess, watched as Crazy Horse crossed from the adjutant's office to the jail. "I could tell by the way he walked into the guard house that he did not know that he was to be placed in confinement," Grouard said later. Noticing Dr. McGillycuddy, Crazy Horse half nodded. In front of the guardhouse, a sentry was marching up and down. Crazy Horse, Captain Kennington, Little Big Man, and several Indians passed the sentry and went through the door. Crazy

Horse had never seen the inside of a jail before. When the Indians with him saw the bars, several shouted "It's the jail!" and came running out. From under his blanket, Crazy Horse drew a knife and began slashing back and forth in an attempt to get out. As he came through the door, his friend Little Big Man pinned his arms behind him. Crazy Horse cut Little Big Man across the base of the thumb and base of the forefinger, and tried to stab Kennington. Little Big Man began to howl, an eyewitness said, "as though he was half killed." Hundreds of Indians on horseback and on foot were now all around the outside of the jail. They were yelling. Some were trying to grab Crazy Horse. The leg irons of the white prisoners inside were clattering. Kennington was shouting, "Stab the son of a bitch! Kill him! Kill him!" The sentry, possibly a forty-seven-year-old private from County Tyrone, Ireland, named William Gentles, unshouldered his rifle and stabbed Crazy Horse twice through the abdomen with his bayonet. A third thrust missed and stuck in the doorsill. Crazy Horse turned completely around on his left foot and fell over backward. He said, "He has killed me now."

A guard of twenty soldiers made a ring around Crazy Horse. His father was one of the first to get to him. "I felt awful sorry for the old man for he loved that son," a member of the guard said later. On either side, pro- and anti-Crazy Horse Indians shouted and sang war chants, "bending and swaying like crouched tigers ready to spring at each other's throats," according to one eyewitness. The sound of shells being chambered and hammers being cocked was everywhere. Another member of the guard later said that it was lucky Crazy Horse was stabbed and not shot, because a single shot would certainly have started a fight. Dr.

McGillycuddy said, "I wedged my way in between the guard and found Crazy Horse on his back, grinding his teeth and frothing at the mouth, blood trickling from a bayonet wound above the hip, and the pulse weak and missing beats, and I saw that he was done for." Captain Kennington tried to lift Crazy Horse by the shoulders and return him to the guardhouse. Unanimously, the Indians stopped him.

Touch the Clouds, Crazy Horse's seven-foot Miniconjou friend, asked that Crazy Horse be allowed to die in an Indian lodge. Dr. McGillycuddy carried the request to General Bradley, adding that violence might result from putting Crazy Horse in the jail. Bradley said, "Please give my compliments to the officer of the day, and he is to carry out his original orders, and put Crazy Horse in the guard house." Dr. McGillycuddy relayed this to Kennington, who tried again. American Horse, who had recently conspired against Crazy Horse's life, protested that Crazy Horse was a chief, and could not be put in prison. Dr. McGillycuddy returned to Bradley and told him it would be death to try a third time. Bradley finally agreed to compromise and allow Crazy Horse to be taken to the adjutant's office, a small room with a desk, a kerosene lamp, and a cot. Several Indians carried him in a blanket and set him on the floor. He refused to lie on the cot.

It was then about five o'clock in the afternoon. Dr. McGillycuddy gave him a shot of morphine. Also present in the adjutant's office were Captain Kennington, another officer, an interpreter, Touch the Clouds, and Crazy Horse's father. All other Indians were ordered to leave the fort by sunset. The only light in the adjutant's office came from the kerosene lamp, which smoked. About ten o'clock in the evening, Crazy Horse asked to see Agent Lee. Still thinking that he might be killed, Lee looked at his wife for advice. She nodded yes. Over the protest of their friends, he went. Crazy Horse told Lee that he did not blame him. The first shot of morphine wore off, and Dr. McGillycuddy gave him another. Crazy Horse said that his people preferred hunting buffalo to living at the agencies, that they fought the soldiers because they were attacked, that he only wanted to be let alone, that he had come here just to talk. He was conscious and unconscious again. His father said, "Son, I am here." Crazy Horse said, "Father, it is no use to depend upon me; I am going to die." His father and Touch the Clouds both cried. Crazy Horse tossed back and forth. At 11:30, after a final struggle, he died. Touch the Clouds went over to the body lying on the floor and pulled the blanket over the face. He pointed to the blanket and said, "That is the lodge of Crazy Horse." Then he said, "The chief has gone above."

Almost instantly, news of the death spread to the Indian camps. The sleepless people at the fort, and the eight-hundred-man garrison which had been ordered to stay on the alert all night, heard the death wail rise all at once from the darkness for miles around. Frank Grouard, William Garnett, and another interpreter went to wake Lieutenant Clark, who had asked to be told if anything happened during the night. Clark was sleeping so soundly that they had to take him by the arms and legs and swing him; Garnett suspected he had taken something to make him sleep. When Clark heard the news, he said, "You go to bed. You are all played out. You are all afraid of him." Garnett answered that the soldiers were all afraid of him. In his diary, Agent Lee wrote the next day, "My part in this transaction is to me a source of torture." He also wrote that when he talked to General Bradley, "He did most of the talking. I felt so miserable that I could scarcely say anything . . ." Lieutenant Clark filed an official report stating that in the opinion of the physicians Crazy Horse must have stabbed himself with his own knife—which opinion Dr. McGillycuddy, for one, certainly did not have. The report filed by General Bradley gave a similar impression. No one ever received the $200 reward offered for Crazy Horse's capture; the Army ruled that Crazy Horse had not been captured.

Later that fall, the Army started moving the Sioux east to the Missouri, and got them partway there the following spring. After a couple of months, the Sioux turned around and came back west without permission. The Spotted Tail people stopped at what is now the Rosebud Reservation, and the Red Cloud people stopped at what is now the Pine Ridge Reservation. Private William Gentles died that following year of asthma. When he was dead, the Army may have found it convenient to name him as the man who stabbed Crazy Horse, in order to draw attention from someone else. Dr. McGillycuddy became Indian Agent at Pine Ridge, and began a long series of feuds with Chief Red Cloud. A man named Crow Dog shot and killed Chief Spotted Tail to advance his own political career, and served four years in jail for the crime. Nellie Larrabee was remarried, to a man named Greasing Hand, who then took the name Crazy Horse. Black Shawl never remarried, and lived until the late 1920s. Sherman turned down several chances to run for President. Lieutenant Clark died suddenly in Washington, D.C., in 1884; he was thirty-nine.

Nine or ten years after Crazy Horse was killed, interpreter William Garnett found out that Woman Dress had lied about Crazy Horse's supposed plan to kill General Crook at the council. Baptiste Pourier found out, too, and he told Woman Dress, "You are a liar and you are the cause of a good man's death." To this accusation, "Woman Dress said not a word," according to Garnett. When Garnett ran into Crook in 1889, he passed this along. "I ought to have gone to that council and I should not have listened to Clark," Crook said. "I never started any place but I got there."

Wailing, Crazy Horse's parents took his body by travois from the adjutant's office all the way back to the Spotted Tail Agency, the place he had hoped to move to. There they put it on a platform on a hill within sight of the post. They remained beside the grave for three days straight. Agent Lee's wife made up a basket of "good food and a bottle of hot coffee," and Lee took it up to them. He also brought a carpenter and some posts and rough planks, and built a fence to keep the wolves away. Later, Crazy Horse's body was moved. Some people say he was placed in a crevice in a bluff and buried under a rockslide. The list of his alleged burial sites is long. Because he possibly said that his bones would turn to rocks and his joints to flint, Indian boys used to search the hills for his petrified remains. No one knows for sure where Crazy Horse's bones lie.

In the Black Hills, near the town of Custer, South Dakota, sculptors are carving a statue of Crazy Horse from a six-hundred-foot-high mountain of granite. The rock, called Thunderhead Mountain, is near Mt. Rushmore. The man who began the statue was a Boston-born sculptor named Korczak Ziolkowski, and he became inspired to the work after receiving a letter from Henry Standing Bear, a Sioux chief, in 1939. Standing Bear asked Ziolkowski if he would be interested in carving a memorial to Crazy Horse as a way of honoring heroes of the Indian people. The idea so appealed to Ziolkowski that he decided to make the largest statue in the world: Crazy Horse, on horseback, with his left arm outstretched and pointing. From Crazy Horse's shoulder to the tip of his index finger would be 263 feet. A forty-four-foot stone feather would rise above his head. Ziolkowski worked on the statue from 1947 until his death in 1982. As the project progressed, he added an Indian museum and a university and medical school for Indians to his plans for the grounds around the statue. Since his death, his wife and children have carried on the work.

The Black Hills, sacred to generations of Sioux and Cheyenne, are now filled with T-shirt stores, reptile gardens, talking wood carvings, wax museums, gravity mystery areas ("See and feel cosmos—the only gravity mystery area that is family approved"), etc. Before I went there, I thought the Crazy Horse monument would be just another attraction. But it is wonderful. In all his years of blasting, bulldozing, and chipping, Ziolkowski removed over eight million tons of rock. You can just begin to tell. There is an outline of the planned sculpture on the mountain, and parts of the arm and the rider's head are beginning to emerge. The rest of the figure still waits within Thunderhead Mountain—Ziolkowski's descendants will doubtless be working away in the year 2150. This makes the statue in its present state an unusual attraction, one which draws a million visitors annually: it is a ruin, only in reverse. Instead of looking at it and imagining what it used to be, people stand at the observation deck and say, "Boy, that's really going to be great someday." The gift shop is extensive and prosperous; buses with "Crazy Horse" in the destination window bring tourists from nearby Rapid City; Indian chants play on speakers in the Indian museum; Boy Scouts, Girl Scouts, local residents, and American Indians get in free. The Crazy Horse monument is the one place on the plains where I saw lots of Indians smiling.

Korczak Ziolkowski is not the only person ever to feel strong emotion at the thought of Crazy Horse. Some, both Indian and non-Indian, regard him with a reverence which borders on the holy. Others do not get the point at all. George Hyde, who has written perhaps the best books about the western Sioux, says of the admirers of Crazy Horse, "They depict Crazy Horse as the kind of being never seen on earth: a genius in war, yet a lover of peace; a statesman, who apparently never thought of the interests of any human being outside his own camp; a dreamer, a mystic, and a kind of Sioux Christ, who was betrayed in the end by his own disciples—Little Big Man, Touch the Clouds . . . and the rest. One is inclined to ask, what is it all about?"

Personally, I love Crazy Horse because even the most basic outline of his life shows how great he was; because he remained himself from the moment of his birth to the moment he died; because he knew exactly where he wanted to live, and never left; because he may have surrendered, but he was never defeated in battle; because, although he was killed, even the Army admitted he was never captured; because he was so free that he didn't know what a jail looked like; because at the most desperate moment of his life he only cut Little Big Man on the hand; because, unlike many people all over the world, when he met white men he was not diminished by the encounter; because his dislike of the oncoming civilization was prophetic; because the idea of becoming a farmer apparently never crossed his mind; because he didn't end up in the Dry Tortugas; because he never met the President; because he never rode on a train, slept in a boardinghouse, ate at a table; because he never wore a medal or a top hat or any other thing that white men gave him; because he made sure that his wife was safe before going to where he expected to die; because although Indian agents, among themselves, sometimes referred to Red Cloud as "Red" and Spotted Tail as "Spot," they never used a diminutive for him; because, deprived of freedom, power, occupation, culture, trapped in a situation where bravery was invisible, he was still brave; because he fought in self-defense, and took no one with him when he died; because, like the rings of Saturn, the carbon atom, and the underwater reef, he belonged to a category of phenomena which our technology had not then advanced far enough to photograph; because no photograph or painting or even sketch of him exists; because he is not the Indian on the nickel, the tobacco pouch, or the apple crate. Crazy Horse was a slim man of medium height with brown hair hanging below his waist and a scar above his lip. Now, in the mind of each person who imagines him, he looks different.

I believe that when Crazy Horse was killed, something more than a man's life was snuffed out. Once, America's size in the imagination was limitless. After Europeans settled and changed it, working from the coasts inland, its size in the imagination shrank. Like the center of a dying fire, the Great Plains held that original vision longest. Just as people finally came to the Great Plains and changed them, so they came to where Crazy Horse lived and killed him. Crazy Horse had the misfortune to live in a place which existed both in reality and in the dreams of people far away;

he managed to leave both the real and the imaginary place unbetrayed. What I return to most often when I think of Crazy Horse is the fact that in the adjutant's office he refused to lie on the cot. Mortally wounded, frothing at the mouth, grinding his teeth in pain, he chose the floor instead. What a distance there is between that cot and the floor! On the cot, he would have been, in some sense, "ours": an object of pity, an accident victim, "the noble red man, the last of his race, etc. etc." But on the floor Crazy Horse was Crazy Horse still. On the floor, he began to hurt as the morphine wore off. On the floor, he remembered Agent Lee, summoned him, forgave him. On the floor, unable to rise, he was guarded by soldiers even then. On the floor, he said goodbye to his father and Touch the Clouds, the last of the thousands that once followed him. And on the floor, still as far from white men as the limitless continent they once dreamed of, he died. Touch the Clouds pulled the blanket over his face: "That is the lodge of Crazy Horse." Lying where he chose, Crazy Horse showed the rest of us where we are standing. With his body, he demonstrated that the floor of an Army office was part of the land, and that the land was still his.

Crazy Horse was my gran'father!

7

NOTES from a 6,000-mile ramble on the plains:

Stopped to fish on Blackfeet Indian Reservation. Couldn't find lake at first—drove past the turnout. Went back and saw little hand-lettered sign: "Mission Lake." Long way down dirt road. Wind at my back so strong that my dust trail was actually in front of me. My van full of dust—dust gritting between my back teeth. Parked, set up fly rod, put on waders. Whitecaps on lake. Waded in—whitecaps splashing against me. Hard to cast. Two Indians appeared on bank carrying two shopping bags. They took out Bud tallboys, opened them, took out hand line wrapped around empty beer can, started whipping the line bolo-style, casting into lake. One Indian walked over to where I was, asked, "What're you using?" I said, "Well, right now I've got on a weighted hare's ear nymph in size 12 tied with olive dubbing instead of brown and a little gold ribbing around the body. What're you using?" He said, "Leeches."

Caught nothing—no strikes. Gave up. Back on the highway, truck in front of me missed gear, stopped suddenly on incline. I hit brakes, said, "Jesus Christ!" Stopped close enough to read his bumper sticker, which said, "We Are One In The Spirit."

Stayed in the Bell Motel in Glasgow, Montana. Ate at a restaurant called Sam's Supper Club: two cold Rainier beers in bottle, relish tray (hot peppers, celery), prime rib (fatty and excellent), potatoes in a cheddar-cheese sauce with chives, homemade maple-walnut ice cream for dessert. Wind blowing grit into the intersections in waves. Trains behind the motel at night. Horrible yellow "European Bathing Gel" in motel shower.

Next day drove to Fort Union. Ranger leading tourists around the fort site. One woman tourist to another: "I had so many clothes in my closet I broke the closet rods!" Group standing around the ranger half-attentive, dreamy. Gal in peach shorts and a white top raised a baby to her shoulders and held him there, white arms in a classical pose.

Sat in park overlooking Missouri–Yellowstone confluence a long time and thought. Wind whipping across sandbar on opposite shore, sand blowing across water. Pelicans (!) flying in a roller-coaster type of formation over water. Lone deer grazing across the Missouri, very red in setting sun. I clapped hands; a second later, hearing me, he looked up. Ate sandwich. Prairie dog pestering me.

Left after sunset, intending to camp in Teddy Roosevelt Park, since camping at Yellowstone–Mo. not allowed. Crossed bridge over Mo., one-lane railroad bridge with boards for cars to drive on alongside rails. Van's wheels trolleying. Buttes lit up by sun, about the height of a cruise ship, blue sky and mare's-tail clouds above. Soon after bridge, came upon oil-drilling rig in full operation, nine-thirty at night. It was tall and lit with bars of fluorescent light to top. They were pulling pipe from well. Foreman had the kind of whistle that people who can really do it are born with and have been showing off since grade school. Piercing, piercing whistling rasping through teeth, could easily be heard over engine. Two-three guys would hook cable to end of pipe, foreman would whistle, cable would pull pipe up, men disconnect section, whistle, move section, whistle, section deposited with other sections in huge rack on rig. Then pull next section. Men working hard—absorbed, mobile. Clouds of diesel smoke blowing back from engine's stack over all the men in the wind.

Campsite unfindable in dark. Drove up and down same road five times. No light anywhere but my headlights. Finally pulled over, slept. Kept parking lights on. Every half hour or so, a car would go by singing like a sewing machine. Next morning woke and saw campsite across the road.

Bright sun. Cottonwoods just starting yellow in the valley of Beaver River west of Wibaux, Montana. Wibaux once greatest primary shipping point for livestock in West. Population now: 740. Everywhere, wheat fields. Coming over rise on dirt road near Beach, N.D.—all you'd need to paint landscape would be gold for wheat and blue for sky. Strips of summer fallow stencilled on the side of a butte all the way to the caprock. From a car, summer-fallow strips on rolling earth wave like stripes on a flag.

Badlands along Little Missouri River. Land cut vertically as many ways, in as many shapes, as erosion can cut it. North Dakota State Highway 22—a road so straight and empty I set a book on the steering wheel and read. Bear Butte State Park, South Dakota; Crazy Horse born near here. The Black Hills: winding roads, motor homes, smell of gift-shop candles. Eastern Wyoming. Grass long and mussed by wind. Clear water in creeks. Horsehead oil pumps pumping. Storm clouds piling up against Black Hills to east. Searchlight beams of sun coming through holes in clouds. Above the plain, a perfect double rainbow. Sign on bridge: "Beaver Creek." This is where Crazy Horse wanted his agency to be.

I talked to:

Gas station attendants. Whenever I stopped for gas, I always asked the name of the local high-school team. I never found a person working in a gas station, convenience store, or truck stop who didn't know. In Deer Lodge, Montana, the team is called the Wardens; Deer Lodge is the home of the state prison. In Havre, Montana, the team is the Havre Blue Ponies. In Newcastle, Wyoming, it's the Newcastle Dogies. In Brush, Colorado, it's the Brush Beet Diggers. Beaver, Oklahoma, has the Dusters; Oakley, Kansas, the Plainsmen; McCamey, Texas, the Badgers; Tucumcari, New Mexico, the Rattlers; Matador, Texas, the Matadors. Colby, Kansas; Eads, Colorado; Hondo, New Mexico; and Pecos, Texas, all call themselves the Eagles. Chappell, Nebraska; Rush, Colorado; and Chugwater, Wyoming, all are the Buffalos. At a gas station near an Indian reservation in Montana, a white gas-station attendant told me that Indian basketball teams are easy to beat. He said all you have to do is punch one guy, and then the whole team will attack you and get kicked out of the game.

A Hunkpapa Sioux woman named Doreet. I picked her up hitchhiking with another woman and two men. Doreet sat in the front seat and told me that her brother recently found a stone serpent head while diving in the river, that she had a young son named Eagle on His Journey, that a medicine man had predicted that Journey (his nickname) would be born either retarded or dead, that the medicine man was wrong. In the back, Jason, Derek, and I didn't get the other woman's name, talked in Sioux and sometimes asked me questions like "So, bro, what do you think of the Sioux people?" Of a nearby butte, Doreet said, "That's Devil Butte. High-school kids go up there and try to arrange these white rocks to spell out their initials, but by morning the rocks always rearrange themselves into the shape of a devil's head." Doreet was big, pretty, with scars up both arms. She was wearing a Cornell T-shirt. I asked her, "Did you go to Cornell?" She said, "Where's that?" I pointed to the name on her shirt. She said, "Oh, probably—I've been all over the country."

Two young guys named John and Tom. They gave me a ride to the site of Sitting Bull's cabin in Tom's red four-wheel custom deluxe Dodge pickup. (I had been to the site before, with Jim Yellow Earring, but I wanted to go back, to make sure the trees over the monument were actually bur oaks.) It was pouring rain. As I looked for the turnoff, my van slid off the road. John and Tom drove up, regarded me in silence, helped me get unstuck, and told me they'd take me to Sitting Bull for some money. I got in their truck. I asked them what they were doing out here.

John: "Drinkin' and driving around."

Tom: "Nothin' else to do when it rains like this."

J: "What do you want to go back there for, anyway? It ain't that much different from anyplace else."

T: "We take people to Sittin' Bull all the time. People like you, come back here in their two-wheel-drives, get stuck—"

J: "Indians down in Bullhead give 'em directions, don't say nothin' 'bout gettin' stuck."

T: "Indians don't care about gettin' stuck. They got nothin' to do anyway. Government pays 'em just to lay around."

J: "Last winter some guy in a Cadillac all the way from California gave us a hundred dollars to take him to Sittin' Bull. Snowdrifts were ten feet deep. He just wanted to see it, take a picture."

T: "We make a lot of party money takin' people out to Sittin' Bull."

The floor of the truck was shin-deep in beer cans. They finished the twelve-pack, pushed the box out the window. The truck roared and ripped down the last descent to the river valley. The front wheels threw fist-sized pieces of prairie through the windows. John and Tom rolled the windows up. In some parts of the flatland along the river, water came above the wheel wells. Grasses waved in the wake the truck left. "This ain't tough—not for *my* pickup," Tom said. We sped right up to the Sitting Bull monument. I hopped out, walked over, plucked a leaf from the bur oak above it.

My old friend George Scott. He is a rancher who lives southwest of Casper, Wyoming. (He is the same one who told me about the "early-man tools.") George and I became friends in college. In the riots in the spring of 1970, he and I ran from the cops together, and later went to the Red Cross first-aid station and pretended to have been tear-gassed so that the beautiful hippie-girl volunteers would bathe our eyes with cool compresses. Summer, 1970, I worked as a hand on his family's 14,000-acre ranch. Today

George is married and has two children. With his older brother, Charlie, he runs a second, much larger ranch which his family bought in 1971. George is tall, red-haired, freckled, with deep squint lines at the outside corners of his blue eyes. He drinks six or seven Pepsis a day. All the men in his family stick their tongues out to one side and bite them when they concentrate, like boys building models in old-time illustrations.

I spent four nights sleeping in my van in George's driveway. His driveway is long, dirt, with ruts that keep redefining themselves to one side or another. After leaving his house, it passes his brother Charlie's house, the bunkhouse, an equipment barn, a horse barn, and a long, low cow barn with a green roof. Alongside the driveway are tractors, pickups, a three-wheel motorcycle with a shovel strapped across the back, tanks of gas and diesel for ranch vehicles, bent pieces of irrigation pipe which somebody ran over by mistake, horse trailers, kids' bikes, stray hay bales, sleeping or running dogs, and an old sheepherders' wagon, which looks like a mini covered wagon. Beyond George's house, the driveway crosses an irrigation ditch and heads off into fields of alfalfa and Sudan grass. Nights I spent there were quiet, except when I bumped the inside of my van in my sleep and started the dogs barking.

George's wife, Milcey, made us breakfast at six, and he and I were usually off driving somewhere by seven. The ranch's homeplace is the capital of tens of thousands of acres stretching in a patchwork for more than fifty miles. We drove through pastures big enough to have their own rainfall pattern. Along a straightaway, a coyote raced the truck, his tongue flapping beside him like a tie. I saw a golden eagle the size of a building ornament sitting in a field doing nothing. Across the plain, a herd of antelope ran, and then pivoted all at once like a school of fish. A single antelope stood in the line of shadow of a telephone pole. George did a lot of work through small bird-watching binoculars. He would drive to a ridge, look for cattle, drive to another ridge, look again. Near a cabin where a hay hand named Eggleston killed himself one winter, we stopped and fished for brook trout in the Little Medicine Bow River. The spot was so ancient that I wondered what its name had been eight thousand years ago. The windowsills of the cabin were piled with worked pieces of stone—choppers, grinders, scrapers, points—which had been found around there. Then George drove to a place where he wanted to build a three-hundred-yard fence to keep cattle from drifting, and met with an agent of the Bureau of Land Management, who had to okay the fence before it was built: like a lot of range-land, this pasture is on long-term lease from the federal government. George wanted to build a four-strand fence, but the BLM would allow only a three-strand fence, because a BLM biologist had ruled that this land was primary antelope habitat, and four-strand was too liable to cut antelope up. At the side of the road, leaning against their vehicles, George and the BLM agent discussed this, and also maybe ten other topics. The sun rose higher and crossed their faces. George applied and reapplied chapstick to his lips. Lip cancer is something ranchers worry about.

Another day, George rounded up some yearling calves for sale. He told me he had a wild horse for me to ride at the roundup. I said, "That's just fine—I've stomped down many a bronc in my day!" Russell Brown, George's nineteen-year-old top hand, laughed. We went to the corral and caught and saddled the horses. I wasn't much help. The horses did not want to get in the trailer. Russell mounted his horse, rode off, and rode back at full gallop toward the trailer. At the last second, he jumped from the saddle and swung on the trailer roof as the horse went in. The others followed easily after that. George's kids, Jessica and Chris, rode along in the back seat of George's crew-cab Ford pickup. Chris: "Dad, Jessie keeps repeating my words!" The truck was working hard to pull the loaded trailer up hills. Suddenly—*whompf!*—the radiator hose blew. All the coolant hit the engine block in a tumult of steam. We got out and ate our bologna sandwiches on white bread and drank Pepsis by the side of the road while George called Milcey on the radio. The wind blew so hard the bread got stale in our hands. Then we listened to oil-rig workers placing nervous requests over the radio for Oil Sorb, a product used to soak up oil spills. Milcey came with a new radiator hose and jugs of coolant. Soon we drove on.

George and Russell were talking about a white-face yearling that had run off earlier in the summer. They hadn't seen him in two months, but they'd heard from a neighbor that he was in the vicinity. As we came over a rise, in the road ahead was a white-face calf. "That can't be him," George said. He took out his binoculars and read the number of the calf's ear tag. "I don't believe it!" Russell and George opened the horse trailer, took out their horses, unlimbered their ropes. Whiteface stood in the road with a dawning sense of dread, then turned and ran. George and Russell took off like a drag race. The calf dodged, cut back; George threw his loop, missed; Russell came whipping through sagebrush, threw, stopped short, the rope twanged, the calf's hind feet flew up in the air. The roped calf was up instantly, bawling hoarsely, shaking his head. George rode over and roped him. It took two horses to move him, stiff-legged, crow-hopping, bellowing, to the trailer. Russell held him while George backed the trailer up to the side of a bank so the calf could walk in. They maneuvered the calf to the door. George undid the rope from his saddle horn, and the calf dodged around the other side of the trailer and pulled Russell's horse up against it. George grabbed the calf and Russell undid his rope. The calf bellowed, bucked, kicked the outside of the trailer. George had him by the head, then he only had him by the foot, then the calf was loose and running across the prairie, this time trailing two ropes. Russell borrowed Jessica's rope and chased him again. After another big struggle, the calf was in the trailer. He stood there panting, eyes crazed.

We reached the place for the roundup and unloaded the horses. Russell and George were instantly gliding up this hill and that, collecting little black specks of cattle into a bigger and bigger mass. Jessica, Chris, and I rode along the creek bed looking for strays. My horse did nothing I wanted. Finally I went back to the corral and got off and left him as if he were a car. George and Russell brought the yearling herd and its cloud of dust into the corral. Later two cattle trucks came, and the drivers put coveralls over their regular clothes and hazed the yearlings into the trucks. The drivers poked with cattle prods and shouted, "*On* the bus! *Git* on the bus!" Then all the yearlings, including the whiteface who almost got away, were taken to Torrington, Wyoming, and sold at auction to a feedlot for 65 cents a pound.

Another morning, stopping the truck occasionally for me to get out and open fence gates, George said, "The cattle in this field are our best herd. We've been trying for a long time to come up with a way to select our best cows and put them in a pasture with our best bulls, and this bunch Charlie finally selected with a new computer program he wrote. We've got two computers on the ranch. I hardly do anything with them, but Charlie spent three hours every morning—he got up at five—and then he'd work two or three hours every night, and he finally came up with a program that would tell us which cows produced the best calves. Each of these cows has her own computer card. The software companies sell several different ranch programs, but none of them really do what we wanted. We think the program Charlie wrote is better than any you can buy. See, the commercial programs all rate calves in terms of weaning weight—that's the calf's weight at about six months. But we wanted a program that used weight gain per month instead. That's what's important in a calf—how fast he puts on weight, rather than how much he weighs at any one time. Our ranch is a cow-calf operation. Most cattle ranches in Wyoming are. We raise calves for sale to feedlots, which fatten them up to market weight. What's really hurt the beef-cattle industry is this recent idea that red meat is bad for you. I agree, actually, that corn-fed feedlot beef has too much fat, and I wouldn't be surprised if it caused some of that stuff they say it does. But that's just a result of the feedlot system in this country, along with the fact that people nowadays want meat so tender you don't have to chew it. That type of meat is not what beef is, really. We eat a cow of ours about every other month, and it's not tender. Grass-fed beef is good, but it's tough. Charlie wants to start a campaign to get people to eat grass-fed beef as a health food. It's got all the protein, but the cattle haven't been eating antibiotics and the meat isn't fat. That's the kind of project Charlie likes to work on—that, and computers, and irrigation systems, and machinery. He does that, and I work with cattle. I like beating on things and making them do what I want."

We turned down a fence line through high sagebrush. The truck drove over bushes as high as the hood, and the smell of crushed sage rose. Suddenly there was another smell, very strong. George hit the brakes. "What was that?" We got out. Right next to the fence was a dead calf. Its lip was up off its teeth and its side was a metropolis of maggots. George bent over and noted the number of the calf's ear tag in a green notebook. Then he got back in the truck. He said, "One fact you learn in ranching is that things have a tendency to die."

Other people:

A guy working in a wheat storage yard in Limon, Colorado. He was standing in the doorway of a warehouse, with wheat spilling out around his ankles. Above him, wheat poured from a long pipe-on-wheels into the back of a grain truck. I watched him work for a while. Then I asked him what the pipe-on-wheels was called. He said, "A grain auger." He chinned himself on the side of the truck and looked in to see how full it was. He told me, "A grain auger is like a conveyor, only it uses a screw instead of a belt. We're moving wheat from this warehouse to that elevator. We just loaded out all the wheat in that elevator. That'n holds 280,000 bushels. This warehouse holds 250,000. Right now, wheat is $2.60 a bushel. So, in here we got between half and three-quarters of a million dollars' worth of wheat. This is hard red number-one wheat. This'll go to a bakery. Some of this wheat is five years old, some is six years old, some is eight years old. Some is even older—

Russian grain-embargo wheat that we didn't sell to Russia back when Carter was President. If you watch it carefully, wheat will keep indefinitely. The way we watch it is we have temperature sensors that go down into the wheat, and we make sure the temperature at this time of year stays right at forty to fifty degrees. When it goes above that, you know you're getting rot or insects." He turned and waded back into the wheat and chopped at it with a shovel.

A table of coffee drinkers in a Colorado cafe. They were wearing Cenex caps, khaki work shirts, black rubber boots. One guy had a T-shirt that said, "Peter Marshall Golf Classic." Another guy was leaning back in his chair and swatting here and there with a flyswatter.

"I just got done shingling the doghouse roof. I'm exhausted."

"Did you see here in the papers where Billy Dawson— *thwap!*—well, he wasn't angry, but I guess you could say he didn't like it too much that these people were goin' through his pasture and litterin' and so forth. Seems to me we never used to think a thing about people goin' through our pasture, lookin' for arrowheads or just walkin'. Jake, did you ever think you shouldn't go into somebody's pasture, or did you ever think if you didn't ask they might get mad?"

"Noooooh! Why, I'd just walk in and—"

"It's these damn antelope hunters. I don't mind feeding the antelope half as much as I mind the damage those antelope hunters do."

"You know, I went to Meet the Teams at the high school last night and I really enjoyed myself. I hadn't had a chance to see the new band uniforms. My, they are nice."

"Seems to me we didn't ever have to worry about people abusin' our pastures until all these—*thwap!*—Texans came in here with their big hats and their belt buckles—"

"—And the suitcase farmers. They'd come in and plow up a bunch of ground and when it didn't rain they'd pack up and leave the dust to blow on the rest of us."

"Hey, Dad? Dad? *Dad!*"

"Yeah?"

"My gum's pretty good."

"—all these Texas farmers that moved in here in the forties and started plowin' up the prairie and borrowin' money—"

"I was just talking to Stancil down at the bank and he said they aren't lending money for hay. Of course, right now that's what everybody needs to buy. So I suppose that means that they just aren't lending money, period."

"—these big farmers that came in from out of state and started borrowin' money—a $5,000 tractor, a $25,000 combine, a $125,000 house—and then any time it went a couple years without rain they'd be cryin for the government to help, and they're still doin' it today [*thwap!*]."

In the West of the Pecos Museum, in Pecos, Texas, I met a woman named Phyllis. She showed me the bullet holes in the windowsill, the floor, and the door of what used to be a saloon before the museum took over. She said, "Of course, there were other shootings in here besides just the famous ones. There used to be some pretty raunchy characters come in this saloon. There was an old sheriff here named Louis Roberson, and if they got too raunchy for him, why, he shot 'em. Most people know Pecos as a cowboy town. They also know us for our cantaloupes. The sun and soil here grow the sweetest, best cantaloupes in the world. Used to be, farmers all around Pecos raised cantaloupes and shipped 'em out on the Southern Pacific to California or back East. Then about fifteen years ago everybody's wells just started to dry up. All the well water came from the Ogallala Aquifer, which is a big natural reservoir that's been there underground for millions of years. It stretches from here up through the Texas panhandle to Kansas all the way up to South Dakota. Farmers and ranchers all over who used that water had to sell out—they couldn't afford new wells, or they couldn't afford the power to pump up from so deep. There's not nearly as many cantaloupe farms here there used to be, and the creek beds are dry most of the year. Some people say now that the Ogallala Aquifer may be coming back up, that it's not so bad as we thought. But here in the old Orient Hotel courtyard there's an artesian well that used to have enough pressure to pump up to the third floor. I don't believe we'll ever see that again."

In Turkey, Texas, I met a woman named Mrs. Homer Lang. Turkey is in north Texas, just below the panhandle, and it was the hometown of country-music star Bob Wills, the King of Western Swing. Turkey's schools closed in 1973, when its district consolidated with nearby Quitaque, and today a few classrooms of the empty school building hold the Bob Wills Museum. Mrs. Lang was minding the museum, and knitting. She told me, "Just look all you want to. Then sign the register." I saw the original sheet music of the Bob Wills classic, "Stay a Little Longer," and a photo of Bob Wills and the Texas Playboys standing next to a giant loaf of Playboy bread, and a suit that once belonged to Bob Wills, and a photo of Bob Wills's horse, Punkin. No one had signed the register for eight days. Mrs. Lang said, "Nobody calls me Mrs. Lang except people tryin' to sell me something over the telephone. Most everybody around Turkey calls me Aint Zona. I never did know Bob Wills, myself. I've seen him when I was a girl. Now, Homer—my husband, he died three years ago this April—Homer knew him real well. He used to cut Homer's hair. Bob Wills went to Amarillo and took a six-week course in barbering and then he come back here and worked at Floyce Ham's barbershop in town. He was playin' dances in Turkey when he was twelve. I never did go to dances when I was a girl, and when I got old I didn't start. My mother always said you could make harm out of anything. Now, Homer did go. They used to clear out space next to the M System store and people would come from all around. The road was lined car-to-car plumb up to the hilltop. These days, everything in Turkey closes up on a Saturday night. My second son? He was the overseer on the roads? He always believed Turkey would come back on the map someday. Turkey used to have three hardware stores, three banks, three drugstores, three cafes, three lumberyards. Now there's houses empty, with the yards all gone back to shinnery—shinnery, that's sandpiles, weeds, bushes, land not good for nothin'. I worked twenty years in a cafe in town. We didn't have no radio, no television. Homer went to Fort Worth to enlist for World War I and they turned him back. They said they had already signed the Ar-*miss*-tice. My kids was pretty good-size before I ever got a refrigerator and they was up great big before I ever got an air conditioner. I was raised up a Democrat, but they ain't no party now. I still vote straight Democratic ticket. Lyndon Johnson, they say he was wrong with Vietnam, and I don't know about none of that, but he was for the poor people. I took a trip back East two years ago and I went to New York—that's the dirtiest place I was ever in, but then I didn't go down but one street—and then I went to Washington, D.C. I seen a lot of things. I saw the machine they set down on the moon. I saw the biggest bakery in the world. I saw Reagan's apartment. I was never much for having people do for me, but they took me special through Mrs. Reagan's kitchen. It was solid chrome. I don't believe you should set down and study on yourself. I've made seventy-five quilts in the last three years. I knit lap robes like this here. I lack about 125 of making fourteen thousand pies. Last night I made apricot and apple. My daughter's mother-in-law, she's a member of Church of Christ, she told me, 'Zona, the world is comin' to an end.' That was two years ago now. She talks to my granddaughter, and my granddaughter came to me and said, 'Mawmaw was prophesyin' that the world is comin' to an end.' I told her, 'I don't believe so, but it don't matter if it is. You're gonna set on your own bottom before the Lord no matter what.' We don't none of us know what's comin'. We don't have no *i*-dee."

The radio:

Maybe, when you're driving on the plains, you'll tune in Bob Wills and the Texas Playboys singing "Bring It on Down to My House, Honey (Ain't Nobody Home but Me)." Maybe you'll hear Roy Acuff doing "The Fireball Mail." Maybe you'll hear "Reckless Love and Bold Adventure," by Rose Maddox, or "Courtin' in the Rain," by T. Texas Tyler, or "Hang the Key on the Bunkhouse Door," by Wilf Carter, or "Cypress Grove Blues," by Doc

Watson, or "All of the Monkeys Ain't in the Zoo," by Tommy Collins, or "I'm a Natural Born Gamblin' Man," by Merle Travis, or "You Don't Know What Lonesome Is," by the Sons of the Pioneers ("I've got all the lonesomeness that the common law allows / You don't know what lonesome is 'til you get to herdin' cows"). Maybe you'll hear a good bluegrass song, like "Blue-Eyed Darlin'," by Bill Monroe and the Bluegrass Boys, that comes at you like a truckload of turkey gobblers. Or maybe a scary song, like "The Rubber Room," by Porter Wagoner, or a funny song, like "We Didn't Sink the *Bismarck*," by Homer and Jethro, or a talking song, like "To a Sleeping Beauty," by Jimmy Dean.

More likely, though, what you'll hear is "Hold on to the Night," by McGuffey Lane; "Hold On Hold Out," by Jackson Browne; "Hold on to Your Love," by Neil Young; "Hold on to My Love," by Jimmy Ruffin; "We're Gonna Hold On," by George Jones and Tammy Wynette; "Hold On Loosely," by .38 Special; "Holdin' On to Yesterday," by Ambrosia; "Holdin' On to the Love I've Got," by Barbara Mandrell; "Hold On (Don't You Be Sad Tonight, Love Will Be There)" by Gail Davies; "Hold On," by Santana; "Hand to Hold On to," by John Cougar-Mellencamp; "Baby, Hold On," by Eddie Money; "I'll Keep Holdin' On," by Jim Capaldi; "Hold On, Baby, Hold On," by Kansas; "Hold on to Your Dreams," by Billy Thorpe; or "Hold on Tight to Your Dream (*Accroche-toi à Ton Rêve*)," by the Electric Light Orchestra.

Weather:

On the northern plains, a radio announcer said, "It's going to get pretty windy tonight, so if there's anything you don't want to blow away, you'd better tie it down."

Clouds sped across the sky, and their shadows kept up across every kind of terrain. In 1846, Francis Parkman observed that a herd of buffalo being chased by Indian riders was "like the black shadow of a cloud, passing rapidly over swell after swell of the distant plain." Next to the road, horses grazed with their tails standing straight out in the wind, and dust devils spun across unplowed ground. Up ahead, in North Dakota, storm clouds came all the way down to the ground like an overhead garage door. Inside the storm, the ceiling was low, and the light was like the North Atlantic's. Fifteen minutes of driving put me back under blue skies again.

In a state park in southern Wyoming, I sat on a low sandstone ridge next to ruts made by travellers on the Oregon Trail. Next to the wide, five-foot-deep rut in the rock made by wagons and oxen is a narrow, three-foot-deep rut made by human feet. About 350,000 people travelled the two-thousand-mile trail from the settlements to the West Coast. About 34,000 died along the way. I watched as a rainstorm moved down the Platte River valley from the northwest. When the rain passed, the limbs of the wet trees were darker and their leaves were greener. By comparing weather descriptions in the daily journal entries of thirty-four travellers on the trail in 1849, one scholar has charted the storms that crossed the plains from April to July of that year.

I drove south into Colorado during the night, and six or more thunderstorms followed me. Any direction I looked, there were flashes—like the Fourth of July in New Jersey seen from an airplane. A flash as far away as the horizon lit for an instant long hallways of clouds. Lightning in the distance straight ahead sent reflections shooting all the way up the tarry wheel tracks on the pavement.

In New Mexico and west Texas, the hard white sky is screwed onto the earth like a lid, and the wind is as hot as a gust from a blow dryer. In Texas, the rate of evaporation makes twenty-two inches of rain there the same as fifteen inches at the Canadian border. Southward, the prairie grasses get more and more sparse; sage, greasewood, prickly pear, and mesquite take over. Mesquite trees have eight-inch thorns, delicate leaves like a locust tree's, and roots which go down 175 feet. Longhorn cattle grazed on mesquite, and dropped the seeds along the way on drives to the north. Today you can trace the old cattle trails from the air by following the mesquite. When mesquite takes over a field, little else will grow. Around each low tree, the earth is brown and bare. I began to see oil wells here and there among the mesquite, and pipelines, and tall, narrow heater-treater tanks. On the far southern plains, the oil towns of Plainview and Midland and Odessa rise like off-shore drilling rigs. In prosperous years, the push buttons of local pay telephones are smudged with oily fingerprints, and Laundromats have "Do Not Wash Rig Clothes Here" signs. In bad years, you see a lot of yard-sale signs and plywood windows. Between McCamey and Fort Stockton, Texas, I passed buttes fading up into hazy sky, land as flat as a piece of paper, buzzards jumping up off the shoulder reluctantly, a hawk raising dust with his wingbeats as he chased something around a bush, heat shimmers dancing, and a spider as big as a hand crossing the pavement. In Fort Stockton, I stopped and ate some Mexican food and stayed in a Motel 6 where they charged extra for a key to turn on the television and I saw a flea. The next morning I got in my van and headed back to Montana.

8

SOMETIMES I wasn't sure whether I was on the Great Plains or not. Around the edges it was hard to tell. In the Southwest, I figured that when the plants started looking too pointy I was heading into the desert. On U.S. Highway 64 near Cimarron, New Mexico, I passed a sign which said: "You are now at the Great Plains–Rocky Mountain Boundary. The Cimarron Range, one of the easternmost ranges of the Sangre de Cristo Mountains," but I kept going anyway. I wanted to see the little town of Lincoln, New Mexico, where the outlaw Billy the Kid shot some people about 110 years ago. The roads went along mountain canyons, through old Spanish and mining towns one after the next. Billy the Kid worked as a cowboy, but he was more a townie than a frontiersman. He was born Henry McCarty, possibly in New York City, possibly in 1859. His mother and stepfather ran a restaurant in Santa Fe. The shootings which made him famous by the age of twenty-one had mainly to do with a feud that developed between a lawyer and the owner of one of the general stores in Lincoln. In general, most famous Western gunmen were town people. They slept in boardinghouses, not under the stars. Wyatt Earp, who served as a lawman in Dodge City and other places, owned saloons, operated gambling halls, and died in Los Angeles. After a career on various sides of the law in places like Ogallala, Nebraska, and Las Animas, Colorado, and Mobeetie, Texas, the gambler and gunman Bat Masterson spent his last years in New York City as a sports columnist for the *Morning Telegraph*, where he died at his desk of a heart attack. Western gunfights were alcohol-related, or else involved battles over gambling, prostitution, or political preferment. They were closer in spirit to drug wars in the Bronx than to duels of honor.

The main street in Lincoln is narrow, and the little houses are close together. The town is in a valley and has no place else to go. It probably looks much the same as when Billy the Kid was here. The feud, sometimes called the Lincoln County War, was between a lawyer named McSween who lived on one side of the street and a former Army major named Murphy who ran a general store on the other side. Both were also incipient cattle barons competing for government beef contracts. Billy the Kid was among the McSween faction. From minor beginnings the feud quickly grew through several ambush killings, until finally the Murphy faction had their friends from the nearby Army fort surround McSween's house with cavalry backed up by a twelve-pound cannon. The house was then set ablaze. Billy the Kid was inside along with McSween, Mrs. McSween, and a number of McSween gunmen. He played the piano in the parlor as the flames burned closer. The attackers let Mrs. McSween escape to safety. Then the men came out shooting, except for McSween, who was unarmed. He caught nine slugs and died. Billy the Kid and a friend named Tom O'Folliard escaped unhit. A sign in front of the site of the McSween house tells some of this story; charred beams and adobe bricks still lie beneath the grass.

At large, Billy the Kid moved beyond the confines of the feud to more general shootings and stock thefts. Pat Garrett, the Lincoln County sheriff, eventually caught him, and he was convicted of murder and taken to Lincoln to be hanged. Since there was no jail to put him in, he was shackled and held in Garrett's office, on the second floor of the courthouse. One of the guards, deputy Robert Ollinger, showed Billy the Kid the double-barrelled shotgun he would shoot him with if he tried to escape. When Ollinger went across the street to the hotel for supper, Billy the Kid worked free of his cuffs, grabbed a gun from guard J. W. Bell, shot him, and walked to the window carrying Ollinger's shotgun. Ollinger came running at the sound of the shot, and Billy the Kid called, "Hello, Bob!" Then he shot him with both barrels. He said, "Take that, you son of a bitch! You will never follow me with that gun again!" Then he broke off his leg shackles with a miner's pick and (he must have had a musical streak) danced on the balcony. Then he jumped on a horse, rode down Main Street, yelled "Three cheers for Billy the Kid!" and galloped away.

Lincoln's main street would be a good place to yell that from. It is barely bigger than a road on a stage set, and it disappears picturesquely around a bend. The courthouse still stands. There is a marble marker on the ground at the spot where Robert Ollinger fell. The second floor still has a balcony—wooden, recently painted, with a railing. It is the only balcony in town, which it overlooks like a pulpit. I, too, went across the street to the hotel and had supper. The menu featured home-baked bread and sole; New Mexico is like the Vermont of the West. Later I had to drive miles out of town to find a gas station. All of the town of Lincoln is a historic district, which discourages new construction. Because Billy the Kid danced on it, the courthouse balcony endures.

New Mexico has towns over three hundred years old. None of them is on the Great Plains. The little towns back in the canyons were hiding from what used to be out here: Apache, Kiowa, and Comanche, mainly. As I came out of the pinon foothills, the flat openness still seemed to suggest swarms of screaming mounted warriors. For centuries after General Francisco Vásquez de Coronado first explored the southern plains in 1541, the Spanish kept sending parties of soldiers and missionaries this way. Often, they did not return; pieces of captured Spanish armor survived as heirlooms in Indian households long after the Spanish were gone.

Sucking on milkshake cups full of crushed ice, I drove north in the heat, to Bent's Fort on the Arkansas River. The Arkansas runs for 1,459 miles from the Colorado Rockies across the plains to the Mississippi. Traders from the Mississippi valley travelled up it on their way to the Spanish settlements of the Southwest. Bent's Fort, built in 1833 with adobe walls fifteen feet high and seven feet thick, was to the southern plains what Fort Union was to the northern. Its builders, Charles and William Bent, of the mercantile firm of Bent, St. Vrain and Company, chose to trade here to avoid the power of the American Fur Company to the north. Rather than sell the fort to the Army, William Bent blew it up in 1849; the National Park Service has since reconstructed it, including the cactus which once grew on top of the walls. The fort is not far from the present town of La Junta, Colorado. When I got there on an afternoon

in August, it was filled with men and women wearing buckskin and broadcloth and calico in styles which were common
in 1850. They had come to Bent's Fort for a black-powder
rendezvous.

Black powder is the gunpowder old muzzle-loading fire-
arms used. Black-powder people, as they are sometimes
called, are hobbyists with an interest in black-powder
guns—specifically, guns of the period 1800–60. For most
black-powder people (they prefer the name "buckskinners,"
or "skinners"), enthusiasm for that era extends to everything
else about it: clothes, tools, skills, trade goods, history,
figures of speech. Some call each other "Hoss" and refer to
buffalo as "buffler" because supposedly trappers in 1840
did. Buckskinners number in the tens of thousands, and
they hold rendezvous all over the country (although mainly
in the West). The original rendezvous, back in the 1820s,
were gatherings held in some Rocky Mountain valley where
fur trappers met traders recently arrived from the settlements with pack trains of goods, and everybody traded
and drank and gambled and brawled. A modern rendezvous is a family event. People sleep in tipis and purge
the campsite of all signs of the twentieth century; at
Bent's Fort, the cars and trailers hide in a weed-screened
lot a quarter mile or so away. Debates on what one may
or may not bring to a rendezvous often include reference
to historical texts. Powdered lemonade mix is okay; it
existed in 1840, when it was known as "crystallized
essence" of lemon. Mosquito netting accompanied the fan-
cier travellers of the 1840s, so it, too, is defensible. A
person who prefers to sleep on an air mattress might cite
this passage from *Up the Missouri with Audubon*, by Edward
Harris:

We struck our camp on the River shore under 6 Cotton
Wood Trees growing in a clump, and after making a good
fire, Michaux and one of the Hunters started after Deer,
having still an hour or more of daylight. We had hardly any
time to refresh ourselves with a little bread and cheese,
before they brought in a fine yearling Buck . . . It was not
long before some of the choice morceaux were roasting before the fire . . . We all agreed it was the best Venison we
ever tasted, and none failed to do ample justice to the repast.
Our beds were soon blown up and wrapped in our blankets
with our guns by our sides, we were soon asleep.

Audubon and company called their air mattresses "India
rubber beds." The year was 1843.

In the shade of the fort's walls, I talked to Bill Gwaltney,
a seasonal Park Service ranger from Texas, in charge of
activities at the rendezvous. Bill Gwaltney was wearing a
Missouri River boatman's shirt with bloused sleeves, white
cotton broadfall trousers from an Amish clothing-supply
house in Indiana, and a strand of red-and-blue glass beads
of a design about three hundred years old. "What's so funny
about being a buckskinner is the contrast between then and
now," he said. "If you go into a Wendy's hamburgers
dressed in your rendezvous gear, people look at you like
you're crazy, when in fact you're not. A black-powder rendezvous is a positive, out-of-doors experience, a family experience. It generates respect for Native Americans. The
fur-trade period was fascinating for lots of reasons. The
trappers who came West brought technology to the Indians,
but the Indians gave the trappers spiritual and survival
knowledge in return. The fur-trade period was an opportunity for us to learn from Native Americans, and in the
end we turned that opportunity down. I prefer a rendezvous

without any reminders of the modern era at all, but there can be some leeway. Take yourself, for example: your canvas shirt, denim trousers, leather belt, notebook, pencil; about the only thing you wouldn't've had back in 1840 would be the hard rubber soles on your hiking boots. I am opposed to air mattresses at a rendezvous, personally. If you have to have them, cover them with a hide or a blanket. Same goes for coolers. And then there's other things which are just ridiculous—rawhide beer-can holders, for example. People say the trappers would've used them if they'd had them. That's a cute saying, but I don't buy it."

In the center plaza of the fort, vendors had set out displays of black-powder items for sale on blankets: knives made of half a sheep-shear, jugs, rose-pink hand-blown glass bottles from Mexico, riding quirts, strike-a-light bags of flint and steel and tinder, little knives like the ones Indian women used to wear around their necks to kill their attacker or themselves if they were about to be raped, hand-carved tipi pins, animal legbones for making knife handles, turtle shells, door knockers made of deer hooves, bunches of sweet grass for burning, tiny powder horns with silver stoppers for fine-grained priming powder, polished stones, porcupine-quillwork barrettes, and throwing tomahawks like the one Gerard Baker and I fooled around with when I visited Fort Union.

It turned out the guy with the tomahawks even knew Gerard Baker. He said, "Shoot, ol' Gerard's District Ranger at the northern unit of Teddy Roosevelt National Park now." On the plains, that happened to me often; I ran into people who knew Gerard Baker all over. They'd say, "Gerard's an old buddy of mine. He's the fella that taught me how to jerk buffalo meat," or "Gerard's the guy that got me into flint-knapping," or "Gerard and me are gonna trap an eagle this fall." If anyone nowadays could be called a genuine plainsman, it is Gerard Baker.

Men in coyote-skin hats and buckskin were walking around the plaza and hailing each other by their black-powder names: "Hey, Long Shadow, what you know good?" "White Eyes, how you been?" "Hey, Bijou, ol' hoss, how you makin' it?" To talk, they often got down on their haunches and hunkered. A man with long gray-and-black hair hanging straight down, wire-rim glasses, a calico shirt, and stiff buckskin trousers was telling several listeners about a woman gunsmith of the 1830s named Anne Patrick. Then the discussion turned to buffalo hunter Billy Dixon's famous mile-long shot at the Battle of Adobe Walls in 1874, and whether the Indian he was shooting at was killed or just had the wind knocked out of him. After a while I butted in to add that Billy Dixon's hair was supposed to be almost nine feet long. Then the man with the wire-rim glasses, who gave his name as Moses McTavish, told me all kinds of things about buffalo hunters. He said they were always dying of skunk bites. With his knuckles he drew a map in the dust of the Staked Plains of Texas, a mostly flat place with no landmarks where the hunters often got lost. He said that a lot of buffalo hunters were as dumb as a rock.

Moses McTavish asked me if I wanted to see his tipi. We went out the side gate of the fort, down a long, gentle slope, and across a grassy depression where the Arkansas River used to run before it moved. On the other side, a grove of big cottonwood trees grew far apart, in what botanists call a gallery forest. The people at the rendezvous had picked this spot for their campground; canvas tipis as white as water-cooler cups stood among the trees. A few tipis had blue smoke coming from their tops. In front of one, a round mirror hung from an iron holder shaped like an upside-down L. Others had cooking pots hanging over fires from tripods. Beneath a canvas awning strung between two trees, several guys leaning back on their elbows were passing a small jug. Here and there, picketed horses grazed. Little kids as barefoot as any in 1840 played in the trodden-down grass.

Moses McTavish and I ducked through his tipi door and sat cross-legged on buffalo robes around the fire pit in the center. Moses McTavish reached under a deer hide, lifted the lid of a cooler, and brought us out a couple of cans of Coke—Classics, of course. Then he filled his clay pipe with Prince Albert tobacco mixed with mullein weed for his bronchitis and lit it. He said, "This is a Crow lodge. Some people prefer Sioux lodges, some Cheyenne, some Comanche. I like Crow because of its shape—the tipi poles of a Crow lodge extend so far above the covering that the whole thing looks almost like an hourglass. You could tell the tribe from the shape of the tipis from miles away. Cheyenne tipis kind of angled forward to the door. Sioux were like Cheyenne, but without the two flaps above the door. Comanche tipis were more squat and conical. Indian women could take a tipi down in a few minutes and put it up in an hour. If my wife and I hustle, it takes us fifteen minutes just to unload it all from the trailer. It takes us two and a half hours to get everything up and where it belongs. This tipi has I forget how many square yards of canvas, sixteen poles, fifteen pegs, twenty stakes, five different ropes, a canvas liner—that's just some of it. You see those cords running along the inside of the tipi poles? Well, when it rains real hard, water will run down the poles, and when it gets to a bump or a knot on the wood it will stop there and drip on you. Those cords are so the water has something smooth to run along all the way to the ground.

"Tipis take on color from the wood you burn in your fire. Cottonwoods make poor firewood—they turn tipis a kind of smutty brown. Willow gives 'em a nice soft yellow color. Pine burns pitchy and turns 'em black. Quaking aspen hardly smokes at all. The Crows liked willow because they took great pride in how light-colored their tipis were. You don't ever go off and leave a fire burning in one of these. And you don't want wood that sparks. At a rendezvous several years ago, a tipi caught fire and burned to the ground in a minute and a half, and one rendezvous person was killed."

We finished the Cokes, and Moses McTavish put the cans away out of sight. "My real name is Lee Walsh," he said. "I used to be a food chemist for Trenton Foods. Then I made printed circuits for Gulton Industries. I've worked as an anthropologist, classifying bones. Once I worked on a skeleton with a stone arrowhead in his lumbar vertebrae. Now I do this. I go to eleven rendezvous a year. I spend three months of every year in a lean-to. My wife's got a good job."

On my way out, I stopped at the Bent's Fort information kiosk, where a uniformed park employee with a name tag that read "McGee" sat alone. I asked if he was going down to the rendezvous. He said, "No, I'm not. I know what it is to chop wood and haul water and shit outside and I don't want to have a thing to do with it."

The Arkansas River used to be one of the most treacherous on the Great Plains, a multi-channelled torrent of liquid sand that often drowned people and animals when it was in flood. Driving east along the Arkansas valley from Colorado into Kansas, I saw only trickles of water for two hundred miles. At Dodge City, where I stopped, cowboys sometimes spent days trying to coax their herds into the river. A Dodge City hotelkeeper named "Deacon" Cox owned a swimming cow which he would lend to trail bosses with stalled herds. The cow avoided the slaughterhouse for years because of her willingness to jump in and lead the others across. Today a swimming cow would be hamburger with a hidden talent. A person strolling through the dusty bed of the Arkansas near Dodge City might never guess at the river that was there.

Dodge City has had at least three booms in its history. The first began in 1872, when it was the western terminus for the Santa Fe Railroad and the center of trade for buffalo hunters on the middle plains. In 1872 and 1873, millions of hides and seven million pounds of buffalo tongues were shipped east from Dodge City. The second boom was a few years later, when Dodge became the destination of cattle herds heading for the railroad from Texas. Every business from barbershops to dance halls grew on Front Street along the railroad tracks. Doc Holliday briefly practiced dentistry there after his escape from the Fort Griffin lynch mob. In the Long Branch Saloon, Cock-Eyed Frank Loving shot and killed Levi Richardson; in Webster's Saloon, the cowboy Bing Choate was killed by the gambler Dave St. Clair; at the door of the Opera House at the corner of Front Street and First Avenue, Mysterious Dave Mather shot and killed Assistant City Marshal Tom Nixon. Women named Mollie Hart and Lizzie Palmer and Sadie Hudson and Bertha Lockwood became involved in hair-pulling battles and stabbings. Bat Masterson, who was sheriff in 1877, appears in the town

GERARD BAKER, historian, plainsman, and Park Service ranger

KENNETH McKENZIE, the man who built Fort Union and was its most famous bourgeois

JOHN JAMES AUDUBON in later life. He may have looked like this when he visited Fort Union in 1843

JOHN JACOB ASTOR, whose American Fur Company made his first fortune

CHARLES LARPENTEUR, longtime trader on the upper Missouri

WILLIAM CLARK

MERIWETHER LEWIS

FOUR BEARS, chief of the Mandans. George Catlin
painted this portrait in 1832. Four Bears died in the
smallpox epidemic of 1837

RUDOLPH FRIEDRICH KURZ; a self-portrait from his Western sketchbooks. Note naked person in upper right

FRANCIS PARKMAN, American historian and author of *The Oregon Trail*

JIM BECKWOURTH, mountain man, trader, storyteller

KIT CARSON, the 5′4″ mountain man, explorer, and scout

JIM BRIDGER, King of the Mountain Men

WOVOKA, the Paiute Indian whose vision inspired many tribes to dance the Ghost Dance in 1890

SITTING BULL

BUFFALO BILL CODY, scout, showman, entrepreneur

Sioux Indian policeman at Pine Ridge Reservation, c. 1890

EDWARD C. "TEDDY BLUE" ABBOTT, cowboy, cattleman, co-author of the classic *We Pointed Them North*

GRANVILLE STUART, pioneer Montana cattleman who lost half his herd in one blizzard during the Big Die-Up of 1887

THE MARQUIS DE MORÈS, a few years after he returned to France from the plains

MAJOR JAMES McLAUGHLIN, Indian agent, author of *My Friend the Indian*

TEDDY ROOSEVELT, during his Dakota days

Nightlife in Cheyenne, Wyoming Territory, during the cattle boom

(*above*) Family of Norwegian homesteaders, with elaborate sod house in background

(*left*) Publicity photo of LAWRENCE WELK, "the most popular musician in U.S. history"

(*left*) CLYDE BARROW and
BONNIE PARKER, South-
western outlaws and
murderers

(*above*) FRANK HAMER,
Texas lawman who
pursued Bonnie and Clyde
and ended their career

DR. JOHN HENRY "DOC"
HOLLIDAY, dentist, gambler,
gunman

WYATT EARP, lawman, saloon
owner, author, prizefight referee,
as he looked in 1886

WILLIAM BARCLAY "BAT" MASTERSON, lawman, gambler, sportswriter

(*above*) BILLY THE KID

(*left*) LITTLE BIG MAN, Oglala Sioux warrior and comrade of Crazy Horse who held his arms when he tried to escape

DR. VALENTINE T. McGILLYCUDDY,
Army surgeon, Indian agent, friend to
Crazy Horse

GENERAL GEORGE S. CROOK

LIEUTENANT WILLIAM PHILO CLARK,
"White Hat," the officer at Fort
Robinson assigned to keep tabs on
Crazy Horse

GENERAL JESSE M. LEE. As a
lieutenant, escorted Crazy Horse from
Spotted Tail Agency to captivity at
Fort Robinson

GENERAL WILLIAM T. SHERMAN

GENERAL PHIL SHERIDAN

(*above*) BAPTISTE POURIER and WILLIAM GARNETT, interpreters, important sources on the last days of Crazy Horse

(*left*) SPOTTED TAIL, orator, diplomat, leader of the Sioux at Spotted Tail Agency

WOMAN DRESS, who lied to General Crook about Crazy Horse

FRANK GROUARD, interpreter, scout, self-invented character

NELLIE LARRABEE, Crazy Horse's second wife

HE DOG, Oglala Sioux chief, friend and comrade to Crazy Horse. Lived to be a hundred years old

Korczak Ziolkowski, the sculptor who began the carving on Crazy Horse Mountain

(*above*) Le War Lance on West Broadway in New York City

(*left*) Chiefs Red Cloud and American Horse, in 1891

(*above*) GEORGE SCOTT, Wyoming rancher
(*right*) RUSSELL BROWN, his top hand

RICHARD READ, the last
man lynched in Kansas

KATHLEEN CLAAR (1900–87), of Oberlin, Kansas,
founder and curator of the Last Indian Raid in
Kansas museum

(*top*) ALAN and LINDI KIRKBRIDE, Wyoming ranchers and (Lindi) peace activist

(*above*) Bill, Wyoming

(*right*) JUANITA ROBINSON (Mrs. Virgil Robinson, Jr.) of Nicodemus, Kansas

JOHN ST. JOHN, Governor of Kansas who welcomed black emigration, then changed his mind

BENJAMIN "PAP" SINGLETON, the Moses of the Black Exodus, who led thousands of blacks from the South to new homes in the West

GENERAL GEORGE A. CUSTER, at the end of the Civil War, when he was about twenty-six

ELIZABETH BACON CUSTER, his wife, c. 1885, almost ten years after her husband's death

(*above*) THOMAS JEFFERSON

(*right*) Two MOON, Cheyenne chief, and unidentified children. He said the Battle of the Little Bighorn lasted "as long as it takes a hungry man to eat his dinner."

JOHN LEDYARD, explorer, who died of impatience in Egypt. Leader and sole member of Jefferson's first expedition to the American West

CATHERINE THE GREAT of Russia, who thwarted Ledyard's plans

Abandoned anti-ballistic-missile system command center on the plains near Ledger, Montana

census of 1880 living with a nineteen-year-old named Annie Ladue, identified by the census taker as a "concubine." In all the years of the cattle boom, fewer people were shot or stabbed in Dodge City than die violently in New York City in three days; what gave Dodge its fame, partly, was the fact that the town had several weekly newspapers chronicling each gunfight and its aftermath in detail.

Dodge City's third boom began more recently, when the town was the fictional setting for several TV series, including *Gunsmoke*, one of the most popular series ever. Fans of those shows wanted to see what the original Dodge City looked like. By then, not much of old Dodge was left—a fire destroyed the buildings on Front Street in 1885—so the town built a new museum and reconstructed some of the old saloons and businesses on a nearby site. Much of the land where the dangerous part of Dodge City once stood is now under a long parking lot for visitors and tour buses. As I pulled in, a thunderstorm hit so hard that raindrops were bouncing back up off the pavement. In the museum's gift shop, a woman just off a tour bus undid her clear plastic scarf and said to a man, "Look, honey—figurines."

Dodge City has lots of tourist attractions, including my favorite museum combination of all time: on Fifth Avenue, just across the street from the town's old Boot Hill Cemetery, a single building houses the Kansas Teachers' Hall of Fame and the Famous Gunfighter's Wax Museum. ("Each, a separate attraction," says the brochure which they also share.) The Kansas Teachers' Hall of Fame is free, and contains portrait photos and short testimonials to honorees like Marie Harden Reynolds, a vocal and instrumental music teacher from Pittsburg, Kansas, who inspired many of her former students to become music teachers, and Ward

L. Kiester, former principal of Basehor Rural High School, and Clare Kaufman, from Gridley, whose students remember her star-gazing field trips, and Alice V. Tuttle, an elementary-school teacher from Garden City ("If we could bottle her patience and sell it, we would be very wealthy," said a former student), and J. Harvey Douglass, a former industrial-arts instructor from Winfield, author of *Units in Woodworking* and *Projects in Wood Furniture*. In the other half of the building, the Famous Gunfighter's Wax Museum (admission $1.85) has life-size replicas of Wild Bill Hickock, Calamity Jane, Billy the Kid, Clay Allison ("Alcoholic New Mexico cattleman who killed 32 men and died in a fall from a wagon while drunk"), Grat Dalton ("Member of the awful Dalton gang of killers and robbers"), and, on a purple velvet pillow, the severed head of Joaquin Murrieta, a California outlaw who "tied Chinamen together by their queues, made them dance to the tune of a pistol, and shot their eyes out."

A three hours' drive north of Dodge City is the town of Oberlin, Kansas. Years ago, I stopped in Oberlin to visit the Last Indian Raid in Kansas Museum, and met the curator, Kathleen Claar, a white-haired woman with a habit of shyly touching her listener's elbow to point out exhibits she liked best. In 1978 I went back to write a *New Yorker* article about the town's celebration of the centennial of the raid. Indian descendants of the Cheyenne who killed about forty settlers on the prairie around Oberlin were supposed to attend the celebration, but at the last minute they couldn't make it. The article I wrote appeared. Something I wanted to include in the article but didn't get a chance to was a trip Kathleen Claar and I took to the site of Hawkeye, a now-vanished town near where she used to live. We met at a cafe in Oberlin called Lindy's, got in my rent-a-car, drove west on the highway, and turned off onto a gravel road. It was early fall. We passed a field of tall sunflowers with their heads all turned the same direction, like a crowd at a ball game. The sky was an enamel blue. "If I had a dollar for every time I've been down this road," Kathleen Claar said. "It was my husband's mail route and I used to drive it all the time. Right over there was where his family's land started. Old Henry Claar—my grandfather-in-law—was a ladies' man. What's the word I'm looking for—he was *overbearing*. All the Claars were like that. My daddy Pickens farmed not too far from here. He didn't homestead. He farmed the homestead that my grandfather left him, but he had itchy feet and couldn't stay in one place too long and out here he didn't stick. One time I saw my daddy kneeling down in the field with his head in his hands and tears was streaming down his face and I said, 'What's wrong, Daddy?' and he said, 'We should've never come out here. Nothing goes right for me in this state. I hate Kansas.' So, later, when I was living in Idaho and I met Lawrence Claar and he wanted me to come back here, I said no. See, I didn't want to come back to the state that had made my daddy cry.

"I lived in a sod house from when I was two and a half until I was four. It was just a one-room house made of blocks of sod cut from the prairie. I remember it—bugs and snakes and mice were always dropping down from the ceiling. The ceiling was made of brush, branches from the creek, fodder—you know what fodder is?—like cornstalks, weeds, anything. Mama used to hang sheets over the tables and beds so that things wouldn't fall on them. Then we got the idea of putting a big piece of muslin across the whole ceiling. We'd keep it up there for a year or so until it got too filthy and rain-stained and then take it down, tear it into strips, wash it, dry it, sew it back together, and put it back up. To decorate the windows, we used to cut up red and green wrapping paper that Mama would save through the year—heavier-quality wrapping paper than they have now. We kids used to try to come up with the prettiest design. I was the youngest of eight in the family, and even today I'm still the baby when my older sister is around.

"In the middle of that field of milo is where Claar's Roadhouse used to stand. It was like an inn and had stables and barns. It was a great big old three-story building. The people who bought the land some years ago tore down everything. Then they came to ask me where the well that old Henry had dug was at and I wouldn't tell them. I said, 'This place should have been a historic monument and you tore out all those trees that took years to grow.' The soil around here doesn't look very much like it used to. See those draws and washes? That didn't use to be here. Didn't use to be any gullies, or not as many as there are now. What caused it? Men's greed. They wanted to plow up everything, put in wheat and other crops, and they ruined a lot of land that used to be good grazing land. During World War I the price of wheat went way up and everybody thought they were going to be rich. Now a lot of the land is just wore out."

At a corner where two dirt roads met, we stopped at a little cemetery behind a fence. A flock of sparrows burst from a row of pruned juniper trees as we went through a gate under a black wrought-iron arch that said "Hawkeye Cemetery." The grass was mown and wet; someone had just watered. Beyond the fence, wheat and milo fields stretched away on every side. Kathleen Claar showed me the graves of her husband, his parents, her daughter, her granddaughter, and her grandson. She said she had raised her grandson after his parents divorced, and he was killed in a car accident in Trinidad, Colorado, while waiting to ship out for Vietnam in 1972. She said his death was the one she hadn't gotten used to yet. She showed me a stone marked "Unknown Dead" on the grave of an apprentice boy who stole a horse up in Nebraska and was killed by pursuers who found him hiding in a nearby barn. She showed me the grave of an in-law who loved California and whose last wish was that his ashes be buried in a California prune box. Then she led me to a marker all by itself on the other side of the cemetery ground. She said, "Did you ever hear about the last man lynched in Kansas? Well, this was him. His name was Rick Read. He was lynched in 1932 after he raped and murdered an eight-year-old girl. The Reads lived right next door to us and I used to see him all the time when I was driving my mail route. He had these big long arms hanging down and sometimes he used to just come out of the bushes when I was driving on the road and come toward the car, and the lust on that man's face! I used to drive away as fast as I could and not stop until I was a long way away and then get out of the car, I was shaking so bad. He was jailed in Colorado for a similar offense a long time before, when I was a schoolteacher there, and later when they paroled him I said, 'We will all live to regret this day.' After they lynched him I didn't want to visit his family but we had to. They were friends—his sister still is a close friend of mine—and his poor old mother, her cheeks were so red from crying you could see the blood right through them. His dad was a member of the Odd Fellows Lodge and so was he—he went through right before my husband—and his poor old dad said he wanted his son to have an Odd Fellows funeral. My husband turned pale and then another Read boy said, 'Dad, you forget how he died.' They wanted us to go in and look at him and oh, Lord, I didn't want to, but my husband said, 'You've got to—they were good friends of your mother and father.' So my husband took me by the hand and led me in and my goodness I'll remember that sight as long as I live. They must've used a rope this big on him, there was a big purple groove around his neck. When they went to bury him the people were so mad they would have dismembered the body and no preacher would preach the sermon, but at the last minute a preacher showed up who believed that every man was entitled to a Christian burial—he was a relative of mine but I'd never liked him very much—and he preached the most beautiful sermon I ever heard. He said, 'If you had a man in your community as crippled in body as this man was in spirit you would all have so much pity on him you'd take him into your homes and care for him.' All the women started to weep and I cried myself and some men cried, too, and you could feel all the hatred and violence just dissolve up into the air."

This time, the Last Indian Raid in Kansas Museum was closed for the day when I got to Oberlin. I called Kathleen Claar from a phone in the Pizza Hut, but she wasn't home. Being in a place I'd already written about felt strange to me, so I got back in my van and continued north into Nebraska. Later I sent Kathleen Claar a postcard. She sent me a Christmas card. We talked on the phone. She said that we should go back to Hawkeye, and that she had a lot more to tell. Just before Christmas 1987, at the age of eighty-seven, Kathleen Claar died, and joined her husband and family and the last man lynched in Kansas in the old Hawkeye cemetery in the wheat fields.

I slept in my van outside the town of McCook, Nebraska. The next morning I went on, over Interstate Highway 80, across the forks of the Platte River (the first river with any water I'd seen for days), and into the west-central part of the state. I was now in one of the blankest spots on the American map, a big section showing almost no rivers or roads or towns. This is the Nebraska sandhill country, the original model for the mapmakers' Great American Desert—a land of grassy rises receding into the distance like a sea in a heavy chop. There was so little to look at that when a crow flew past in front of me and dropped something from its beak I turned around and went back to see what it was: a fetal duckling, featherless, blue, with bulging sealed eyes and tiny webbed feet.

Near Crawford, Nebraska, I stopped at the site of the old Red Cloud Indian Agency. Nothing is left of it now but a few foundations. The plain below where the buildings once stood is as empty as when Crazy Horse surrendered there. In this part of the state, the sandhills give way to John Ford–type scenery—open prairie with moving cloud shadows, lines of green winding along the creek and river valleys, splintery buttes rising from low uplands dotted with pines. Above the buttes, the mile-high white clouds were as flat on the bottom as paperweights. Fort Robinson, where Crazy Horse died, is just the other side of the White River. The fort is a state park now. Cottonwood trees buzzing with locusts line the old parade ground. The feeling is like that of a small-college campus. In Crazy Horse's day, the fort, just a few rows of buildings, had no trees at all.

In the library of the Fort Robinson Museum, as I was going through the Crazy Horse file, a young man with brown hair and green eyes and a white shirt with the cuffs rolled up asked me what I was doing. I told him, and he said I should be careful to believe only eyewitnesses on the subject of Crazy Horse's death. He said his name was Ephriam Dickson III and he was working at the fort for the summer as a historian. He was a junior in college. Ephriam Dickson had read everything ever written that contained a mention of Crazy Horse. We walked over to the adjutant's office, which has been reconstructed on its original site, and talked for three hours about whether Dr. McGillycuddy's account is reliable, when exactly General Crook left the fort on the day before Crazy Horse was killed, whether Crazy Horse was stabbed with a regular bayonet or a trowel bayonet (regular, Ephriam Dickson said), who Frank Grouard really was, and whether Agent Lee later lobbied unsuccessfully for the Medal of Honor for bringing Crazy Horse to the fort from the Spotted Tail Agency (Ephriam Dickson agreed that he had). He also said that he was sure William Gentles was not the soldier who bayonetted Crazy Horse, and that he was going to look through more military records until he learned who did. I said that until now I had thought I might be the only Crazy Horse scholar in the world. Ephriam Dickson smiled and said, "No, you're not."

On to southeastern Wyoming, to the horse and cattle ranch of Alan and Lindi Kirkbride. Lindi Kirkbride is an anti-war activist who once took a trip to the Soviet Union sponsored by a group called A Run for Peace with other Western ranchers and farmers to promote reduction of nuclear weapons. I had read about her in the newspaper and wanted to meet her. She has auburn hair and freckles and a good laugh, which she showed when I asked her if many Russians wear different-color socks. The Kirkbrides work a ranch started by Alan's great-grandfather in 1889 and live in a brick house on a rise with a six-mile view from the living-room bay window. Lindi Kirkbride gave me good directions over the phone and met me at the door. She said, "This is our way to travel—to have you guys come here and visit us." Then she asked me to sign a guest book, where I saw the names of reporters from *The* London *Sunday Times*, *People*, *The Progressive*, a Japanese newspaper, an East German film crew, and CBS News. We sat on the couch and had peanut-butter Girl Scout cookies and tea while her four-year-old daughter, Anduin, kept us company. "Which do you think is the most white on me, my white on my dress or on my shoes?" Anduin asked.

Lindi Kirkbride told me that from the plane Moscow didn't have near as many lights as New York, that they met the head of the Soviet state farms and lots of other bigwigs, that they were on TV many times, that an NBC News crew followed them, that she hated breakfast because it was just some awful pieces of salami, that the Moscow subway had the longest escalators she'd ever been on in her life, and that she met a schoolteacher who told her, "We have the kindergarten so well under control, we're now working for a cure for the common cold." She said that the Russians really snowed her and that when she came back she was much too glowing. She said the trip made her understand how really really special living in a democracy is. She said it made her like the Russians both more and less. She said, "The people at A Run for Peace thought sending farmers and ranchers would be a good idea because of our closer relationship to the earth—yes, Anduin, you can write your name, but *not on the couch!*"

Alan Kirkbride came in from somewhere he'd been working. He is tall, blond, with black-rimmed glasses and tan arms. The name over the pocket of his cutoff Army shirt was his own. He cocked his head and looked at me. We talked for a few minutes. Then he said, "I like you." He took me on a drive around his ranch. He stopped the truck and said, "Let's take a look at these grasses. This tall one here is bluestem. This'll grow eight feet high if it gets enough water. Bluestem is what used to grow everywhere farther east, in places like Iowa. This low, skinny grass here is prairie sandreed. If cattle graze this in the summer, they'll take it right out. We graze it more in the winter. This is threadleaf sedge. It's the first thing to green up in the spring. I've seen this greenin' up the tenth of March. Once this was up, the Indian ponies had something to eat, and the Indians could travel. This is little bluestem. Cattle don't eat that so much. This is eriogonum. Technically, it's not a shrub or a grass—it's an herb. It's green in the spring, gold in the summer, and red all winter. This is Indian ricegrass. Stock loves this, but it isn't a real abundant grass. This is blue grama grass. It's a low-growing little grass, but it's nutritious. The whole plant, seeds and all, cures over the summer and makes great winter feed. Grama grasses are what the fifty million buffalo ate. That tall plant over there is soapweed. Cattle love to eat soapweed blossoms. It's a member of the yucca family. That copper-colored bush growing up in the rocks has a great name—mountain mahogany."

We got back in the truck and drove to the lip of a canyon. Sometimes it is hard to believe how many ups and downs such a flat-looking place can have. The Kirkbrides' ranch includes some of Horse Creek, a stream almost small enough to jump across, which has carved a broad canyon several stories deep in places. We drove down a coulee to the canyon floor. From a one-lane bridge I could see small trout holding in the tea-colored water. "I only do this once or twice a year," Alan Kirkbride said. "But let's take a look at the golden-eagle nest." We went along the canyon a ways and stopped within sight of an eagle nest of sticks and branches built into the rock wall. The nest had enough wood in it for a football-rally bonfire, and it extended from the rock in a sketchy half sphere. In the middle of the nest we could just see the top of the eagle, looking out like a man in a cupola. "He stays around here all winter," Alan Kirkbride said. "Sometimes I see him when it's twenty below with a forty-mile wind, and he'll be all hunkered down on top of a phone pole, waitin' for a prairie dog or somethin'. I respect the hell out of that."

The Kirkbrides asked me to stay to dinner, but by now I was addicted to driving. I went on north until I got tired, and stopped on the banks of the North Platte River, not far from Register Cliffs, a big hump of rock sticking from the prairie where travellers on the Oregon Trail sometimes wrote their names as they passed by. There are hundreds of names on the rock, some carved, some lettered in a mixture of hog fat and tar used to lubricate the wooden wagon axles. In the morning I walked around the rock reading the names: "J Foreman" "I R Kennedy May 19 1850 Dubuque, Iowa" "Thyrza Hoe Pelling 1859 Wagon." Francis Parkman, who made a trip along the trail in 1846, described the emigrants as "a crowd of broad-brimmed hats, thin visages, and staring eyes . . . Tall, awkward men, in brown homespun; women, with cadaverous faces and long lank figures . . ." They "tormented" him with questions about what his name was, where he was coming from, where he was going, what he was doing. Francis Parkman was Harvard '44, of an old Boston family; one gets the feeling that people named Thyrza Hoe Pelling were not exactly his speed. Some of the 140-year-old printing on the rock looks only slightly faded. Hog fat and tar may be a medium for the ages.

From there I took some highways and then a little road running thirty-five miles across not much of anything just to see the town of Bill, Wyoming. It was a Saturday afternoon. The one store in town was closed, as was the post office. I did not see a single person in Bill, Wyoming. All along the road, mile after mile, long trains of coal cars rolled by at a steady twenty-two miles per hour. The machine that fills the coal cars does every one exactly the same, piling each load into an identical little peak. In the whole landscape, the coal train was the only moving thing.

When I crossed into Montana, I felt I was almost home, even though I still had five hundred miles or more to go. By now I was getting kind of burned out from driving so much. To pass the time, I was reduced to thinking about things like what would I do if I had a hundred million dollars. Suddenly I entered the land of grasshoppers. They started whirring up all around like little firecrackers and ricocheting off the windshield by the dozen. All along the windshield wipers they got wedged under with legs and wings in disarray. We have been the scourge of many Great Plains species, but we haven't made a dent in the grasshoppers. About the only condition they can't live with is damp. They like to sun themselves on pavement too hot to walk on in shoes. No car had come down the road for a while. The hoppers would wait to jump until I was right over them; then they would bounce off the bottom of the car. It sounded like I was driving in a popcorn popper. This went on for hours.

Then there were flocks of birds—mountain plovers, mostly. They were olive and taupe-colored above, sooty-white underneath. They always took off in a way that showed the white. Sometimes they rose before the car by the hundreds in an endlessly opening curtain, like a scene from an African wildlife movie. The winter-wheat harvest had begun, and two-thousand-bushel grain trucks full to the top were spilling wheat along the roads. The birds came to eat the wheat. Lots of them had been run over, and rolled to parchment on the asphalt. No matter how flat they got, somehow one wing always remained upright to flap in the draft.

From the fields on the benchland, I drove down into the valley of the Missouri River, to the town of Fort Benton. Just upstream, the Great Falls of the Missouri begin; in the days when steamboats travelled the river, Fort Benton was as far up as they could go. At first, Fort Benton was a fur-trading post, and then in the 1860s it was the main shipping point for miners working the gold strikes in the mountains to the west. Some historians maintain that Fort Benton was the wildest town in the West. Unfortunately, unlike Dodge City, it had no newspapers during its early days, so nobody really knows. For river people all along the Missouri and Mississippi valleys, Fort Benton was the end of the line. It attracted the usual Wild West crowd; one historian says that on a Saturday night you couldn't see the wood planking of the sidewalks for the discarded playing cards. Army officers suspected that it was from Fort Benton's traders that the Sioux and Cheyenne obtained many of their bullets and rifles. Today the sedate center of a prosperous farming country, Fort Benton has about as many people as when it was a wide-open river town. Next to the levee where no steamboat will probably ever dock again, the Missouri still slides by. Downstream, where it disappears around a bluff called Signal Point, it is still backlit with the beckoning promise of a highway. Six dams now block the river between Fort Benton and St. Louis.

In 1882, the Grand Union Hotel in Fort Benton was the biggest and classiest hotel between Seattle and Minneapolis. Its linen and its china patterns are on display in the local museum. The turreted three-story brick hotel building still stands. At the time I was there, investors were planning to fix it up and reopen it. I looked through the glass of the locked main door into the lobby with its black-and-white tile floor and oak registration desk. One night when the hotel was new (according to a display in the museum), the night manager shot and killed a cowboy who tried to ride his horse up the stairs just beyond the desk. Now the scene of the shooting was filled with mattresses stood on one end, headboards, a handcart, a wooden chair taped with electrical tape, tread-worn snow tires, an oil painting of the hotel towering above the smokestacks of steamboats docked beside it, a vacuum cleaner, and a bouquet of different-length curtain rods in a green plastic wastebasket.

Up the street from the hotel was where the dance halls, hurdy-gurdies, and gambling parlors used to be—places with names like Mose Solomon's Medicine Lodge, the Occidental, the Break of Day, the Exchange, the Board of Trade, and Dena Murray's Jungle. On the site of the Cosmopolitan, run by Fort Benton's most famous madam, Madame Moustache, I found a clothing store called the Toggery. I tried on several pair of pants there and listened in the dressing room as a clerk and a customer talked about how they had decided to sell their ranches after thirty-four and thirty-five years, respectively. They didn't have any pants I liked. I sat by the river and swatted mosquitoes for a while. Then I drove up to Signal Point Golf Course, on the plains above the town. Almost no one was playing. "All the farmers are harvesting," the girl in the pro shop said. I rented clubs, and sliced my tee shot about half a mile down the airport runway alongside the first hole. The fairways were a chalky brown, with big green circles where the sprinklers reached.

Fort Benton was my last stop, except for gas. The closer I got to the Blackfeet Indian Reservation, the more crosses marking fatal car accidents appeared beside the road. In a convenience store on the reservation I got a fill-up and a microwave burrito. They made me pay for the gas in advance. About forty kids and teenagers were crowding around the video games. At the pump next to me was a pickup truck with a green armchair in the back, and a man asleep in the chair. Dogs were strolling around loose, and the rows of houses and trailers had board fences on one side against the wind. Past the convenience store, the road rose toward the mountains in the west until it turned up a canyon and left the Great Plains behind.

9

NICODEMUS, Kansas, is a town with a population of about fifty in the western part of the state. Like many other towns on the Great Plains, Nicodemus was founded in the 1870s; unlike any other that still survives, it was founded by black homesteaders. In 1877, a small group of emigrants from Kentucky and Tennessee, including the families of Randall Smith, Lewis and Henry Williams, Sam Garland, Manuel Napew, and a Baptist minister named Silas Lee, arrived in Graham County, filed homestead claims, and laid out a town. They began too late in the season to break sod and put in crops, and they were short on draft animals, equipment, seeds, and money. Their first winter was hard. They lived in shelters dug into hillsides. Some of the men got jobs on the Kansas Pacific Railroad thirty-five miles away. In the spring, with just three horses between them, they had to do a lot of cultivating and planting by hand. Emigrants continued to arrive, and the town grew. By 1880, it had a population of almost five hundred. By 1887, it had churches, stores, an academy, a band, and two newspapers, one called *The Western Cyclone*. A man from

Nicodemus who became State Auditor in 1883 was the first black to hold major office in Kansas.

The people who founded Nicodemus were part of a movement of tens of thousands of blacks who left the South in the late 1870s for new homes in the West. The movement started because many recently freed slaves were poor, mistreated by whites, and disappointed that freedom was so little of an improvement. In Southern states where Democrats had returned to power, blacks had just lost the vote. Some white Southerners opposed to Reconstruction were not convinced it should be a serious offense to shoot blacks; several of the West's famous white outlaws got their start that way. Benjamin "Pap" Singleton, a black carpenter from Nashville who helped so many to emigrate that he was sometimes called the Moses of the Colored Exodus, compared the white Southerners to "a muddy-faced bellowing bull." Singleton could not read or write, but he travelled all over distributing circulars (which the railroads and Western land companies were printing in volume at the time) about the halcyon new lands on the Great Plains. His Tennessee Real Estate and Homestead Association was one of several "colonization councils" which attracted members by the thousands. He helped to found black colonies in several Kansas counties, and by the end of 1878 had sent 7,432 people to the state. Black people all over the South became excited at the thought of this new promised land. In Vicksburg, a convention of cotton planters urged them to preserve "intact until completion, contracts for labor-leasing which have already been made."

Because of the career in Kansas of the famed abolitionist John Brown, that state was especially attractive to black emigrants. At first, Governor John St. John made a speech welcoming the new arrivals. Then, possibly because of urging from S. J. Gilmore, land commissioner for the Kansas Pacific Railroad, who said of the blacks, "Indications are that we will be over run with them next year," Governor St. John began to discourage black immigration, and said that conditions in Kansas were not as promising as the blacks had been led to believe. The Kansas Pacific sent blacks who wanted to emigrate a form letter advising that all the good lands were taken, that no laborers were needed, that the weather was chancy for farming, and that each family should bring $500 in cash. It was probably the only time in history that a railroad ever told the truth of the situation to a prospective settler.

But the effect of railroad propaganda was not easy to undo, and advertising circulars continued to spread by way of Pullman porters, itinerant preachers, and steamboat employees. The blacks who decided to emigrate soon acquired the name "Exodusters." Their exodus had its own songs, like "The Land That Gives Birth to Freedom":

> . . . We have held meetings to ourselves
> To see if we can't plan some way to live.
> (*chorus*)   Marching along, yes, we are marching along,
> To Kansas City we are bound.

The movement reached a flood in 1879, when between fifteen thousand and twenty thousand blacks arrived in Kansas within a four-month period. They built shantytowns on the outskirts of Leavenworth, Topeka, Atchison, and Kansas City. Their towns had names like Rattlebone Hollow, Juniper Town, and Wyandotte City. Atchison passed an ordinance against the importation of paupers. Leavenworth refused to allow steamboats carrying blacks to land.

Many blacks died in the shantytowns; in Wyandotte, in the spring of 1879, they were said to be dying at a rate of fifty a day. Back East, Freedmen's Relief Associations were set up to help them. Blacks still planning to come heard unhappy reports from those who had preceded them, and the exodus, which by then had brought perhaps forty thousand to the West, suddenly stopped. Soon, two-thirds of the black immigrants had left the state. The black farming colonies eventually died out. Today, on the Great Plains, Nicodemus is the only artifact of the black exodus which remains.

I first learned of Nicodemus at the Fick Fossil Museum, in Oakley, Kansas. This museum has a good collection—a pterodactyl wing, claws and all; sea lilies, in bas-relief; an eighteen-foot-long, buck-toothed prehistoric fish called Portheus Molossus; a plesiosaurus fin with bite marks on it—from the world-famous fossil beds nearby. Mr. and Mrs. Earnest Fick, who gave the money for the museum, found thousands of prehistoric shark teeth around their ranch, and Mrs. Fick used the teeth to make oil-painting collages. The museum has many of her shark-teeth artworks on display, as well as a display of telegraph- and telephone-pole insulators, with names like Double Petticoat, Green Milk Glass Beehive, Pilgrim Hat, Roman Helmet, Baby Signal, Bavarian China Telephone, and a display about four emigrant girls who were captured by Cheyenne Indians, and a wagon, and an old-time telegraph office, and a photograph of a local man who was once first in the state fair in Grooming, and a display of photographs of disasters in the area, including the blizzard of 1912, the hailstorm of 1923, the floods over the Tux Smith bridge in 1951, the Page City grain elevator "bulging" in 1956, and the last Union Pacific passenger train to Oakley in 1971. The display about Nicodemus told a little of the history of the town, with photographs. The history ended, "Today, the once-prosperous town of Nicodemus is no more."

Because I am interested in ruins, I decided to drive over to the town site. Nicodemus is eighty-two miles from Oakley; surprisingly, Rand McNally still showed it on the map. When I reached the place where I had expected to find just a few foundations by the roadside, I found instead a living town: houses, streets, gardens, a township hall, a baseball field; a Baptist church, and a barbecue place called Ernestine's. Cars, many with out-of-state plates, were parked all over. At Ernestine's, you ordered through a side door and sat at picnic tables outside. I had a sagging paper plate of ribs, cole slaw, and white bread, and a Dr Pepper. At the next table, a large white man wearing overalls and barbecue sauce to the eyebrows told me that Nicodemus was in the middle of its annual Founders' Day Weekend celebration, that he and his wife were from the nearby town of Bogue, that people had come from all over the country, and that tomorrow was the parade. His name was Buzz Mauck. He said he would take me to meet a man named Alvin Bates who had lived in Nicodemus all his life and could tell me anything I wanted to know. I got in the back seat of the Maucks' older-model sedan and rode along bouncy streets and into the driveway of a small, one-story house where Buzz Mauck rolled down his window and yelled, "Alvin!" A short, light-brown man came out and walked up to the car and said, "Hello, Mr. Mauck, how are you doin'?"

"Mr. Mauck! Shoot, I'm Buzz to you," Buzz Mauck said. Then he said, "Alvin, I've got a man here who wants to talk to you about Nicodemus." Turning to me, he said, "Go ahead." I got out and talked while Alvin Bates kept his eyes at shoulder level and agreed politely with the questions I asked. After a few minutes I got back in the car and Buzz Mauck drove me back to my van.

You don't see many black people on the Great Plains. In the nineteenth century, there were a lot of black or part-black plainsmen, like Jim Beckwourth, the fur trapper and trader who lived for many years with the Crow Indians, or Desirée, the Missouri River pilot who once took an American Fur Company keelboat from Fort Union to St. Louis by himself, or Britt Johnson, the teamster who rode alone hundreds of miles beyond the frontier to retrieve his wife and two children captured by Kiowa Indians, or Isaiah "Teat" Dorman, the interpreter with the 7th Cavalry, who was killed at the Little Bighorn, or the 10th Cavalry, the all-black brigade which finally ran down and defeated the most elusive of the Comanche bands, or Isom Dart, the famous horse thief and rustler who was killed by the hired gunman Tom Horn, or Bose Ikard, the bronc buster and all-around cowboy who took some of the first trail herds north out of Texas, or Bill Pickett, the rodeo cowboy who used to throw steers off their feet by biting their front lips and falling to the ground. Today, once you get north of Oklahoma, you almost never see a black face at all.

When I returned to Nicodemus the next morning, even more cars—from Denver, Topeka, Wichita, Los Angeles, San Jose, St. Louis, Baltimore—were parked on driveways and lawns. Everything was quiet. By midmorning, people from nearby towns were at the rest area on Highway 24, unloading horses and hitching them to wagons for the parade. Along the main street, people began to bring lawn chairs from their houses and set them up. For a while, being there felt like horning in on a family reunion. Then the crowd started to grow. Local white people and black people called out greetings to each other with the distant heartiness of ship captains hailing. A guy in khaki shorts was carrying a video camera. At one o'clock, the parade began. It was like a parade in someone's living room. Its front was followed closely by its back. There was applause. Then people stood around. Kids were chasing each other and playing. Mothers stood above kids in strollers and talked about them. I ate a hotdog and drank some lemonade with six sisters named McGhee, from Wichita, Kansas. Soon everybody went into the township hall to see a program. Admission was a dollar for adults and fifty cents for children. People sat on chairs against the walls, leaving the floor in the middle open. Many stood at the near wall, around the door. I was next to the biggest of the McGhee sisters, who said she was the manager of a supermarket. We discussed her store's check-cashing policies. The crowd was more black than white; in front of me, a white rancher with a creased neck and a straw Stetson hitched up his jeans and sat on his heels. In the center of the floor, a seven-year-old girl and a twelve-year-old girl began a dance that looked impromptu. "What I want to see is some of this here break dancing," the rancher said to a girl beside him.

Next came a fashion show of ladies' hats designed by Billie Singleton of Topeka. The hats were big, in dramatic shapes, burgundy and gray and black and white. Mrs. Avalon Roberson modelled them. She put on each hat and strolled around the room so everybody could see it. She got applause all the way around. Then Mrs. Juanita Robinson, of Nicodemus, introduced her daughters Kathleen, Karen, Kaye, Kolleen, Krystal, and Karmen. Her other daughter, Kimberleen, who was pregnant, watched from the audience. First, Karmen, wearing (Juanita Robinson told us) a white suit with a slit skirt, a navy handkerchief, a black-and-white blouse, white ankle boots with a chain on the side, and a black-and-white hat with a veil, walked to the middle of the floor and stood with her left hand on her hip and her face turned to the side. Then Krystal, wearing a white lace dress, a white lace coat with balloon sleeves, and a white hat with navy lining and a veil, came and stood next to her sister the same way. Then came Kolleen, in a casual dress with black-and-off-white-striped pockets on the side, white nylons, black shoes, and a black hat. Then Karen, in a two-piece red suit, a white lace blouse, a red hat with a veil, and white shoes. Then Kathleen, in a purple silk dress with black stripes, a black hat, and black shoes. Then Kaye, in a black-and-blue triangle dress, a black belt, black shoes, blue nylons, and a black hat. When they were all lined up, they held that pose for a moment. Then the song "When Doves Cry," by Prince, began to play on the loudspeaker, and they began to dance. I looked past the people sitting on chairs against the wall, the women with their pocketbooks on their knees, past the portrait of Blanche White, who was like a mother to the kids in the town, through the tall open window, past the roadside grove of elms which Blanche White's 4-H Club planted in the 1950s, past the wheat-field horizon, and into the blank, bright sky. Suddenly I felt a joy so strong it almost knocked me down. It came up my spine and settled on my head like a warm cap and filled my eyes with tears, while I stood there packed in with everybody, watching Mrs. Robinson's lovely daughters dance.

And I thought, *It could have worked!* This democracy, this land of freedom and equality and the pursuit of happiness—

it could have worked! There was something to it, after all! It didn't have to turn into a greedy free-for-all! We didn't have to make a mess of it and the continent and ourselves! It could have worked! It wasn't just a joke, just a blind for the machinations of money! The Robinson sisters danced; Prince sang about doves crying; beauty and courage and curiosity and gentleness seemed not to be rare aberrations in the world. Nicodemus, a town with reasons enough to hold a grudge, a town with plenty of reasons not to exist at all, celebrated its Founders' Day with a show of hats and a dance revue. The Robinson sisters wove between each other, three-by-three. People cheered and whistled. The rancher who had wanted to see some break dancing clapped. To me, and maybe to some others in the room, the sight of so many black people here on the blue-eyed Great Plains was like a cool drink of water. Just the way they walked was something different and exciting. For a moment I could imagine the past rewritten, wars unfought, the buffalo and the Indians undestroyed, the prairie unplundered. Maybe history did not absolutely have to turn out the way it did. Maybe the history of the West, for example, could have involved more admiration of hats, more unarmed get-togethers, more dancing, more tasting of spareribs.

Joy! I leaned against the sturdiness of the McGhee sister by my side. From the wooden floor came a dust that smelled like small towns. Thoughts which usually shout down joy in me were nowhere in sight. I read in some magazine once that the most important word in American movies is "home"; that Americans, being immigrants, have strong associations with that word. The Robinson sisters turned and did a move that was mostly from the knees down. I was in the middle of America, in the middle of the Great

Plains, in the midst of history, in the valley of the Solomon River, in the town of Nicodemus: in my mind, anyway, home. "Home on the Range," a song whose first verse ("Oh, give me a home . . .") is familiar to millions, has a less familiar second verse, which goes:

> Oh, give me the gale of the Solomon vale
> Where life streams with buoyancy flow,
> Or the banks of the Beaver,
> Where seldom if ever,
> Any poisonous herbage doth grow.

All around me, I observed an almost total lack of poisonous herbage. The life streams were flowing with buoyancy. I was no longer a consumer, a rate payer, a tenant, a card holder, a motorist. I was home. The world looked as I wanted it to. My every breath was justified. I felt not the mild warmth of irony, not the comfort of camp, not the cheer of success and a full bank account; just plain, complete joy.

What a humming engine this feeling was! Joy like this is so rare in me as to be endangered. Did people use to feel like this all the time? Was this what those old-timers were looking for, and finding, on the Great Plains? Certainly, no man was ever happier than the first plains Indian to ride a horse, when time and space changed in an instant, and two feet were replaced by four, and a ridge that used to be a long, hot walk away was suddenly as near as a thought, a little leaning forward, and a tap of heel to flank. How it felt riding uphill, and how it felt leaning back over the haunches going downhill, and then the smooth feeling on the straightaway when the trot stretched into a gallop! Instead of seeing the upraised tails of the back ends of disappearing buffalo, the Indian was suddenly part of the herd itself, observing what they looked like when they ran, picking the ones he wanted to eat, driving his arrow all the way through them into the ground, then walking his horse back over miles to see how many he'd got. Wrapped in a buffalo robe at night, he must have had a physical memory in his whole body of the horse moving beneath him. The Minniconjou Sioux John Fire Lame Deer, in his book *Lame Deer, Seeker of Visions*, says: "For bringing us the horse we could almost forgive you for bringing us whiskey."

And how great the fur trappers must have felt, sometimes, seeing this land when it was still completely wild! A trapper with a good gun and two mules and a partner to share the watch at night was liable to leave the settlements for the West and never come back. Trappers who weren't killed were changed so that they never wanted to sleep in a house again. Kit Carson went West when he was seventeen, and travelled enough of the wilderness to earn him an airline mileage bonus today. Jim Bridger, sometimes called the King of the Mountain Men, first crossed the plains at eighteen, did not return to the settlements until he was thirty-five, stayed a short while, then went back. He told people that not once during those seventeen years had he tasted white bread. And how much fun the cowboys must have had, mixed in with the pain of their job! They were America's first continental citizens, seeing south Texas and Canada in a single season, carrying everything they needed with them on their saddles, stopping in towns with nicknames like the Gomorrah of the Cattle Trail (Ogallala, Nebraska), Hell on Wheels (Sherman, Wyoming, among others), and the Holy City of the Cow (Cheyenne, Wyoming). How pleasant to dance at the Cottage Saloon in Miles

City, Montana, with Connie, the Cowboy Queen, who wore a $250 dress embroidered with the brands of every cattle outfit between the Yellowstone and the Platte! And imagine the time the early railroad passengers had, shooting buffalo from the windows of the moving train, filling the compartment with smoke, shouting, laughing, then retiring to the saloon car! And how on-top-of-the-world it must have felt to be a town builder, sitting in a wagon above a cottonwood-lined river valley and seeing the promised land!

Probably the happiest man ever to ride the plains was also probably the most famous. In her book *Boots and Saddles*, Elizabeth Custer, wife of General George A. Custer, said, "My husband used to tell me that he believed he was the happiest man on earth, and I cannot help thinking that he was." Custer graduated last in his class from West Point in 1861, was jailed there after graduation for neglect of duty as Officer of the Guard, was released through the intercession of his classmates, fought many battles in the Civil War, became the youngest major general in the history of the Army by the end of the war, was appointed to the 7th Cavalry, fought several engagements with Indians on the plains, was court-martialed and suspended from duty for a year for ordering the shooting of deserters while on a forced march across Kansas primarily to see his wife, was reinstated after ten months through the intercession of General Sheridan, led an Army expedition to the Black Hills (in violation of a treaty with the Indians) in 1874, discovered gold, told the newspapers, started a gold rush, was removed from command for making unsubstantiated allegations of corruption against President Grant's brother before Congress, pleaded on his knees before General Terry to be allowed to serve in the Indian war which had followed the gold rush, was reinstated through the intercession of Generals Sheridan, Sherman, and Terry, led the 7th Cavalry in pursuit of Indians in the summer of 1876, continued the pursuit past where his orders said to stop, discovered a village on the Little Bighorn River in southeast Montana, attacked the village, and died, with about 265 of his command, at the hands of thousands of Sioux, Cheyenne, and other warriors. The event was the crescendo of a century of history on the Great Plains. Among the millions of words circling invisibly above the granite memorial on the low ridge where the bodies of Custer and some of his men were found is an account of Custer's death which Sitting Bull gave to a newspaper reporter. "He killed a man when he fell. He laughed," Sitting Bull said. Although Sitting Bull did not see that himself, I like to believe it. I like to believe Custer even had fun dying.

At West Point, Custer entertained his classmates with comical mistranslations of French assignments and silent pantomimes in his pew during chapel. All his life, he enjoyed heedless and extreme practical jokes. Whenever he received orders to move, he celebrated with "wild demonstrations of joy," smashing chairs and whirling his wife around the room. She thought he was a riot; once, when she was with guests in the parlor, and he wanted her to come to him in his study, he made her laugh uproariously with a note which read, "Do you think I am a confirmed monk?" The Great Plains, which he called "the fairest and richest portion of the national domain," were his playground. In the field, he sometimes travelled with his own cook, a cast-iron cookstove, a sixteen-piece Army band, and a pack of staghounds—one named Lucy Stone, after the woman-suffrage leader. Whenever buffalo crossed the line of march, Custer was liable to forget everything and take off after them. During one such chase, he accidentally shot his horse through the head, leaving himself stranded and alone in hostile territory miles from his command.

In his only book, *My Life on the Plains*, which is mostly about the plains Indian campaigns of 1867–68, he tells of finding the bodies of twelve men who had been caught by hundreds of Sioux. As it happened, these men, led by Lieutenant Lyman Kidder, had been looking for him. They were a special detail sent by General Sherman with orders for Custer, who was wandering as usual at his own inspiration far from where he was supposed to be. The fate of these men caused him no guilt; rather, as he followed the trail they had left trying to escape, he thought, "How painfully, almost despairingly exciting must have been this ride for life!" The bodies were so mangled as to be unrecognizable, shot with "twenty to fifty" arrows each, limbs hacked, genitals cut off and stuffed into mouths, eyes cut out and laid nearby on rocks, etc. "How painfully, almost despairingly exciting . . . !"

Custer's life demonstrates the power of a person having fun. Why, for example, were his superiors never able to restrain him successfully, or to keep this repeat offender away from important command? Maybe because they secretly looked up to him; maybe because a career of cavalry charges and danger and glory was something they had dreamed about as boys; maybe because he more closely resembled the soldier they had dreamed of being than they now did. Or maybe they simply loved him—Custer was good at being loved. The congressman who appointed him to West Point remembered him as "beautiful as Absalom with his yellow curls." Several now-forgotten Army officers did a better job fighting Indians on the plains, but Custer's fame is the victory of fun and myth over complicated history. Pursuing his boy's dream of a life on the Great Plains, a land which was itself a dream in many people's minds, Custer finally ran into the largest off-reservation gathering of Indians ever in one place on the continent, and gave them what was possibly the last really good time they ever had.

Later the Indians said that their encampment along the Little Bighorn stretched for miles, that they knew the soldiers were coming after them that summer, that Sitting Bull had foreseen the victory days in advance with a vision of "soldiers without ears falling upside-down into camp," that the first attack came at the southern end of the camp, that they chased the soldiers there into defensive positions on a ridge, that then they saw flags coming over a hill to the east of camp, that Custer and more soldiers came pouring over the hill, that Crazy Horse said, "That's where the big fight is going to be," that Crazy Horse led the first charge against Custer, that the soldiers dismounted and retired back up the rise in good order, that some soldiers held the horses while others shot, that the Indians tried to kill the horse-holders first, that soon the dust and smoke made it difficult to see, that warriors on horseback flew through the dust like shadows, that eagle-bone whistles were shrieking, that Indians shot and sometimes even scalped each other in the confusion, that the battle "looked like thousands of dogs might look if all of them were mixed together in a fight," that the Indians so outnumbered the soldiers they could have killed them with their horses' hooves, that the soldiers were covered with white dust, that many soldiers were killed with hatchets and stone clubs, that the fight lasted "about as long as it takes for a hungry man to eat his dinner."

Myth adhered to every Indian who was there. Well into this century, warriors who had fought Custer were famous on their reservations. (After World War I, some were reluctant to admit Indian veterans to their warrior societies, on the grounds that that war was "just shooting.") Indians recounted the Little Bighorn in songs, stories, drawings, paintings, and interviews with white reporters. The way people never forget where they were when President Kennedy was shot, Indians remembered what they were doing—eating, minding the pony herd, visiting a friend, greasing for a swim in the river—on the morning when the 7th Cavalry attacked. A man named Iron Hawk said that as he prepared for battle he was shaking so much and the pony he was holding was jerking so much that it took him a long time to braid an eagle feather into his hair. A woman named Mrs. Spotted Horn Bull (her husband was later to die with Sitting Bull) was in the hills digging turnips with many other women from the camp that morning; a mural-sized canvas tipi liner which she later painted of the event shows her and her digging stick and the turnips at the top of the picture, and the battle below. The Sioux holy man Black Elk, who was thirteen at the time, said that as he walked among the dead soldiers the smell of blood made him sick, but "I was not sorry at all. I was a happy boy." A warrior named White Bull told an interviewer, "It was a glorious battle, I enjoyed it."

A person can be amazingly happy on the Great Plains. Friends have told me the joy they felt, say, driving from Sheridan, Wyoming, to Hardin, Montana, or buying a turkey from a Hutterite religious colony near the Canadian border, or watching TV on New Year's Eve in the Trail

Dust Motel in Matador, Texas. So I know the way I felt in Nicodemus watching the Robinson sisters dance wasn't just me. Joy seems to be a product of the geography, just as deserts can produce mystical ecstasy and English moors produce gloom. Once happiness gets rolling in this open place, not much stops it. And if the Great Plains are like that today, what must they have been like in the nineteenth century, when man didn't have to share the stage with laws or institutions or machines. The Great Plains provided an obligingly blank backdrop for Custer, for the Sioux, for gamblers and buffalo hunters and river pilots and outlaws and trappers and cowboys. People pursued happiness here so fiercely that sometimes they touched it just as it was disappearing; and when their "real" lives were over—when Custer was dead, the Indians subdued, the open range fenced, the easy money gone—Great Plains adventures became theater. Only a few years after Little Bighorn, Buffalo Bill Cody, the former Army scout better known as an impresario, hired some of the same Indians who had fought Custer to reenact the battle in his travelling Wild West Shows. In arenas all over Europe and America, Custer died thousands of times more. The Wild West Shows also featured cowboy gunfights, trick shooting and roping and riding, stagecoach robberies, buffalo, bucking horses, etc. Old-time plainsmen who would never have "real" fun again were paid to have imitation fun.

Wild West Shows toured until the 1950s, but by then they had competition from rodeos, cowboy-and-Indian movies, and Westerns on radio and television. When I was a kid, every boy and some girls knew who their favorite cowboy was—usually Gene Autry, Roy Rogers, or Hop-along Cassidy. In the late 1950s, there were thirty Western series on prime-time television. Nobody makes Westerns for series TV anymore, and Western movies are rare. Like the plains themselves, the genre has been mostly forgotten or abandoned. Western movies are box-office death, supposedly. The dust which choked the Custer battlefield would tend to rule out any movie on the subject at Walt Disney Studios, which has four guidelines for screenplays: no snow (winter scenes are out), no headlines (recent news stories are out), no rural (the action must take place in an urban area), and no dust (Westerns are out).

10

ONCE, the whole country faced west. For Thomas Jefferson, exploring the western part of the continent had the same fascination that exploring space had for later Presidents. When Jefferson designed his house, Monticello, he gave it a long porch and terrace from which he could view the western horizon. In 1803, he sent an expedition headed by Meriwether Lewis and William Clark to explore the enormous tract of trans-Mississippi wilderness recently acquired from France in the Louisiana Purchase. The expedition was to follow the Missouri to its source, look for easy water routes across the continent, continue to the Pacific, and return. Particularly on the high plains, Lewis and Clark camped at places where nothing as important has happened since. On some of the bleaker reaches of the upper Missouri, they were the harbingers not of civilization but of future visits by Lewis and Clark buffs. Today the names they gave to geographic features commemorate themselves, their sweethearts, enlisted men with the expedition, Clark's slave, the President, Sacajawea's baby son, and several otherwise-forgotten members of the Jefferson Administration.

The Lewis and Clark Expedition was actually Jefferson's

third try at sending explorers to the American West. His second try was a decade earlier, when, as Secretary of State, he wanted to send a party headed by the French botanist André Michaux. Michaux got as far as Kentucky before President Washington had him recalled for his part in a French scheme to get America to declare war on Spain. Jefferson's first try was in 1785, when he was living in Paris as United States Ambassador. There he met a man named John Ledyard, who was, as Jefferson said, "of a roaming disposition." Ledyard was born in Groton, Connecticut, in 1751. He had failed to finish at Dartmouth because he was always off in the woods exploring, and he had sailed with Captain James Cook on his famous voyage of discovery to the South Pacific in 1776. Ledyard was obsessed with the idea of crossing the North American continent. In Paris, he and Jefferson came up with a plan for Ledyard to explore the West by heading east: that is, Ledyard would go from Paris across Europe, across Russia, across the Pacific in a Russian ship, down the west coast of North America to the latitude of the Missouri, and down that river to the Mississippi and the United States.

Jefferson loved this idea, but first he had to get Ledyard a passport from the Empress Catherine to travel in Russia. Jefferson sent his request by way of diplomats he knew who knew her, and she took months to respond. When she did, she said, "Everything that has been written about this expedition is completely false and a chimerical dream." Jefferson decided to wait and ask again. Meanwhile, Ledyard became so impatient that he went to London and got passage on a ship sailing to the American Northwest. Before setting out, he bought "two great Dogs, an Indian pipe and a hatchet" for the journey. Soon after the ship left the harbor, it was overtaken by a customs boat and forced to return because of unpaid debts.

To Jefferson's later request, Catherine replied through his go-between, the Baron von Grimm of Saxe-Gotha, "I have told you all I had to say about Mr. Ledyard." In London, Ledyard finally decided he was going anyway, although by then winter was coming on. He raised money with the help of an English nobleman and an American diplomat, sailed to Ostend, travelled to Hamburg, Copenhagen, and Stockholm. On the way, he lost one of his dogs. From Stockholm, he had intended to go by sled across the frozen Baltic Sea to Finland. Unfortunately, that winter was warm, and the Baltic froze only enough to prevent ships from sailing. So, rather than wait a few months for the Baltic to become navigable, Ledyard walked around it. In the middle of winter, he went up one side of the Gulf of Bothnia, down the other, across Finland, and over to St. Petersburg. The northernmost part of the trip took him almost to the Arctic Circle. In all, it was a walk of about twelve hundred miles. He arrived in St. Petersburg in March of 1787.

Still in need of a passport to cross Russia, he somehow managed to get one after a few months with the help of a Russian Army officer who was a favorite of the Grand Duke Paul, who did not like Catherine. From St. Petersburg, Ledyard went on to Moscow, followed the Volga River to Kazan, crossed the Ural Mountains, and continued, in various conveyances, to Tobolsk, Omsk, Tomsk, and Irkutsk. By then he was about 3,100 miles from St. Petersburg. From Irkutsk he went two hundred miles to Kachuga on the Lena River, and floated fifteen hundred miles down it to Yakutsk. There, a local Army commandant ordered him to wait until spring to continue on to the Pacific, still five hundred miles or so away.

What happened next, apparently, was that Catherine found out Ledyard had gone ahead with his trip despite her refusals, and she hit the ceiling. Soldiers came after him, found him in Irkutsk, where he had returned for some reason, arrested him, put him in a carriage "with his linen quite wet from the wash-tub" (in the words of an Englishman who was there), and drove him all the way back to Moscow. According to Jefferson, Ledyard "was put into a close carriage, and conveyed day and night, without ever stopping, till they reached Poland," but it is hard to believe this is literally true. In any event, Ledyard's captors must have made good time over the four-thousand-odd miles; Ledyard later wrote his cousin, "This journey was performed in 6 weeks: cruelties and hardships are tales I leave untold." In Moscow, authorities held an inquisition to find out if he was a spy. Then he was taken to the Polish border, told never to come back to Russia, and released.

The experience almost ruined his health, which he partially regained in Poland in the care of some Jewish women who may have found him crying by the side of the road. Then, before the year was out, Ledyard went to Egypt to get a caravan together to explore the interior of Africa. On the day he had planned to leave Cairo on the journey, some people who were to take him up the Nile decided to wait because the winds were wrong. The delay made Ledyard so upset that he became sick to his stomach. For relief, he took an emetic, which caused him to vomit so violently that he burst a blood vessel and died. He was buried in the sand. As Jefferson later wrote, "Thus failed the first attempt to explore the western part of our Northern continent."

That Catherine the Great should obstruct John Ledyard on his way to explore the region of the Great Plains is appropriate, because the Great Plains are linked more closely to Russia than to any other country. Among the Soviet Union's 8,650,000 square miles are many which resemble the Great Plains in latitude, treelessness, and rainfall. The steppes of southern Russia—a six- or seven-hundred-mile-wide belt of prairie stretching eastward from Hungary for thirty-five hundred miles or more—are colder than the southern plains and drier than the northern. They are at least as windy and empty. On a map of the Soviet Union, town names thin out to the east of the lower Volga River, just as they do in America west of the Missouri. Both the plains and the steppes are ruled by continental weather systems, with similar extremes of temperature, and similar thunderstorms interrupting months of blue skies. The fine windblown loess soil of the Great Plains is like the *chernozem*, or black earth, of the steppes. Many of the same plants flourish there as here. In fact, some of the most successful weeds on the Great Plains came from Eurasian Russia with settlement in the nineteenth century. Before white men, the Great Plains had no Russian knapweed, no goat grass, no cow cockle, no summer cypress. Corn cockle, which grows with winter wheat and makes bread taste bad when it gets ground up in flour, came from Russia. So did cheatgrass, that stick-like plant that takes over pastures and is not eaten by cows. Russian pigweed, which has spread from the Canadian plains to North Dakota and Montana, came originally from Siberia in 1886.

On the steppes, as on the plains, plants live in the wind. One Russian import which has done particularly well here is the Russian thistle, also called Russian cactus, saltwort, prickly glasswort, or wind witch. On the plains, its most common name is the tumbleweed. Its seedlings appear in dry, sandy soil in the spring, and for a couple of months they are edible to livestock. When the weather gets warm, they become hard, woody, prickly bushes which crowd out other vegetation. In early fall, the stalk breaks loose from the ground, and the plant rolls away on the wind. A single plant may have from 10,000 to 100,000 seeds, which fall off as they ripen all through the winter. The winds can take the plant for miles in many directions, and the seeds it drops stay vital for several years. As the ground freezes over the winter, many species of plants on the Great Plains come loose and become tumbleweeds. The Russian thistle is the best traveller, and the toughest tumbleweed for farmers to control.

Because tumbleweeds spend a lot more time in the wind than in the ground, they are not much use for cover, shade, or holding the soil in place. On the plains, from the point of view of humans, the tumbleweed's main function is poetic. They roll and bounce on the wind, they fly through the air like half-filled weather balloons, they pile up in throngs against fences and buildings. The poet Anselm Hollo has written that a tumbleweed "looks like the skeleton of a brain." Everywhere on the plains you see Tumbleweed Motels, Tumbleweed Cafes, Tumbleweed Liquors. In the Tumbleweed Bar, the jukebox is likely to have the song "Tumbling Tumbleweeds," by the Sons of the Pioneers, one of the most popular Western tunes ever. *Tumbleweeds* is a favorite syndicated cartoon strip, and in at least one prairie town Tumbleweed is the nickname of the travelling marijuana dealer. Tumbleweeds blow before the Kansas tornado at the beginning of *The Wizard of Oz*. They are a signature of hundreds of old Westerns: the saloon doors swing back and forth, a tumbleweed rolls across a deserted street, the marshal and the bad guy walk slowly toward each other. In southern Russia, too, Russian thistles blow all over—in Turkestan, in the Crimea, on the Khirgis Steppe in Kazakhstan. Russians don't call them Russian thistles, but *perekati-pole*, which means "roll-across-the-field."

Exactly how and when these plant species came to the Great Plains is not certain. Probably, they accompanied the tens of thousands of German Catholics, Mennonites, Hutterites, Amish, and others who left southern Russia for the Great Plains in the 1870s. Almost all of these immigrants were people who had been adrift in Europe since the Protestant Reformation 350 years before. Basically, the German Catholics were persecuted for saying that the Reformation went too far, and the Mennonites, Hutterites, and Amish for saying that it didn't go far enough. The last three groups were a type of radical Protestant sometimes called Anabaptist, because they did not believe in infant baptism. They believed that only adults who knew what they were getting into should be baptized. They also did not believe in swearing oaths, dancing, drinking, or gambling. At various times, certain sects among them were also opposed to marriage of cousins, tobacco, filing lawsuits, Fourth of July celebrations, buttons on clothing, circuses, and singing hymns in harmony. Most important, the Anabaptists believed in nonresistance, which meant they refused to serve in any war.

All these groups were in Russia in the first place because Catherine the Great had invited them. In addition to making John Ledyard miserable, Catherine also waged a series of wars with Turkey, which won for Russia new lands along her southern border. Catherine was German herself, and she wanted these sober, German-speaking farmers to secure her conquests by settlement. To convince the Mennonites to leave their homes in Polish Prussia, she promised them religious toleration, military exemption, 175 acres of land per family, tax exemptions, transportation payments, a loan of five hundred rubles per family, and government support until the first harvest. At least six thousand Mennonites took her up on it. They settled the steppes so successfully that their numbers grew to forty-five thousand in less than a century. Then, in 1870, Czar Alexander II withdrew the special privileges which Catherine had offered them. They and half a million other German-speaking colonists were now supposed to become full Russians at last. They would have to serve in the Army, and their children would have to speak Russian in Russian schools. The emissaries the Mennonites sent to St. Petersburg to protest this order could protest only in German, which one minister said proved the Czar's point. The Mennonites were upset about losing their military exemption, and the German Catholics, who were not war resisters, did not want to lose their German schools. All the German colonists started thinking about other countries where they might move.

Right away, representatives of the American railroads showed up. If Germans made the best farmers, these Russian Germans were thought to be the best of all. The Santa Fe Railroad, which ran through Kansas, got into a bidding war for the Mennonites with Nebraska's Burlington and Missouri. Both railroads offered almost everything that a farmer could want—free hay, roads, buildings, railroad passes, shipping. The B & M eventually even offered free land, but most of the Mennonites chose in favor of the Santa Fe, mainly because they liked the Santa Fe's immigration agent, a tireless man named C. B. Schmidt, who spoke German and finally got kicked out of Russia for his skill at convincing people to leave.

Hoping for the same military exemption their group once had in Russia, several Mennonite elders went to Washington to discuss the matter with President Grant. They were surprised to find him surrounded by none of the pomp that surrounded the Czar. Grant met them in a worn black frock coat and listened politely. As it happened, General Custer was there to see Grant at the same time. Custer, who was of German ancestry, spoke to the Mennonites in German, and later took them to a play, and they liked him—a man whose views on war could not have been more different from their own. General Grant made the Mennonites no promises. Canada, which was also eager for Mennonite settlers, enacted a law specifically exempting them from military service, but the U.S. Congress never did. However, such laws passed the legislatures of Kansas, Nebraska, and Minnesota—which meant little, since it was not usually the business of the states to raise armies. Of the ten thousand or so Russian Mennonites who came to America, the majority settled in south-central Kansas and built villages often with the same names and street plans as the villages they had left in Russia.

As it turned out, the Russian Mennonites made ideal plains farmers. Which figured, since they had already been practicing on the steppes for nearly a hundred years. They knew how to build houses from sod, how to use manure and grass for fuel, how to be content on an isolated frontier. The same plagues of grasshoppers that sometimes attack the plains attack the steppes; the Mennonites drove them from the fields with flails into the surrounding grass, then set the grass on fire. Most important, the Mennonites knew what to plant. Each Mennonite family had brought a bushel or more of Crimean wheat with them from Russia. This wheat, a hard, red, short-stemmed variety later called Turkey Red, was resistant to heat, cold, and drought. It was the right crop for the plains, and the Mennonites knew to cultivate it with four plowings, to make the soil hold moisture better. With this wheat and this technique, Mennonite farmers were able to move from the river valleys onto the drier, windier tablelands where no one else had yet figured out how to farm.

A problem with hard wheat was that it was more difficult to mill than the soft wheats. Millers in Minneapolis and the East did not like it, and paid less for it. So the Mennonites built their own mills. Their Turkey Red wheat kept them in business through drought years when many other plains farmers were going under. In the 1890s, the Mennonites attracted the attention of an employee of the U.S. Department of Agriculture named Mark Alfred Carleton. He was interested in finding good varieties of crops for dryland farming; his title was Cerealist in Charge of Grain Investigations. Carleton noticed the success of the Mennonites' Crimean wheat, and of another possibly Russian wheat called Red Fife which had been growing well on the Canadian plains. He decided to take a trip to Russia. His superiors were reluctant to send him with no knowledge of the language, so he learned it. He left for Russia in the summer of 1898, and travelled to parts of the steppes which were even colder and drier than the plains, figuring that grains from there would be more than strong enough for

America. On the Khirgis Steppes, in the real Russian boon-docks, Carleton obtained from a farmer named Gnyezdilov a variety of wheat called Kubanka. When he brought it back, it proved even better for some kinds of dryland farm-ing than Turkey Red. Another variety of wheat which Carleton found, the Kharkov, worked well on the northern plains, and both varieties were also highly resistant to black stem rust, a grain parasite which wiped out many wheats on the plains in 1904. Carleton went around to millers, urging them to buy more hard Russian wheat. He also began a campaign to get Americans to eat more macaroni, since hard wheats made good pasta. Eventually, people listened to him. By 1914, farmers on the Great Plains were pro-ducing tens of millions of bushels of Kubanka and Kharkov wheat.

When the Mennonite elders met with President Grant in 1873, he had assured them that the United States was not likely to be in a war for another fifty years. Not counting the brief Spanish-American War in 1898, Grant was only off by a few years. After America entered World War I in 1917, Congress passed the first universal conscription act since the Civil War. This act contained a clause exempting from combatant service "members of any well-organized religious sect or organization at present organized and ex-isting" whose beliefs did not allow them to participate in war. The act said that such people would be given non-combatant service, but did not spell out what that service would be. About half of the Mennonites who were drafted agreed to perform noncombatant service. The other half said that any service at all which aided the conduct of war was wrong. They reported for induction and then refused to wear uniforms or follow any orders, so the Army imprisoned many of them. The Kansas City *Star*, the Chicago *Tribune*, and much of America reviled them. The fact that members of this isolated, strange sect spoke German did not improve their standing in public opinion. Mobs painted their meeting houses yellow or burned them down. Several Mennonites were tarred and feathered. Teddy Roosevelt said the Mennonites were not fit to live in America. Eventually, seventy-six Mennonites, the grandsons of men who had left Russia rather than serve in the Czar's Army, were court-martialed, given terms of from ten to thirty years, and sent to the Army prison at Fort Leavenworth.

World War I changed the Great Plains more than any event in recent history. At the war's start, America, Canada, and Russia were the leading wheat-exporting nations of the world. Largely because of seeds brought from the steppes to the Great Plains, America was now selling as much wheat to the world's major wheat-importing nations in Western Europe as Russia was. When the Turkish Navy blockaded the Dardanelles in 1914, it stopped the flow of Russian wheat down from the Black Sea. Suddenly, like one kidney when the other is removed, the Great Plains had to work twice as hard. Farmers began to plow up land they had not considered planting before, and hundreds of thousands of acres of marginal land went under new lightweight tractors. By 1920, there were twice as many plowed acres on the southern plains as there had been in 1910. The price of wheat went from around $1 a bushel in 1914 to $2.10 a bushel in 1917. Farmers became rich, bought better equipment and more land, acquired more debt.

Prairie is much easier to plow under than it is to restore. When the war ended and the price of wheat fell, plains farmers did not respond by taking land out of production.

Instead, many of them used their new equipment to plant as much as possible, partly in an attempt to outrun the debt which buying the new equipment had entailed. Farming the plains became a speculative venture. People who lived elsewhere bought plains land and planted wheat on it during vacations in the fall; then, if the price was high enough, they returned to harvest in the summer. Much of the plains was dry during irregular rainfalls in the 1920s. 1931 was wet, and a good year for wheat production but a bad year for prices. Then, in 1932, the rain stopped. People had been farming the plains long enough to know that drought returned in regular cycles. This time, much of the native sod of grasses and roots which had held the soil in place since the last Ice Age was gone.

So began the first of the great modern eco-catastrophes. 1933 was drier than 1932. Early in '34, planting seemed ridiculous; plows turned up a dust as dry and fine as corn-starch. In February, the wind began to blow and the dust began to fly. In mid-April, a giant dust cloud, black at the base and tan at the top, rose from the fields of eastern Colorado and western Kansas and began to move south. Inside the cloud, darkness was total, and remained for hours after the cloud passed. People in the cloud's path thought the end of the world had come, and went to churches to await it. The storm left dead birds and rabbits in its wake, and drifts of dust six feet deep against the sides of houses. On May 10, another dust storm came up, on a wind from the west. This one blew all the way to the Eastern Seaboard, and blocked out the sun in New York City for five hours. People came home from work in an eerie half-light like the light during an eclipse. Dust got into the threads of water bottles and inside watch cases. Great Plains dust showered ships three hundred miles out in the Atlantic. All of Chicago was inches deep in it. That one storm dropped an estimated twelve million tons of plains topsoil on the city. All year, the dusters kept blowing. They were identified by color: brown dust storms came from Kansas, red ones from Oklahoma, and dirty-yellow ones from Texas and New Mexico. Farmers watched their fields disappear before their eyes. Tumbleweeds blew up against fences, caught the dust, and were buried. Fence lines were so deep in dust that cattle with mud-coated lungs could stagger away over them. People crammed wet newspapers around windows and doors and slept with wet handkerchiefs over their faces. Lung disease was everywhere. In the winter, snow mingled with the blowing dusters. These were called "snirt" storms.

In the Fick Fossil Museum, in Kansas, is a photograph of a towering dark-brown cloud with tucks at the bottom rolling across the earth. The caption reads, "The Grandfather of Them All—First Duststorm of 1935." This may be the same storm that inspired a famous American folk song. On April 14, 1935, a black dust storm from western Kansas blew down into the Texas panhandle. The songwriter Woody Guthrie, who was living in Pampa, Texas, took a look at the approaching storm and wrote "So Long, It's Been Good to Know You."

In Washington, D.C., dust hung in the air of the congressional hearing room as officials of the Department of Agriculture asked for more money for soil conservation. Dust came into the Oval Office and settled on President Roosevelt's desk. By the fall of '34, Roosevelt had approved a drought-relief program, Congress had passed emergency crop-support measures for farmers in the plains states, and the Department of Agriculture had begun paying ranchers for skinny, dust-sick cattle no one else would buy. One soil-conservation idea which Roosevelt came up with and liked a lot was planting a line of trees in a twenty-million-acre windbreak, or "shelterbelt," all the way across the Great Plains from Canada to the Gulf of Mexico. This idea was widely laughed at, and agricultural and forestry experts persuaded Roosevelt to modify the program so that individual farmers could plant shelterbelts around their fields and houses instead. The rows of wind-bent cottonwood, hackberry, elm, honey locust, and pine that you often see to the windward of abandoned or long-gone farmhouses are the mark Roosevelt left on the Great Plains.

Some farmers plowed deep furrows around their fields to stop them from blowing, stretched snow fences, and met in churches daily to pray for rain. By the hundreds of thousands, others left. Because so many were from western Oklahoma, these people were called Okies, but refugees came from every Great Plains state. A person who stuck it out in Williams County, North Dakota, noted later, "The people who moved away then never came back." The years of the Dust Bowl were the beginning of some of the plains' biggest farm holdings, as surviving farmers bought the others out. In some counties, the blowing was so bad that farmers could find nobody to sell to. The federal government eventually bought millions of acres of windblown land and began trying to restore it to grass. The Comanche National Grassland, in Baca County, Colorado, is one of the results. A land company which had once tried to get people to buy farmland in Baca County had advertised it as part of "what is known as the 'Rain Belt' " of eastern Colorado; in the 1930s, much of Baca County blew away.

Of the farmers who survived, many got government help,

through crop support or other payments. They learned to hold on to their topsoil by contour plowing, leaving crop stubble standing in their fields after harvest, strip farming, and planting windbreaks. In 1941, the rains came back, world war made the price of wheat go up again, and some farmers again made lots of money. After the war, a recent invention called the deep-well turbine pump, which could move water much more efficiently than the old centrifugal pump, showed farmers on the southern plains that they were sitting on a great reservoir of groundwater, and they began to mine it for irrigation at a rate which now threatens to drain it within fifty years. Geologists named this reservoir the Ogallala Aquifer. Its water has turned a number of Dust Bowl counties greener than they ever were before. When it runs dry, the desert which came in the 1930s to depopulate the farms and eat big holes in the prairie will return.

Today the Great Plains are more than linked to Russia; they are also, in a sense, aimed at it. The propellants which deliver American nuclear missiles to their targets are solid fuels which all happen to absorb moisture from the air during storage. Solid rocket fuel is often made of explosives, like nitrocellulose, and oxydants, like ammonium perchlorate, suspended in a neutral substance, like aluminum powder with a polymer binder. Solid fuels are safer and easier to handle than liquid fuels. Unfortunately, the solid part of the fuel absorbs water vapor as readily as it did the explosive chemicals, and once the fuel gets even a little wet, it changes. Modern ballistic missiles control their flight not by flaps and fins but by directing the flow of thrust out the back end. For this to work, the fuel must burn at a regular rate. Fuel that has been wet burns erratically; in particular, it develops fissures, or "grain cracks," which combustion follows. A bad grain crack can burn at such an angle as to melt through the outside of the missile and cause it to tumble. Even more vulnerable to moisture than the fuel is the circuitry of the missile's on-board computer and guidance system. The easiest way to wreck a nuclear missile would be to keep it in a damp basement. For this reason, the Air Force prefers arid places for its land-based missile installations. The driest part of America which is the farthest from major population centers and the closest (via the Great Circle route above the Arctic) to the Soviet Union happens to be the northern Great Plains. Of America's 2,750 or so land-based nuclear warheads, about 1,850 sit on top of Minuteman and MX missiles there.

Driving on the prairie near Great Falls, Montana, or Minot, North Dakota, or Cheyenne, Wyoming, you might not realize right away that you are in a weapons system. A nuclear-missile silo is one of the quintessential Great Plains objects: to the eye, it is almost nothing, just one or two acres of ground with a concrete slab in the middle and some posts and poles sticking up behind an eight-foot-high Cyclone fence; but to the imagination, it is the end of the world. The sign on the fence does not mention the destructive power of thousands of Hiroshimas sitting just a few yards away. It does say that this is a restricted area, and that deadly force may be used to prevent intrusion. In the lonesomest stretch of prairie, you could find no faster way of meeting people than rattling that fence for a minute or two. Attached to the fence are sensors which set alarms ringing in Air Force control centers whenever anything bumps against it. Cattle, horses, antelope, and big tumbleweeds set off alarms from time to time. Depending on where the alarm comes from and how many false alarms they've been getting recently, security forces then jump in vans or armored vehicles and head for the silo at full speed.

Beneath the concrete slab—the silo door—is the tip of a Minuteman II, a Minuteman III, or an MX missile. The Minuteman II carries a single warhead, the Minuteman III carries three independently targeted warheads, and the MX up to ten. The missiles are between fifty-seven and seventy-one feet long and up to seven feet seven inches across. Each silo contains a single missile, as well as support and launch equipment on platforms around the missile. The missile's guidance system depends on the fixed spin of several high-speed gyroscopes. Getting the gyroscopes running is too delicate a task to be left to the last minute, so once they are started up, they run all the time. A flow of sodium-chromate solution in which no organisms can live cools the gyros as they spin at many thousands of rpms. No people stay in the silo. Each group of ten missiles is fired from an always-manned underground launch control center nearby. The main color inside the silo is a *2001: A Space Odyssey*-white. There are no chairs. On top of a computer console or in a corner might be a cloth bag of commercial dehumidifying salts. Night and day beneath the prairie, the gyros hum. The air in the sealed-up silo holds a faint smell of the Old Spice after-shave which the last Air Force maintenance people to visit wore.

If you did not follow the last twenty years of the arms race, here is how some of it went: From the sixties through the mid-seventies, the Soviet Union developed a new generation of long-range nuclear missiles, the SS-17, SS-18, and SS-19, which were thought to be the most accurate missiles in the world. A Minuteman missile silo supposedly cannot survive a nuclear hit at closer than 370 meters; according to CIA reports at the time, the SS-18 was accurate to within 180 meters. American strategists began to fear that the Soviet Union could now destroy most of the Minuteman silos in a first strike, and they popularized their fear with the phrase "window of vulnerability," which they said America now had. To defend against this threat, the Carter Administration wanted to build a new missile called the MX which could carry multiple warheads and which would be deployed on mobile launchers on three thousand miles of track beneath the desert in Utah and Nevada. When Reagan was elected, he did not like the idea of a mobile MX, but instead wanted to house the new missiles in existing Minuteman silos. Debate over the MX went on for years. Meanwhile, the CIA revised its opinion of the Soviet missiles, and said they might not be so accurate after all. Eventually, the MX was built. By the end of 1988, fifty MXs were placed in silos in Wyoming which had been "hardened" with additional concrete and steel. The recent development of other weapons systems like the Midgetman missile, which is small enough to be fired from a truck or an airplane, and new long-range submarine-launched missiles, creates the possibility that the Soviet Union may soon have a window of vulnerability of its own. Since both America and the Soviet Union have concentrated on weapons designed mainly to destroy the weapons of the other, neither country can now afford to wait out a first strike. A missile which is not fired quickly might end up not being fired at all. America used to say that it would absorb a first strike before firing back; today it does not rule out a policy of "launch under attack." Presumably, the Soviet Union does not either. All of which means that any silo you stop to look at on the northern plains probably holds a missile with the locations of ten or more Soviet missiles in its targeting computer. And someplace in Russia, probably in an underground silo in western Siberia along the Trans-Siberia Railroad, a missile knows about this exact piece of nowhere prairie.

The Air Force personnel who look after the missiles in Montana are stationed at Malmstrom Air Force Base, just outside of Great Falls. The public information officers there answer questions by mail about the Minuteman system with a vague line drawing of a missile in a silo. To callers who wish to chat about the missile installations, they reply in the most general terms. Then, in the summer, the base holds an open house for anybody who wants to come, and officers and enlisted men show their visitors around and tell them just about anything they want to know. This event, called Big Sky Days, is usually on a weekend in July. One year, along with about twenty-nine thousand other people, I went. At the gate, an Air Force guy in a short-sleeve blue uniform shirt was directing traffic. Nearby he had parked a Chevy Blazer with the doors open, so he could listen to the radio. "Standing in the Light," by Fleetwood Mac, was playing. Malmstrom is mostly runway. The thousands of cars parked together took up only a little piece of it. In the distance, heat shimmers rose where it seemed to disappear around the curve of the earth.

Big Sky Days was the kind of summer event where people in shorts walk around dazed and asquint. Long lines waited to go up into the camouflage-painted B-52. In a big hangar, Air Force wives and local groups ran booths selling "Rambo Hotdogs" and "Commie Busters" T-shirts. At one booth, kids could get their faces painted camouflage. By the end of the day, about half the kids had. An M-60 tank in the middle of the hangar drew kids by the hundreds. It was like the most popular rock at monkey island. Members of Air Force security in mesh flak jackets and black berets, with automatic rifles across their backs, helped kids climb on and off. By the hangar doors, pilots in flight suits walked up to each other and put their heads together. Then, after a moment, they threw back their heads and laughed big openmouth pilot laughs.

I talked to an airman, name tag D. Moir, whose job for the day was to stand by a vehicle designed for transporting warheads and explain it. "I enlisted to learn aircraft maintenance at a base near where I live back East, and they gave me missile maintenance out here," he said. He told me the name of the vehicle, which was an acronym about six letters long. The vehicle looked like a strange house trailer, and its dark, padded interior smelled like a new TV. An off-duty airman who said his name was Jay kept D. Moir company, straddling a racing bicycle and bumping it back and forth between his knees. Jay was wearing shorts, a T-shirt with the arms ripped off, and white-rimmed sunglasses on a purple cord. "Dwight and I are technicians. We do computer maintenance," Jay said. "There's two kinds of missile technicians—electronic and mechanical. We're electronic. Malmstrom can be kind of a cliquey place. The computer guys usually hang out with each other, and so do the support people—cooks, logistics-and-transport guys, like that—and the mechanics, and the launch officers, and the security cops. Especially the cops. Those guys in the black berets, they may not be that smart. But I'll tell you one thing, they are some gung-ho soldiers. Last week I was with a crew out at an LF—launch facility, that's a silo—and when we radioed back we screwed up and forgot the password, so we just said, 'Well, nothing to do now but wait.' About four minutes later, this helicopter comes over the horizon and sets down and these security guys jump off with the guns pointed *at* us, and they had us down on our noses in the dirt. And they *knew* who we were. But at least it was some excitement. This duty can get pretty boring sometimes. Like every three months or so, they change the target codes in all the Minuteman IIs, and we have to go out and put in the new codes. The codes come in a suitcase-like thing, looks like a big cassette. That's been every day for the last two weeks: loadin' codes. Drive all the way out to an LF, go down, take out the old codes, slip in the new codes, close up, get in the truck, drive back. Loadin' codes, man. In a few months, all the Minuteman IIs are changing over to remote loading, so we won't have to do that anymore. Can't happen soon enough for me. There's silos out there that are three and a half hours from the base by road, one way. And you're not supposed to drive faster than fifty on pavement or twenty-five on gravel—supposedly. Almost everything that has to do with missiles is 'supposedly.' But I'll tell you, you wreck one of those trucks and they take it out of your pay."

To train people to work in missile silos, Malmstrom has one on the base. They call it a Trainer Launch Facility, and it is like a real silo except that the missile it holds is not live. I went down in the silo with a bunch of other people on a tour led by Staff Sergeant John Swift. Sgt. Swift had a freckled face off a cover of *Boy's Life*, aged with a red toothbrush mustache. His eyes roved beyond his listeners as he spoke, like a man at a cocktail party hoping to spot a closer friend. Sgt. Swift led us along the doughnut-shaped platform that encircles the missile. The platform was twelve inches deep in foam-rubber padding, and felt funny to walk on. On it were an air-conditioning unit, a dehumidifier, a coolant pump for the missile's gyros, the circuitry for the security system, a radio receiver, a scrambler, a decoder, and the computers which talk and listen to the missile. The padding was to cushion any jolts to this equipment. Sgt. Swift said the whole platform was suspended from cables which would allow it to bounce three feet in either direction. The support equipment was connected to the missile by a thick, veined cable called the umbilical. No matter how high-tech things get, there is always a big cable lying around somewhere. Sgt. Swift explained the operation of the missile's guidance system so quickly that he might have been speaking Malay. He showed us the pewter-colored tip of the missile—the warhead shell—of titanium alloy. He said that it was ablative. I had not heard that word since Latin class. In rocketry, it means designed to ablate, or burn away smoothly and slowly during reentry into the atmosphere. Improvements in the ways warheads ablate is one reason they have gotten more accurate. Sgt. Swift said that in the event of a near-hit which tipped the silo on its side, it could still fire the missile from an angle lower than ninety degrees. He said that he had been working on these missiles for years, and could tell by the sound when he opened the silo hatch whether the gyros and the support equipment were running right.

The question everybody wanted to know was: "So, how do you fire one of these things?" Sgt. Swift's eyes roved farther beyond us as he began his recitation; the end of the world is a pretty personal subject, after all. He said that each group of ten missiles is controlled from a Launch Control Center—an LCC, also called a capsule—fifty to ninety feet below ground, where two Air Force officers wait on duty around the clock. When they receive an order to launch, they open a safe locked with two combination locks and take out two launch keys, which look like ordinary car keys. They insert the keys in control locks about fifteen feet apart in a computer console. They make sure the order is genuine by checking it against a verification code, they retarget the missiles as the order requires, they give the computer an "enabling code" to free the missiles for firing, and they talk to officers in four other capsules in a conference call via underground cable. One of these officers is the launch leader. The launch leader says, "Stand by for key turn." Everybody waits. At the launch time indicated in the order, the leader tells the officers to turn their keys, and they turn them down and to the right to a position marked "Launch," and hold them for two seconds. In most circumstances, it takes four officers—two in two capsules—turning their keys in close succession to fire one or all of a flight of ten missiles. The key-turns send a signal to the missile which begins its terminal countdown. This lasts a few seconds or as long as several hours, depending on the launch order. The missile "acid dumps"—that is, it activates its batteries by dumping acid into them. The missile is now on internal command and will accept no orders but its own. It drops its umbilical. It blows open the silo door. It fires its engines, and a smoke ring sixty feet across rises from the silo. A surge of smoke and flames follows the ring. The missile comes shooting through the smoke and flames into the sky.

Sgt. Swift pointed out the canisters of explosives overhead whose job it was to blow the silo door. They were as big around as stovepipes and several feet long. The slow, ominous opening of missile-bay doors with which movies like to indicate the beginning of World War III is a fiction. Out here, a bystander would know World War III was coming if he heard a big bang and saw a 110-ton concrete silo door go flying a quarter mile or more across the prairie.

The other question everybody asked was: "How much does all this stuff cost?" Sgt. Swift said that each silo cost about $20 million. In fact, costs having to do with nuclear weapons are hard to pin down. When I later wrote the Office of Air Force History to ask about the total amount spent so far on the Minuteman, they wrote back to say that looking for that information would be too expensive. The first silo of the two hundred in Malmstrom's wing went into the ground in 1961. It contained a Minuteman I missile. In the sixties, the Minuteman I began to be replaced by Minuteman II. In the seventies, many Minuteman IIs were replaced by Minuteman IIIs. Each generation of missile took years to develop, test, and build. From 1962 to 1965, the Air Force probably spent about $2 billion a year on Minuteman I. (A billion dollars then is about the same as $4 billion now.) The next generations of missiles cost at least as much. In the late seventies, all the Minuteman silos were improved with new support equipment, hardened silo doors, emergency power systems, and better targeting computers. Maintenance and testing of the missiles never stops. The Minuteman is an organism which requires a continuous flow of money. Just building the missiles has cost perhaps 100 billion present-day dollars. With the additional costs, the total might be as high as $150 billion spent on the system to date. There are a thousand silos at the six Minuteman bases. A thousandth of $150 billion is $150 million. So you might say that a single silo represents about $150 million in total spending. Montana's Pondera County, which contains many of Malmstrom's silos, produced about $30 million of agricultural goods in a recent year. A single missile silo would equal about five years' worth of all the cattle, wheat, and barley in Pondera County.

The fifty MX missiles recently installed in silos in Wyoming cost about $148 million apiece. Laramie County, Wyoming, where the first MX went in, produces about $40 million of agriculture a year. The total cost so far of the MX is about $15 billion. Before all the hundred projected MXs are in place, the cost may be $25 billion. Add what was spent for the now-abandoned Safeguard Anti-Ballistic Missile system to the amounts for the Minuteman and the MX, and the total approaches $200 billion. In a good year, the four-hundred-odd counties on the Great Plains produce agriculture—beef, cotton, hay, feed grain, much of the world's wheat—worth about $19 billion.

This, finally, is the punch line of our two hundred years on the Great Plains: we trap out the beaver, subtract the Mandan, infect the Blackfeet and the Hidatsa and the Assiniboin, overdose the Arikara; call the land a desert and hurry across it to get to California and Oregon; suck up the buffalo, bones and all; kill off nations of elk and wolves and cranes and prairie chickens and prairie dogs; dig up the gold and rebury it in vaults someplace else; ruin the Sioux and Cheyenne and Arapaho and Crow and Kiowa and Comanche; kill Crazy Horse, kill Sitting Bull; harvest wave after wave of immigrants' dreams and send the wised-up dreamers on their way; plow the topsoil until it blows to the ocean; ship out the wheat, ship out the cattle; dig up the earth itself and burn it in power plants and send the power down the line; dismiss the small farmers, empty the little towns; drill the oil and natural gas and pipe it away; dry up the rivers and springs, deep-drill for irrigation water as the aquifer retreats. And in return we condense unimaginable amounts of treasure into weapons buried beneath the land which so much treasure came from—weapons for which our best hope might be that we will someday take them apart and throw them away, and for which our next-best hope certainly is that they remain humming away under the prairie, absorbing fear and maintenance, unused, forever.

11

WHEN I went for long drives on the plains, I might be on the road for weeks at a time. I could afford to stay in motels only every third or fourth night, so the others I spent in my van. I slept beneath the mercury lights of highway rest areas where my lone car was visible for six miles in any direction and the inside of the men's room looked as if it had been sandblasted with tiny insects, and on the streets of small towns where the lawn sprinklers ran all night, and next to dammed-up waters of the Missouri River where the white top branches of drowned trees rose above the waves. My van had so many pinholes from rust that it created a planetarium effect on the ground when I turned on the interior light. After a day of driving there was usually a lot of dust on the bed, and maybe a stunned grasshopper that had come through the open window.

One night I tried to sleep at a picnic area at the Double Mountain Fork of the Brazos River in Texas, on U.S. Highway 83. Highway 83 runs from Mexico to Canada and is like the Main Street of the Great Plains. Cars went by only occasionally, which somehow made them scarier. The moon was full, and the wind was blowing harder than during the day. I got up and walked around. By moonlight I read a historic marker in the picnic area which said that in 1877 hunters brought more than a million buffalo hides to a trading post near this spot. When I lay down again, the unquiet spirits of a million buffalo were abroad in the windy night. My head kept falling through the pillow. The moon shone, the stars blinked, the trees tossed back and forth, the shadows waited under the picnic kiosks. I got up again and drove until dawn.

In New Mexico I slept well in front of a shuttered vegetable stand on the outskirts of a town. I woke in the morning to blue sky and the sound of small animals playing under my car and scurrying across the roof. On the vegetable stand I saw a sign posted. I went over to see what it said. It said:

PLAGUE
is passed to man by
WILD RODENTS, Rabbits,
and by their FLEAS
. . . Do NOT
Pitch tents or lay
Bedrolls on or near
nests or burrows.
Plague is CURABLE
WHEN TREATED IN TIME.

The best places to sleep were truck stops. At two-thirty in the morning a truck-stop parking lot full of trucks is the capital of sleep. The trucks park in close rows, as if for warmth. The drivers sleep with purposeful intent. The big engines idle; together, the trucks snore. Hinged moisture caps on top of the diesel stacks bounce in the exhaust with a pinging noise. I tried to park as close as I could without being presumptuous. Unlike tourists in rest stops, truck drivers seem careful about slamming doors and gunning engines late at night. Sometimes the truck I had gone to sleep next to would quietly leave and another would quietly pull in. One morning when I woke up a semi-trailer full of pickup-truck camper tops had been replaced by a stock truck. On the truck's door, in big letters, a poem:

> Buck Hummer
> Hog Hauler

In Colorado, Highways 71 and 36 make a big cross on the map when they intersect at the town of Last Chance. Sixty miles to the west, the prairie ends and greater Denver begins, and the uplands are barnacled with houses for a hundred miles along the Rocky Mountain front. Fewer than seventy people live in Last Chance. The wheat fields are eroding, the oil wells are running dry, the only store in town burned down. "However, hope springs eternally in the breasts of our decreasing high school enrollment," a citizen of Last Chance wrote recently. On a night of many thunderstorms, I pulled over to sleep at that intersection. The wind made the streetlight sway, and made its shadows sway inside my van. A full cattle truck came sighing down the road and then squeaked to a stop at the blinking red light. I could hear the animals shifting and bumping inside. They were very likely on their way to one of the largest feedlots in the world, sixty miles north of Denver, where they would stand around with a hundred thousand other cows and eat until they were fat enough to slaughter. The truck sat for a moment. Then the driver revved the engine and found first gear, and the full load of cattle braced themselves for the start. In step, they set their many feet all at once, like a dance revue.

Now, when I have trouble getting to sleep, I sometimes imagine that my bed is on the back of a flatbed pickup truck driving across the Great Plains. I ignore the shouts on the sidewalk and the bass vibrations from the reggae club across the street. The back of this truck has sides but no top. I can see the stars. The air is cool. The truck will go nonstop for nine hours through the night. At first the road is as straight as a laser—State Highway 8, in North Dakota, say—where nothing seems to move except the wheels under me and the smell of run-over skunks fading in and out in my nose. Then the road twists to follow a river valley, and cottonwood leaves pass above, and someone has been cutting hay, and the air is like the inside of a spice cabinet. Then suddenly the wheels rumble on the wooden planks of a one-lane bridge across the River That Scolds at All the Others. Ever since the Great Plains were first called a desert, people have gone a long way toward turning them into one. The Great Plains which I cross in my sleep are bigger than any name people give them. They are enormous, bountiful, unfenced, empty of buildings, full of names and stories. They extend beyond the frame of the photograph. Their hills are hipped, like a woman asleep under a sheet. Their rivers rhyme. Their rows of grain strum past. Their draws hold springwater and wood and game and grass like sugar in the hollow of a hand. They are the place where Crazy Horse will always remain uncaptured. They are the lodge of Crazy Horse.

NOTES

INDEX

Notes

Chapter 1

[p. 4] Queen of the Cowtowns was only one of Dodge City's many monikers. Others were the Athens of the Cow Trade, the Cowboy Capital, the Wickedest City in America, and the Beautiful, Bibulous Babylon of the Frontier. The last two names were the invention of visiting journalists. See *Dodge City, Kansas*, by Charles C. Lowther (Philadelphia, 1940); *Dodge City, the Cowboy Capital*, by Robert M. Wright (Wichita, Kan., 1913), a good book by a man who lived in Dodge from its beginning; *The Cattle Towns*, by Robert R. Dykstra (New York, 1968); and *Queen of Cowtowns: Dodge City*, by Stanley Vestal (New York, 1952).

Air Midwest, at this writing part of Eastern, flies from New York City to Dodge City.

[p. 4] Various complicated routes West were available to travellers going overland in 1849. This itinerary is from *Overland to California in 1849*, by Joseph Sedgley (Oakland, 1877), pp. 5–7:

SATURDAY, March 31.—To-day we left New York, and took passage in the steamboat *John Potter*, at seven o'clock, A.M., and arrived at Amboy [New Jersey] at nine o'clock . . . At half-past nine o'clock we took the cars reserved for us, and traveled over the Camden and Amboy Railroad, and arrived at Camden at two o'clock, P.M., covered with dust. Here we took the ferry-boat across the Delaware River to Philadelphia, where we arrived at five o'clock . . .

MONDAY, April 2.—. . . At ten o'clock we took the cars of the Columbia Railroad, connecting with the Pennsylvania and Ohio Canal. Peach and other trees are in full bloom.

TUESDAY, April 3.—. . . We crossed the Susquehanna River by the canal . . .

WEDNESDAY, April 4.—. . . To-day we traveled up the Juniata River . . . We arrived at Lewiston at eight o'clock and took supper. Left Lewiston at ten, P.M., and continued our journey up the Juniata to Holidaysburg, which point we reached at six o'clock, and took lodgings at the hotel . . .

FRIDAY, April 6.—. . . We took the cars to go over the Alleghanay Mountains, thirty-six miles, to Johnstown . . . The ascent is made by means of ten inclined planes. After crossing the mountains, we took passage in a canal boat for Pittsburg . . .

SATURDAY, April 7.— . . . We arrived at Freeport at twelve o'clock at night, and took lodgings at the Freeport Hotel . . .

SUNDAY, April 8.—The boat not running on Sunday, part of our company, being anxious to reach Pittsburg, chartered a boat belonging to another line to take us there, which place we reached at five o'clock.

After nine days of travel between New York and Pittsburgh, Sedgley's party took steamboats from there to the edge of the frontier.

A good description of a route west from Baltimore is in *Gold Rush: The Journals, Drawings, and Other Papers of J. Golds-*

borough Bruff, edited by Georgia Willis Read and Ruth Gaines (New York, 1944). See also, among many other accounts, *Overland to California,* by William G. Johnston (Oakland, 1948); *Trail to California: The Overland Journal of Vincent Geiger and Wakeman Bryarly,* edited by David M. Potter (New Haven, 1945).

[p. 5] The story of Angus Mackay and the introduction of summer fallow to the plains is told in that classic work of Western history, *Montana: High, Wide, and Handsome,* by Joseph Kinsey Howard (Lincoln, Neb., 1983), pp. 276–77. Part of Howard's account is retold from *Hunger Fighters,* by Paul de Kruif (New York, 1928).

[p. 5] People have gone to extraordinary lengths to coax rain from the Great Plains sky. For example, an experimental cloud-seeding program sponsored by the National Center for Atmospheric Research in Montana used high-speed jets to chase down and seed small clouds which often had a life span of less than thirty minutes. The program had planes equipped with laser probes, suction samplers, and armor plating against hail. In 1910, C. W. Post, the cereal magnate, began an ambitious rainmaking project on his 200,000 acres of the Texas plains. Post had noticed that in accounts of wars which he had read, heavy rains always seemed to follow artillery battles. He believed that with enough explosions he could produce rain. He blew off box-cars and boxcars of dynamite on the plains around his town of Post City, Texas. The dynamite was laid out on the ground and fired at intervals designed to simulate artillery barrages. Post and his staff kept at it for several years, and produced drizzles and one or two rainstorms, which encouraged him. (See *Heaven's Tableland: The Dust Bowl Story,* by Vance Johnson, [New York, 1947], Chap. VIII.)

[p. 6] A discussion of the boundaries, both physiographic and botanical, of the Great Plains is in *Prehistoric Man on the Great Plains*, by Waldo R. Wedel (Norman, Okla., 1961), pp. 20–24, 36.

[p. 7] The fact that banks and insurance companies would not lend money for agriculture west of the hundredth meridian I learned from a historical marker put up by the South Dakota Historical Society on Highway 16 just west of Blunt, South Dakota:

YOU ARE NOW ON THE 100° MERIDIAN

Historically that meridian is significant. For two generations the Insurance Companies and other world wide lending agencies would not, as a matter of agreed policy, lend a shiny dime west of this line. Their reason was that some geographer had labeled it the EAST EDGE of the Great American Desert. Neither the geographer nor the Insurance Companies had been west of 100° . . . This unrealistic, geographically limited loan policy forced South Dakota into the farm loan business. Our Rural Credit business cost us plenty and was a splendid illustration of why a state should not be in the loaning business. But South Dakota has paid all its debts in full. The 100th Meridian is just another bad memory. Historically however the 100° Meridian was a most important one in Western economy.

Dayton Canaday, director of the South Dakota Historical Resource Center, sent me additional information about this subject.

[p. 8] The size of the aquifer beneath the Great Plains is mentioned in an article in *The New York Times*, "Depletion of Underground Water Formation Imperils Vast Farming Region": ". . . the Ogallala Aquifer, a huge deposit of water-laden sand, silt, and gravel that stretches through Nebraska clear down into New Mexico and Texas. Its volume is estimated to be roughly equivalent to that of Lake Huron" (August 11, 1981, II, 4:1).

[p. 8] The fact that the Great Plains export two-thirds of the world's wheat is mentioned in *The Last West*, by Russell McKee (New York, 1974), p. 270: "Fully two-thirds of all the world's wheat exports are shipped from the Great Plains of Canada and the United States, an amount not expected to decline."

[p. 8] The expedition led by Zebulon Pike went west along the valley of the Arkansas River, and saw the landscape created when Great Plains winds blew sand from the bed of the Arkansas into dunes and hills. The Stephen Long expedition followed the Platte, and saw there a similar landscape, which they called the "deserts of the Platte." See *Account of an Expedition from Pittsburgh to the Rocky Mountains in the Years 1819, 1820*, by Edwin James (London, 1823), Vol. II, p. 176.

The theory that it was the particular landscape which Pike encountered along his route which led eventually to the idea of the Great American Desert is discussed in "The Cognition and Communication of Former Ideas about the Great Plains," by G. Malcom Lewis, in *The Great Plains: Environment and Culture*, edited by Brian W. Blouet and Frederick C. Luebke (Lincoln, Neb., 1979), pp. 35 et seq. Professor Lewis also traces the first appearance of "Great Desert" and "Great American Desert" on maps and atlases of the time.

[p. 9] An examination of the advertising and public-relations blitz which attempted to remake the Great American Desert into a garden spot is in *Garden in the Grasslands*, by David M. Emmons (Lincoln, Neb., 1971). Joseph Kinsey Howard also talks about this subject in *Montana: High, Wide, and Handsome*, Chap. XVI et seq. A "wet period" which attracted would-be settlers to the northern plains at the turn of the century is mentioned in *The Rape of the Great Plains*, by K. Ross Toole (Boston, 1976), p. 131. Another, in the 1880s, is mentioned in *The Great Plains*, by Walter Prescott Webb (New York, 1931), p. 341.

[p. 9] Whitman actually used "A newer garden of creation" as an epithet for the prairie states, in a poem of that title. Whitman's poetry often looked "inland to the great pastoral Plains." See *Walt Whitman: Complete Poetry and Collected Prose* (New York, 1982), pp. 524, 282.

[p. 9] The fact that two-thirds of the counties on the Great Plains have lost population since 1930 comes from U.S. Census Bureau figures from 1920 through 1980.

The estimate of the coal reserves under the plains comes from newspaper articles on the subject. An article in *The New York Times* of July 3, 1974 (p. 39:3), says that forty-five percent of the nation's coal reserves is in the Dakotas, Montana, and Wyoming. Those deposits lie in a formation called the Fort Union formation. More deposits are found in Colorado and New Mexico.

[p. 13] The spot where a driver gets a dramatic first view of the Great Plains is on U.S. Highway 89, about five miles east of St. Mary's, Montana.

[p. 14] It was the Stephen Long expedition whose scent moved through a herd of buffalo and frightened animals far in the distance. See James, Vol. II, p. 167.

[p. 15] All of the information about the murder of Thomas Running Rabbit and Harvey Mad Man and its aftermath comes from the Kalispell, Montana, *Daily Interlake* and the Missoula, Montana, *Missoulian*.

Chapter 2

[p. 17] The River of the Souls in Purgatory is mentioned in James, Vol. II, p. 264. The River That Scolds at All the Others is mentioned in *The Journals of Lewis and Clark*, edited by Bernard De Voto (Boston, 1953), p. 88.

For more on the Missouri River system, see *The Missouri*, by Stanley Vestal (New York, 1945).

[p. 18] Among the river Indians, the Mandan in particular were skillful traders. In the days before white men, Indian trade routes brought dentalium shells from the Pacific Coast, obsidian from the upper Yellowstone, horses from the Southwest, pipestone from Minnesota, conch shells from the Gulf of Mexico, native copper from the Great Lakes, etc., to the Mandan villages at the mouth of the Heart River and (later) the Knife River. I learned about this from Eric Holland, a park technician and interpreter with the National Park Service at the Knife River Indian Villages National Historic Site, near Stanton, North Dakota. (See also *Indian Life on the Upper Missouri*, by John C. Ewers [Norman, Okla., 1968].)

[p. 19] The origin of the name Fort Union is found in *The American Fur Trade in the Far West*, by Hiram M. Chittenden (New York, 1935), pp. 329–330, one of the few comprehensive books on the subject of the American fur trade.

[p. 19] Some of the goods offered for trade at Fort Union I learned about in conversation with historian Charles Hanson, of the Museum of the Fur Trade, in Chadron, Nebraska. Others are mentioned by Rudolph F. Kurz, onetime clerk at the fort, in his *Journal*.

The hardtack from Milton, Massachusetts, was made by the G. H. Bent Company, which has been making hardtack, hard crackers, and pilot bread in that town for almost two centuries, and is still in business. Hardtack was used as military and ship's rations. To discourage spoilage, it was baked so dry that it absorbed all the moisture in your mouth like a blotter when you bit it. Hardtack and hard crackers were not usually items of trade, but rather snacks given out with coffee and molasses to get trading started. The crackers tended to break into crumbs when bitten. Cracker fragments crunching underfoot was a common sound in the retail stores at Indian trading posts.

[pp. 19–20] All the information about beaver fur and beaverfelt hats comes from *Hudson's Bay Company 1670–1870*, by E. E. Rich (New York, 1961)—in particular, from Vol. I, Chaps. I–VI. My description of beaver felt comes from a beaver hat I saw on display at Fort Union. As for the importance of the hat, E. E. Rich says, "In the last quarter of the seventeenth century the beaver hat was a social necessity" (Vol. I, p. 49).

E. E. Rich also discusses the rivalry among the English, French, and Dutch for the North American fur trade. For more on the merger of the American Fur Company and the Columbia Fur Company (into what was called the Upper Missouri Outfit of the American Fur Company), see *Across the Wide Missouri*, by Bernard De Voto (Boston, 1947). De Voto goes into the various trading companies and their rivalries in detail.

[p. 21] The number of buffalo Fort Union ate in a year is in *Travels in the Interior North America in the Years 1832 to 1834*, by Alexander Philipp Maximilian, Prince von Wied-Neuwied (London, 1843), p. 191.

The contents of the bourgeois's private larder come from a list titled "Order for Sundry Articles to be shipped by H. K. Ortley Spring 1836 pr Steam boat Addressed to K. McKenzie Fort Union," included in the Appendix to *Chardon's Journal at Fort Clark 1834–1839*, edited by Annie Heloise Abel (Pierre, S.D., 1932).

That one had to wear a jacket to dinner at the bourgeois's table is mentioned in *Forty Years a Fur Trader on the Upper Missouri*, by Charles Larpenteur (Chicago, 1933), p. 56.

A partial list of the different nationalities at Fort Union is in Wied-Neuwied, p. 186.

George Catlin's visit to Fort Union is in *The Plainsmen of the Yellowstone*, by Mark H. Brown (Lincoln, Neb., 1969), p. 90.

Bodmer and Prince Maximilian arrived at Fort Union on June 24, 1833. The Indian Nothing But Gunpowder is mentioned in Wied-Neuwied, p. 306. The musical snuffbox is in ibid., pp. 202, 443.

[p. 21] The reason why no city grew at the confluence of the Yellowstone and the Missouri is discussed in *The Wonder of Williams: A History of Williams County, North Dakota*, published by the Williams County Historical Society (Vol. I, p. 24). My thanks to Thor Garaas of Bigfork, Montana, for lending me his copy.

Williston, North Dakota, sits on top of a deposit of oil called the Williston Basin, which extends north into Alberta, west into Montana, and south into South Dakota.

The fact that Bodmer painted the confluence after he returned to Europe, using sketches for reference, is in *Carl*

Bodmer's America, published by the Joslyn Art Museum, St. Louis, Missouri.

[pp. 22–23] Owen McKenzie's pursuit of wolves is in *Audubon and His Journals*, edited by Maria R. Audubon and Eliot Coues (New York, 1899), Vol. II, p. 84.

The "magnificent black hair" is in ibid., p. 88.

Prince Maximilian's description of the Assiniboin is in Wied-Neuwied, pp. 200 et seq.

Audubon and his party arrived at the fort on June 12, 1843, and left on August 16. The incident with the lark (actually a Sprague's pipit, *Anthus spragueii*) occurred on June 24; see Audubon and Coues, Vol. II, p. 55.

[p. 23] Lewis and Clark's sojourn at the confluence appears in their *Journals* for Friday, April 26, 1805: "After I had completed my observations in the evening [Lewis writes] I walked down and joined the party at their encampment on the point of land formed by the junction of the rivers; found them all in good health, and much pleased at having arrived at this long wished for spot, and in order to add in some measure to the general pleasure which seemed to pervade our little community, we ordered a dram to be issued to each person; this soon produced the fiddle, and they spent the evening with much hilarity, singing & dancing, and seemed as perfectly to forget their past toils, as they seemed regardless of those to come." *The Original Journals of the Lewis and Clark Expedition*, by Meriwether Lewis (Reuben Gold Thwaites, editor; New York, 1959), Vol. I, p. 338.

That the main article of trade at Fort Union was alcohol is mentioned in many sources, including Brown, p. 76.

Strychnine was used on the frontier as wolf poison. Its use and effect in whiskey was told to me by Orville Loomer, a park ranger at Fort Union.

The trader who dragged drunken Indians from the fort was Charles Larpenteur. See Larpenteur, p. 60.

The meeting between Astor and Simpson is in Rich, Vol. III, p. 478. It is hard to believe Astor had any serious intention of discontinuing the liquor trade. Whenever anti-liquor trade bills came up before Congress, he lobbied against them. When they passed, he disregarded them. He was like a tick, and liquor was his anticoagulant. His annual income from the American Fur Company is in *John Jacob Astor*, by Arthur D. H. Smith (Philadelphia, 1929), p. 224. Astor's half a million a year was tax-free in those days before income tax. He left a fortune of $20 million, of which $460,000 went toward the eventual creation of the New York Public Library, where I read of his greed.

[p. 24] Information on drinking at the confluence area comes from *The Wonder of Williams: A History of Williams County, North Dakota*. The death of Bartholomew Noon is in *A Chronological Record of Events at the Missouri–Yellowstone Confluence Area from 1805 to 1896* (a pamphlet), edited by Ben Innis. The story of the town of Mondak is in *Since 1887: A Word and Picture History of Williston and Area* (no publisher, no date. I found it in the Williston Public Library).

[p. 25] A good description of the fort is in Audubon and Coues, Vol. II, pp. 181 et seq. The names of the fort's engagees appear either in that book or in Chardon. Alexander Harvey's shooting of Isidoro Sandoval is in Larpenteur (p. 146). The McKenzie–Bourbonnais contretemps is in ibid., pp. 98–102.

[pp. 26–28] The version of the *Journal of Rudolph Friedrich Kurz* which I read was in the *Smithsonian Institution Bureau of American Ethnology, Bulletin 115* (1937). Ye Galleon Press, of Fairfield, Washington, has also published an edition of this journal. Some of Kurz's drawings and paintings were reprinted in *American Scene* magazine (Vol. 8, no. 3). They give some idea why Bodmer advised Kurz to study more before going to America; Kurz drew competently enough, but his skills as a watercolorist were shaky. At Fort Union, Kurz suffered with the philistine tastes of the bourgeois, Edwin T. Denig. "Mr. Denig thinks a portrait worthless unless the eyes follow a person who gazes upon it, no matter on which side the beholder stands," Kurz wrote.

[p. 29] Some of the facts which Gerard Baker told me about the Hidatsa I found later in other sources, including *Travels in North America, 1822–1824*, by Paul Wilhelm, Duke of Württemberg (Norman, Okla., 1973); "The Horse and Dog in Hidatsa Culture," by Gilbert L. Wilson, in *The American Museum of Natural History Anthropological Papers* (Vol. XV, pt. II, 1924); and *The Reader's Encyclopedia of the American West*, edited by Howard R. Lamar (New York, 1977).

[pp. 30–31] Much of the information about the smallpox epidemic of 1837 comes from *The Effect of Smallpox on the Destiny of the Amerindian*, by E. Wagner Stearn, Ph.D., and Allen E. Stearn, Ph.D. (Boston, 1945). Eyewitness accounts of the outbreak at the posts along the Missouri also appear in Chardon, pp. 121 et seq., and in Larpenteur, pp. 109–12.

The statement that Halsey was a carrier appears in *Leonard's Narrative*, by Zenas Leonard (Cleveland, 1904), p. 44, and other sources.

[p. 31] The preventive policy of the Hudson's Bay Company *re* smallpox is discussed in *Five Indian Tribes of the Upper Missouri*, by Edwin T. Denig (edited by John C. Ewers;

Norman, Okla., 1961), pp. 115, 124, an informative book written by the same man whose tastes in art annoyed Kurz. A more detailed look at the role of the Hudson's Bay Company can be found in "Smallpox: The Epidemic of 1837–38," by Arthur J. Ray, in *The Beaver* [the magazine of the Hudson's Bay Company], Autumn 1975, p. 8. The fact that many of the Assiniboin who survived were ones vaccinated by the Hudson's Bay Company is in Denig, p. 72.

Americans were not completely negligent about trying to provide the Indians with protection against smallpox; both the Lewis and Clark and the Stephen Long expeditions brought supplies of vaccine for that purpose. Unfortunately, in both cases, the supplies got wet and were ruined. And, of course, whether or not the Indians would have agreed to be vaccinated is yet another question. The Commissioner of Indian Affairs finally did send some vaccine upriver well after the epidemic of 1837 had done its damage. See De Voto, *Across the Wide Missouri*, p. 294.

[p. 32] Halsey's letter to his superiors is in Chardon, p. 394.

The appetite of white collectors for Indian skulls is one of the grisly sidelights of Great Plains history. Prince Maximilian describes his disappointment when an Indian killed by Blackfeet near Fort McKenzie had his head clubbed to smithereens by vengeful women and children before Maximilian could "obtain his skull" (p. 275). Audubon went to some effort, as described in his *Journals*, to get the skull from a three-years-dead Indian buried in a tree (Vol. II, pp. 72–73). Larpenteur talks about an Indian named The Shining Man whose skull was sent downriver "in a sack with many others" to fill a "requisition for Indian skulls" made by physicians in St. Louis (p. 344). Collectors who enjoyed this hobby turn up often in Great Plains literature.

The fact that the old Fort Union cemetery was dug up by highway contractors I learned from Ranger Orville Loomer and others. He said that guys were driving around with skulls on their dashboards, and little kids were painting themselves with packets of vermillion found in the graves.

Chapter 3

[p. 36] The epidemic of suicides on the Wind River Reservation which Lydell White Plume told me about later made national news:

> ARAPAHO TEEN FOUND HANGED
>
> RIVERTON, WYO.—THE BODY OF AN 18-year-old Arapaho Indian has been found in an abandoned house on Wind River Indian Reservation, where nine young men killed themselves last year.
> —"The Nation" column, New York *Daily News*, March 20, 1986

[p. 38] I can no longer find the source which stated that Sitting Bull's cabin ended up in the Chicago city dump. I read this in a pamphlet of "Did-you-know" facts about North Dakota in a drugstore in Killdeer, N.D., but when I went back to look for it two years later it was no longer on the newsstand and the druggist did not remember it.

[p. 38] Many of the facts of Sitting Bull's life come from either *Sitting Bull, Champion of the Sioux*, by Stanley Vestal (Norman, Okla., 1957), or *New Sources of Indian History 1850–1891*, also by Vestal (Norman, Okla., 1934). The second book is better than the first, because the second is simply a collection of primary source documents, with no attempt made to spin them into a yarn.

Another important source on Sitting Bull is the mistitled *My Friend the Indian*, by Major James McLaughlin (Seattle, 1970). McLaughlin's antipathy for Sitting Bull runs throughout the book. He calls Sitting Bull "crafty, avaricious, mendacious, and ambitious . . . [with] all the faults of an Indian and none of the nobler attributes . . ." (p. 48).

The fact that Sitting Bull sold his autographs for a dollar each is mentioned in an exhibit in the Klein Museum in Mobridge, South Dakota.

[p. 39] Vestal says that Sitting Bull was born on the south side of the Grand River, "at a place called Many-Caches because of the many old storage pits there, a few miles below the present town of Bullhead, South Dakota." McLaughlin says Sitting Bull was born "within twenty miles of the scene of his death." Other sources place his birthplace farther away.

[p. 40] Many of Sitting Bull's wounds and battles are also chronicled in *Sitting Bull: An Epic of the Plains*, by Alexander B. Adams (New York, 1973).

[pp. 41–42] Information on the Ghost Dance comes from sources already named, and also from *The Reader's Encyclopedia of the American West*, edited by Howard R. Lamar; *Wind on the Buffalo Grass: The Indians' Own Account of the Battle of the Little Big Horn River & the Death of their life on the Plains*, edited by Leslie Tillett (New York, 1976); and *Lame Deer, Seeker of Visions*, by John Fire Lame Deer and Richard Erdoes (New York, 1976).

The fact that one of the Sioux delegates said he saw the whole world in Wovoka's hat is in *Lame Deer, Seeker of Visions*, p. 227.

[p. 43] Few white people of the time seem to have understood exactly what the Ghost Dance was; Agent McLaughlin thought the dance originated with the Aztecs and had to do with the return of Montezuma (*My Friend the Indian*, p. 49).

Sitting Bull was not the leader of the Ghost Dance; he may even have been a bit skeptical about it. He proposed to McLaughlin that they journey to the agencies of the West and look for the Messiah together. (McLaughlin did not go for the idea.) On the other hand, the dancers were guests in Sitting Bull's camp, and he could not allow McLaughlin to make him evict them. McLaughlin wrote that he visited Sitting Bull and said, "Look here, Sitting Bull . . . I want to know what you mean by your present conduct and utter disregard of department orders. Your preaching and practicing of this absurd Messiah doctrine," etc. etc.—an approach which did not give Sitting Bull much of an out.

[p. 44] Upon the rumor that Sitting Bull was about to leave, McLaughlin moved to arrest him partly in fear that he would join with other Indians hiding in the Badlands from the recent buildup of troops at the Sioux reservations. McLaughlin and others believed that Sitting Bull might lead these fugitives in a new Indian war.

Chapter 4

[pp. 47–49] The compilation of statements about Indians is taken mostly from the writings of these contemporary white observers:

Travels in the Interior North America in the Years 1832 to 1834, by Alexander Philipp Maximilian, *prinz von* Wied-Neuwied. (It was he who said Indians swam differently: "We crossed the river near the part where a great number of young Indians were bathing . . . Their mode of swimming was not like that of the Europeans, but perfectly resembled that of the Brazilians," p. 265);

Life in the Far West, by George Frederick Ruxton (New York, 1849);

The Plains of the Great West and Their Inhabitants, by Richard Irving Dodge (New York, 1877);

My Life on the Frontier, by Granville Stuart (Cleveland, 1925);

Account of an Expedition from Pittsburgh to the Rocky Mountains in the Years 1819, 1820, by Edwin James;

Forty Years a Fur Trader on the Upper Missouri, by Charles Larpenteur;

The Oregon Trail, by Francis Parkman (New York, 1978).

The dislike of Indians for meat butchered cross-grain is in *The Indian Tipi: Its History, Construction, and Use*, by Reginald and Gladys Laubin (Norman, Okla., 1957), p. 80. Wild meat is drier than farm-raised; butchering across the grain tends to spill juice.

[p. 48] The Indians' use of their bodies as alarm clocks is in *Warpath: The True Story of the Fighting Sioux Told in a Biography of Chief White Bull*, by Stanley Vestal (Lincoln, Neb., 1984), p. 55: "Indian warriors could determine in advance their hour of rising by regulating the amount of water drunk before going to bed."

[pp. 49–50] The exchange rate of tipi poles for horses appears differently in different sources. R. and G. Laubin, in *The Indian Tipi* (p. 9), say that among the Kiowa Apache five tipi poles equalled one horse.

Other exchange rates are taken from Wied-Neuwied, pp. 244, 251, 340; Kurz's *Journal*, pp. 148, 182; Denig, p. 158; Dodge, p. 362; Stuart, Vol. I, p. 127; "The Buffalo in Trade and Commerce," by Merrill G. Burlingame, in

North Dakota Historical Quarterly, Vol. III, no. 4 (July 1929), p. 273.

The exchange of a horse for eight or ten peyote beans among the Oto Indians is mentioned in James, Vol. III, p. 58; he calls them "intoxicating beans." The dollar value of prime beaver pelts appears in Smith, *John Jacob Astor*, p. 224. The yearly salary of a trapper is in ibid., p. 212. The claim that out West the nickel was the smallest coin is in Kurz's *Journal*, p. 129. Many museums display Indian artifacts decorated with American coins; the Museum of the American Indian in New York has a feather headdress with two eyes made of flattened silver dollars to enable the wearer to see bullets in flight. The story about the Indians (they were Sioux) who dumped the gold and ran off with the buckskin sacks is in Stuart, Vol. I, pp. 252–53.

[pp. 50–51] The wanderings of the Sioux which brought them eventually to the Great Plains are detailed by George Hyde in *Red Cloud's Folk* (Norman, Okla., 1937), Chap. 1. Information about the Crow Indians comes from Denig, Chap. V. The Blackfeet are discussed in De Voto, *Across the Wide Missouri*. I read about the Atsinas in *The Reader's Encyclopedia of the American West*, among other sources. The three kinds of Cree are mentioned in Howard, p. 43.

The Cheyenne are the subject of several books, including *The Cheyenne Indians* (New Haven, 1923) and *The Fighting Cheyennes* (New York, 1915), by George Bird Grinnell, and *Cheyenne Memories*, by John Stands In Timber and Margot Liberty (Lincoln, Neb., 1972). They and the Arapahoes also turn up a lot in *Red Cloud's Folk*, and many other books. The Shoshone were mainly a tribe from the Rocky Mountains and beyond, although bands of Shoshone spent time on the plains; see "The Northern Shoshone," by Robert H. Lowie, in *The Anthropological Papers of the American Mu-*

seum of Natural History, Vol. II, pt. II, 1909. For more on
the Kiowa and Kiowa Apache, see The Indians of Texas, by
W. W. Newcomb (Austin, Tex., 1961). Two good books
about the Comanches are The Comanches: Lords of the South
Plains, by Ernest Wallace and E. Adamson Hoebel, (Norman, Okla., 1952), and Comanches: The Destruction of a People,
by T. R. Fehrenbach (New York, 1974).

The plains tribes also known as the Gros Ventre were
the Arapaho; the Atsina, relatives of the Arapaho who were
sometimes called the Gros Ventre of the Prairie; and the
Hidatsa, also known as the Gros Ventre of the Missouri.

(For a better list of books about the plains Indians, see
The Plains Indians: A Critical Bibliography, by E. Adamson
Hoebel [University of Indiana Press, 1977].)

[p. 52] In this and the next several pages, almost every
sentence comes from a different source. I won't list them
all.

The Crows' claim never to have killed a white man except
in self-defense appears in many sources—e.g., Absaraka,
Home of the Crows, by Margaret Irvin Carrington (Chicago,
1950), p. 7. The Crows may have got on better with white
people than other Indians did because their love for stealing
horses and trading horses made them incipient capitalists.
For revenge, a Crow was more likely to steal a man's horses
than to kill him (see Denig, pp. 150–51). The Crows' sexual
habits drew much comment. Prince Maximilian said, "They
exceed all other tribes in unnatural practices" (p. 175)—a
reputation which did not seem to repel white trappers and
traders.

[p. 53] The spiritual exercises of the Cheyenne appear in
Wooden Leg, a Warrior Who Fought Custer, by Thomas B.
Marquis (Lincoln, Neb., 1957).

[p. 53] The writer Washington Irving, after he became famous for his tales of Dutch New York, moved to Europe and lived there for seventeen years. In England he published perhaps his best-known work, "The Legend of Sleepy Hollow," in a collection called *The Sketch Book of Geoffrey Crayon, Gent.* When he returned to his native land, he wanted to see more of it, and so arranged to accompany an Indian commissioner as secretary on a journey over the Oklahoma prairies in 1832. Later he wrote a book about this trip, *A Tour on the Prairies* (Norman, Okla., 1956), an elegant and vivid account of the southern plains in the days before settlement. It was he (among others) who observed how good-looking the Osages were (*A Tour on the Prairies*, p. 22).

Maria Tallchief was born in Fairfax, Oklahoma, of an Osage Indian father and a mother who was Irish, Scottish, and Dutch. Her marriage to Balanchine is discussed in *Balanchine*, by Bernard Taper (New York, 1963), pp. 229 et seq.

[p. 53] Most of the unflattering descriptions of the Arikara come from Denig, Chap. II; the appellation the "Horrid Tribe" is in Dodge, p. 43.

[p. 54] The horror of Texan–Comanche relations is well documented in Fehrenbach.

The Story of Colt's Revolver: The Biography of Col. Samuel Colt, by William B. Edwards (Harrisburg, Pa., 1953), discusses the contributions of Comanche warfare to the development of Colt's new invention. Hays's Big Fight, on the Pedernales River, in June 1844, was the battle where the Texas Rangers first whipped the Comanche. Captain Samuel H. Walker was the ranger who went to New York to consult with Colt on modifications to the revolver; Walker was later killed in the Mexican War by a Mexican with a lance. Colt's assembly-line manufacturing methods and his salesmanship spread his weapons worldwide. He visited the Russians and told them the Turks were buying revolvers, then visited the Turks and told them the Russians were. He sold to both sides in conflicts all over Europe and South America. He bought Crimean War–surplus muskets and sold them to traders, who sold them to the Sioux, who used them against cavalry armed with Colt's .44 Army model. His best friend was his horse, Shamrock.

The Comanche fans made of scissor-tail flycatcher tails I saw on display in the Panhandle Plains Historical Museum in Canyon, Texas.

[p. 55] The list of Indian foods comes from a number of sources already named. E. T. Denig (pp. 50–51) gives this recipe for goose, as prepared by the Arikara: "They smear over the goose a thick coat of mud (this is over the goose as it is killed with feathers, entrails, and everything entire) after which the fowl is put in a hot fire and covered over with live coals. Here it is left until the clay covering becomes red hot, then sufficed to cool gradually until the fire dies out. The shell is then cracked with an axe, the feathers and skin of the goose come off with the clay, leaving the flesh clean and well done."

Larpenteur (p. 352) says that Indians thought pork was disgusting; the fear among Indians that the federal inspection stamp on pork was a tattoo is in *New Sources of Indian History 1850–1891*, by Stanley Vestal, pp. 196–97.

[p. 57] The tribe which killed fourteen hundred buffalo and traded the tongues for whiskey were Sioux, as observed by the painter George Catlin; see *The Great Buffalo Hunt*, by Wayne Gard (Lincoln, Neb., 1968), p. 30. The Indians who shot buffalo on enemy hunting grounds were Crow;

see *Indian Fights and Fighters*, by Cyrus Townsend Brady (New York, 1904), p. 205. Sir St. George Gore, a baronet from Northern Ireland, was perhaps the most famous of the British noblemen who came to hunt. He spent three years and half a million dollars hunting the plains. He burned all his supplies on the ground near Fort Union and threw what wouldn't burn into the Missouri when he could not agree on a price for Mackinaw boats to take him downriver (Brown, p. 109). Russell McKee, in *The Last West* (p. 237), says that the word "gory" is derived from St. George Gore; every dictionary I've read disagrees.

The Kansas Pacific built west from Ellsworth, Kansas, in 1867; the Northern Pacific crossed the Missouri in 1881. The years in between are when most of the early track laying on the plains was done.

[pp. 57–58] Good books about the buffalo and their destruction are *The Great Buffalo Hunt*, by Wayne Gard; *Heads, Hides, and Horns*, by Larry Barsness (Fort Worth, Tex.; no date); and *The American Bison*, by Martin S. Garretson (New York, 1938).

I conclude that buffalo leather made excellent buffing rags from the following statement in *The Border and the Buffalo*, by John R. Cook (Chicago, 1938), pp. 194–95: "[Mr. Hickey, a hide buyer] said that all of Loganstein & Co.'s hides went to Europe; that the English army accouterments of a leather kind were being replaced with buffalo leather, on account of its being more pliant and having more elasticity than cowhide; that buffalo leather was not fit for harness, shoes, or belting, but for leather buffers it could not be excelled."

Prices for buffalo hides come from "The Buffalo in Trade and Commerce," by Merrill G. Burlingame, pp. 282–83.

[p. 58] The term "buffalo runner" is discussed in *The Buffalo Harvest*, a good firsthand account of buffalo hunting by former hunter Frank H. Mayer (Denver, 1958), p. 26. Buffalo hunters' kneepads are mentioned in Gard, p. 121. Specifications for Sharps buffalo rifles are in Mayer, p. 40. The custom of buffalo hunters to work in parties of four is in Dodge, p. 134.

In *We Pointed Them North*, the cowboy "Teddy Blue" Abbott says of buffalo hunters, "You would see three or four of them walk up to a bar, reach down inside their clothes and see who could catch the first louse for the drinks." (I am assuming that the last one to catch a louse lost and had to buy.) He also says, "Buffalo hunters . . . would sleep with women that cowpunchers wouldn't even look at" (p. 121).

[p. 59] General Sheridan's speech about the buffalo hunters and the Indians' commissary is one of the most oft-quoted in the history of the plains. In Cook, it appears on p. 164.

For use of the terms "festive cowboy" and "festive revolver," see the contemporary newspaper excerpts quoted in *Great Gunfighters of the Kansas Cowtowns*, by Nyle H. Miller and Joseph W. Snell (Lincoln, Neb., 1967), pp. 53, 202, 205, 206, 281.

Much of the information on the longhorns comes from *The Longhorns*, by J. Frank Dobie (Boston, 1941). The fact that there were six million longhorns running loose in Texas is in *The Cattlemen*, by Mari Sandoz (Lincoln, Neb., 1978), p. 54. The sewing-the-eyelids-shut trick is in *From the High Plains*, by John Fischer (New York, 1978), p. 9.

[pp. 60–62] Facts about the cowboys are from Miller and Snell; *Cow Country*, by Edward Everett Dale (Norman, Okla., 1965); *The Long Trail*, by Gardner Soule (New York,

1976); *We Pointed Them North*, by Edward C. "Teddy Blue" Abbott and Helena Huntington Smith (New York, 1939); among other sources.

Information about the rich cattle investors also comes from sources named above. The fact that actors invested in cattle ranches comes from a display in the Fort Benton Museum in Fort Benton, Montana. The fact that foreign interests controlled more than twenty million acres comes from *Heaven's Tableland*, by Vance Johnson, p. 36. Other references are from *The Cheyenne Club, Mecca of the Aristocrats of the Old-Time Cattle Range*, by Agnes Wright Spring (Kansas City, 1961).

Moreton Frewen, who married Winston Churchill's aunt, succeeded in winning her mainly because of his career on the plains. Clara Jerome had been wooed by the top society beaus of two continents—counts, dukes, millionaires—but it was Frewen's description of Wild West adventures which caught her attention when the two met in New York as Frewen was stopping on his way from his Powder River Ranch back to England. (See *Mr. Frewen of England: A Victorian Adventurer*, by Anita Leslie [London, 1966].)

For more on Teddy Roosevelt on the plains, see *Theodore Roosevelt*, by Carleton Putnam (New York, 1958).

Information on the Marquis de Morès is from D. Jerome Tweton's excellent biography, *The Marquis de Morès: Dakota Capitalist, French Nationalist* (Minneapolis, 1972). The fact that the marquise had left-handed and right-handed hairbrushes was told me by a tour guide named Julee at the Chateau De Mores State Historic Site in Medora, North Dakota. She also demonstrated the brushes.

[p. 62] The copy of *The Beef Bonanza; or, How to Get Rich on the Plains*, by General James S. Brisbin (Philadelphia, 1881), which I read in the New York Public Library was a first edition. Someone had highlighted the general's more farfetched projections of riches with a wavering, hopeful, faded line.

[p. 62] Most of the information on the vigilantes comes from *The Vigilantes of Montana*, by Thomas J. Dimsdale (Butte, Mont., 1915).

[p. 63] Accounts of the blizzard of '86–87 are in Howard, Sandoz, Abbott, and other places. Granville Stuart lost half his herd—more than nine thousand cattle—during a storm on January 9–19 (*Forty Years on the Frontier*, Vol. II, pp. 228, 235–36).

Teddy Blue Abbott says that sixty percent of the cattle in Montana were dead by March 15, 1887 (p. 217). A report in the February 25, 1887, *New-York Times* gives a similar estimate.

Leslie (pp. 84–85) says that £10 million of English and Scottish capital were lost in cattle investments in 1880–90.

[p. 63] After losing his ranch, Moreton Frewen's next enthusiasm was promoting a new invention for lubricating railroad machinery; see Leslie, p. 88.

Chapter 5

[pp. 66–69] Lawrence Welk describes being hit over the head in *Mister Music Maker, Lawrence Welk*, by Mary Lewis Coakley, (New York, 1958), p. 67.

All the facts of Lawrence Welk's life come from that book or from *The Lawrence Welk Story*, by Albert Govoni (New York, 1966).

[p. 70] The story of Lawrence Welk's parents' emigrations is in Govoni, pp. 13–14.

[p. 71] David Emmons, in *Garden in the Grasslands*, discusses the efforts of the railroads and other Great Plains promoters to convince people to move to the plains. The disdain of the Burlington Railroad for the Italians and French is on p. 112. The pamphlet for the oppressed of Alsace–Lorraine is mentioned on p. 103.

[pp. 71–72] Of the quality of land available for homesteading, *The Farmers' Frontier*, by Gilbert C. Fite (New York, 1966), p. 18, says, "About 40 percent of the land in Kansas was withdrawn from the public domain, removing it from homestead or preemption entry . . . In Nebraska . . . much of the best land in the Platte River Valley was owned by the Union Pacific."

The North's espousal of the 160-acre homestead is in Emmons, p. 16. From the start there were those who thought the 160-acre homestead was a bad idea. The geologist John Wesley Powell, who did soil and rainfall surveys of the plains for the United States Geological Survey, said in his *Report on the Lands of the Arid Region of the United States* (1878) that farmers on the plains would need holdings of 2,560 acres to survive, that some parts of the plains might never support cultivation, that irrigation was vital, and that land use should consider the sod cover and the topography. He was attacked by mining and cattle interests, railroad promoters, etc. Time, drought, and economics eventually proved him right. See *Beyond the Hundredth Meridian: John Wesley Powell and the Second Opening of the West*, by Wallace Stegner (Boston, 1953).

[p. 72] The fact that people were still filing first-time home-stead claims on the northern Montana prairie through the twenties I learned at the Museum of the Rockies in Boze-man, Montana.

[p. 72] Barbed wire and windmills are two subjects which Walter Prescott Webb discusses in detail in *The Great Plains*. Refinements in windmill design are examined on pp. 337–40.

[p. 73] For more on "rain follows the plow," see Emmons, Chap. 6.

Self-described soil scientist Hardy Campbell was the au-thor of the theory of "scientific soil culture," which taught farmers to plow deep and cultivate and recultivate a "dust mulch" on the surface to conserve moisture. Campbell also happened to be a real-estate promoter and farm-equipment manufacturer. As it turned out, Campbell's methods did not take sufficient account of the problems of marginal land and soil blowing. See *Heaven's Tableland*, by Vance Johnson, pp. 82 et seq.

In eastern Weld County, Colorado, two generations of homesteaders had settled and then starved out by 1921. See *The Great Plains: Environment and Culture*, edited by Brian W. Blouet and Frederick C. Luebke, p. 158.

[p. 75] In the list of names quoted from *The Wonder of Williams* I have made occasional minor changes in punc-tuation and style.

[pp. 78–80] The incident at the Pritchard farmhouse on U.S. Highway 83 was the first time Bonnie and Clyde ever made *The New York Times*, in a one-column AP story on page 4 (June 12, 1933, 4:3). The AP gave Mr. Pritchard's name as Steve, not Sam, and said that Pritchard's daughter-in-law (not daughter) was shot in the hand when she knocked on the door. Bonnie Parker was identified only as the "woman companion" of the Barrows.

A week later, the Barrow brothers wounded three Platte County, Missouri, police officers in a gunfight. On July 24, Buck Barrow and his wife were captured after a gun battle in Iowa from which Bonnie Parker and Clyde Barrow escaped. Buck Barrow died of his wounds. On January 16, 1934, Bonnie and Clyde sprang their partner Raymond Hamilton from the state prison at Huntsville, Texas, in a daytime raid on a work detail. On April 2, they killed motorcycle policemen E. B. Wheeler and H. D. Murphey in Fort Worth, Texas. On April 7, they killed a sixty-three-year-old constable named Cal Campbell who found them stuck in a mudhole near Miami, Oklahoma. On May 24, they were ambushed and killed. In a story on page 1, the correspondent for the *Times* described Clyde as "a smear of wet, red rags," and said that the fingers of Bonnie's right hand were shot away. The *Times* was morally opposed to giving cute nicknames to murderers, as it stated in an editorial in the same issue; in headlines, it identified the pair as "Barrow and Woman."

Other information about Bonnie and Clyde is in *"I'm Frank Hamer": The Life of a Texas Peace Officer*, by H. Gordon Frost and John H. Jenkins (Austin, Tex., 1968). That Buck Barrow was four years older than Clyde is mentioned in *The Album of Gunfighters*, by John Marvin Hunter and Noah H. Rose (Bandera, Tex., 1951), p. 89.

[p. 82] Facts about Como Bluff come from *Marsh's Dinosaurs: The Collections from Como Bluff*, by John H. Ostrom and John S. McIntosh (New Haven, 1966); *O. C. Marsh, Pioneer in Paleontology*, by Charles Schuchert (New Haven, 1940);

and *The Great North Trail*, by Dan Cushman (New York, 1966).

[p. 83] Elephant hunters and bison hunters are discussed in *Prehistoric Man on the Great Plains*, by Waldo R. Wedel. Their carefully made stone projectile points, sometimes embedded in fossil mammoth or bison bones, have been found at a number of sites on the plains. The period called the Early Plains Archaic was from 6000 to 3000 B.C. I identified the points from the rancher's glove compartment by comparing them to Early Plains Archaic points in the Wyoming State Museum in Cheyenne.

[p. 84] The Altithermal is mentioned in *The Great Plains: Environment and Culture*, edited by Blouet and Luebke, p. 12; a more extensive discussion is in Wedel, pp. 18–19, 254.

[pp. 84–85] I first read about the medicine wheels in a column called "Helena's Heavens," by Dorothy Starshine, in the Helena, Montana, *Independent Record*. More about the Sun River Medicine Wheel, including a drawing of it when it was in better shape, is in "Medicine Wheels and Plains Indian Astronomy," by John A. Eddy, in *Technology Review*, December 1977, pp. 18–31.

My thanks to Dorothy Starshine for her help and information on this subject.

[p. 86] All the information on Doc Holliday comes from the very good biography, *Doc Holliday*, by John Myers Myers (Lincoln, Neb., 1973). Sample sentence: "As to some of [Doc Holliday's] bents, it might be conceded that they let criticism in at the front door."

[p. 88] The Anti-Ballistic Missile command center was built by Peter Kiewit and Sons Co., of Omaha, which received a $110.9 million contract from the Army in 1972 for work on the ABM system in Montana (*Times*, February 25, 57:8). Under the conditions of SALT I, the U.S. had to get rid of all of its ABM sites under construction except one; it continued work on the site at Grand Forks, North Dakota, and abandoned the western Montana site. Later, SALT II put further limitations on the ABM, but by then the development of missiles with multiple warheads made the ABM less practical—building additional warheads was cheaper than building missiles to intercept them. In 1975, the Defense Department abandoned the Safeguard ABM program altogether. See *The New York Times*, November 25, 1975, 1:1; *Missiles and Rockets*, by Kenneth Gatland (New York, 1975), pp. 147, 151.

[pp. 89–90] Information about strip-mining comes from *The Rape of the Great Plains: Northwest America, Cattle, and Coal*, by K. Ross Toole; from a tour of the mining operations at Colstrip, Montana; and from conversations with members of the Northern Plains Resource Council in Billings, Montana.

[p. 90] A description of the archaeology boom of the 1940s on the plains is in Wedel, p. 158, and in *Cadillac Desert: The American West and Its Disappearing Water*, by Marc Reisner (New York, 1986), pp. 194 et seq. The more recent surge in Great Plains archaeology I learned about from ranger Eric Holland, at the Knife River Indian Villages, just down the road from the strip mines of the Consolidation Coal Company in Stanton, North Dakota.

Chapter 6

[p. 95] Most of the questions about Crazy Horse which I asked Le War Lance are based on statements made by Indians in *To Kill an Eagle: Indian Views on the Death of Crazy Horse*, by Edward and Mabell Kadlecek (Boulder, Colo., 1981). The question about whether he always dismounted to shoot comes from "Oglala Sources on the Life of Crazy Horse: Interviews Given to Eleanor H. Hinman," in *Nebraska History*, Vol. 57, no. 1 (Spring 1976). This work has been reprinted by the Nebraska State Historical Society as a pamphlet. It is one of the best sources on the life and death of Crazy Horse. Crazy Horse's friend and comrade in battle, He Dog, told Eleanor Hinman, "All the time I was in fights with Crazy Horse in critical moments of the fight, Crazy Horse would always jump off his horse to fire. He is the only Indian I ever knew who did that often. He wanted to be sure he hit what he aimed at. That is the kind of fighter he was. He didn't like to start a battle unless he had it all planned out in his head and knew he was going to win."

Another important source of information about Crazy Horse is the so-called Ricker Tablets—a collection of lined school-exercise tablets containing interviews done by Judge Eli S. Ricker in the early 1900s with old plainsmen (and women) who remembered the frontier. Judge Ricker intended to write a novel about the West, but, as one historian put it, "he became lost in his research." Which is an easy thing to do, I can tell you. Microfilms of the Ricker interviews are on file at the Nebraska State Historical Society in Lincoln. The Sioux medicine man Chipps, or Encouraging Bear, told Ricker that Crazy Horse painted his face with "a zig-zag streak with red earth from the top of his forehead downward and to one side of the nose at the base to the point of his chin" (Ricker Collection, series 2, tablet 18, p. 5). But the Miniconjou chief Joseph White Bull, in Vestal's *New Sources of Indian History 1850–1891* (p. 320), says that Crazy Horse painted his face with white spots, which would seem to support Le War Lance.

[p. 95] Sitting Bull, Red Cloud, Chief Joseph, Spotted Tail, and many other plains Indians visited New York City, usually as guests of the government, who believed that it would be good for them to see the numbers and the power of white men. In 1870, Red Cloud gave a speech (via a translator) to a packed hall at Cooper Union which made him a media celebrity and which was a victory for advocates of a "Peace Policy" toward the Sioux. For several years after Red Cloud's speech, the government gave the Sioux presents and more or less let them do as they liked. This phase ended with the discovery of gold in the Black Hills in '74, and the Indian war which followed. See *Red Cloud's Folk*, by George Hyde, pp. 179 et seq.

[pp. 96–98] The only full-scale biography of Crazy Horse is *Crazy Horse*, by Mari Sandoz (Lincoln, Neb., 1961).

The year and the place of Crazy Horse's birth come from an article titled "The Oglala Lakota Crazy Horse: A Preliminary Geneological Study and an Annotated Listing of Primary Sources," by Richard G. Hardorff, which I found in the Crazy Horse file at the library of the Fort Robinson Museum in Fort Robinson, Nebraska.

The statement that Crazy Horse was one of the decoys at the Fetterman fight appears in many sources, including Sandoz, p. 199, and *Red Cloud's Folk* (citing the Cheyenne chief Two Moon), pp. 146–47.

[p. 97] Short Buffalo's speech about Crazy Horse's fight with the Shoshone comes from Hinman, p. 32.

Details of Crazy Horse's military career can be found in the sources named, and in *Crazy Horse and Custer: The Parallel Lives of Two American Warriors*, by Stephen E. Ambrose (Garden City, N.Y., 1975).

The statement that Crazy Horse killed the ponies of Indians who wanted to go into the agency is in Ambrose, p. 457.

Crazy Horse's surrender was reported in *The New-York Times* of May 8, 1877 (1:5).

[p. 99 et seq.] Much of the information about Crazy Horse's life and death at the Red Cloud Agency comes from these sources:

E. A. Brininstool, "Chief Crazy Horse, His Career and Death," *Nebraska History*, Vol. XII, no. 1 (January—March 1929). I will call this Brininstool A.

Brininstool, *Crazy Horse, the Invincible Ogalalla Sioux Chief* (Los Angeles, 1949). I will call this Brininstool B. Both works contain the accounts of principals and eyewitnesses at the death of Crazy Horse. Brininstool is the most assiduous published collector of information on the subject.

Robert A. Clark, editor, *The Killing of Chief Crazy Horse: Three Eyewitness Views by the Indian Chief He Dog, the Indian-White William Garnett, the White Doctor Valentine McGillycuddy* (Glendale, Calif., 1976). I will call this Clark.

William Garnett, "Report of William Garnett, Interpreter, to Gen'l H. L. Scott and Major J. McLaughlin." This is a copy of a typescript, on file at the New York Public Library. (A version of it also appears in Clark.) I will call this Garnett.

Julia E. McGillycuddy, *McGillycuddy, Agent: A Biography of Dr. Valentine T. McGillycuddy* (Stanford, Calif., 1941). I will call this J. McGillycuddy.

Other sources include some already named: Sandoz, Hinman, Hyde, the Eli S. Ricker Collection, and Kadlecek.

[pp. 99–100] A typescript in the Crazy Horse file at the Fort Robinson library gives the lieutenant's name as "J. Wesley Rosenquest," but William Garnett says, "Red Cloud went after Crazy Horse, and couriers came in with Red Cloud and they wanted supplies, that is grub, and I went out with Lieutenant Rosencrans with some wagons loaded with rations and some beef cattle" (Garnett, p. 1). Other sources agree that the lieutenant's name was Rosencrans. An Indian interviewed by Hinman says that Crazy Horse was met about a day's journey from the fort (Hinman, p. 25).

Agent Jesse M. Lee describes how eagerly the Indians accepted General Crook's promise of a buffalo hunt (Brininstool A, p. 7). Crook offered such liberal surrender terms because he was competing with General Nelson O. Miles, who wanted Crazy Horse to surrender to him at Fort Keogh, at the mouth of the Tongue River in Montana (Clark, p. 23).

He Dog said, "When we started in, I thought we were coming to visit and to see whether we would receive an annuity, not to surrender. But when we got near Fort Robinson, I found we were coming in to surrender" (Hinman, p. 19).

Lieutenant Clark came out and met Crazy Horse about four miles northwest of the agency (Garnett, p. 1).

An account of the surrender also accompanied the story of Crazy Horse's death in the September 7, 1877, *Times* (1:4).

[p. 100] Indians signed treaties either by making their mark or by "touching the pen" when a white man signed for them. Agent Irwin of the Red Cloud Agency complained to his superiors in the Bureau of Indian Affairs that Crazy Horse refused to sign receipts for his annuity goods (Kadlecek, p. 50). I found no evidence of Crazy Horse ever putting his name to anything. Dr. McGillycuddy said, "He never registered or enrolled at any Indian agency" (Brininstool A, p. 41). The promise that Crazy Horse would be able to choose the place for his agency is in Hinman, p. 19 and note 20, and p. 31; also in Clark, p. 26. His choice of Beaver Creek is mentioned in Hinman, p. 24. The requirement that no Indian live farther than three miles from the agency is mentioned in Hyde, *Red Cloud's Folk*, p. 294; Agent Lee's wife, however, says that the Crazy Horse camp was six miles from Fort Robinson (Brininstool B, p. 63). Other sources agree with her. The place where the camp stood is described in Kadlecek, p. 36, and Brininstool A, p. 76.

[pp. 100–1] For a discussion of the intricacies of Indian agency administration, see Kadlecek, pp. 29–36 and notes. The distance from Fort Robinson to the site of the Red Cloud Agency headquarters I measured on my car odometer. *Red Cloud's Folk* is the source of information about Chief Red Cloud; *Spotted Tail's Folk*, also by George Hyde (Norman, Okla., 1961), is the main source on Spotted Tail. In 1909, Red Cloud gave an interviewer an account of the Battle of the Little Bighorn which purported to be firsthand (Tillett, *The Wind on the Buffalo Grass*, pp. 91–92), but all evidence points to the fact that neither he nor Spotted Tail was there (see also *Red Cloud and the Sioux Problem*, by James C. Olson [Lincoln, Neb., 1965], Chap. 12).

[pp. 101–2] Of Clark's role at Fort Robinson, Agent Jesse Lee wrote, "Lieutenant Clark was stationed at Camp Robinson, near Red Cloud Agency, having a general oversight of the recent hostiles, especially Crazy Horse and his Oglalas, and it was his duty to keep General Crook informed as to anything of interest" (Brininstool A, p. 8).

Sherman's letter to Sheridan is in the National Archives Record Service, Office of the Adjutant General, Letters Received: M666 R281, Index 492. (My thanks to Ephriam Dickson III for telling me about it and sending me a copy.)

[p. 102] Dr. McGillycuddy later wrote to William Garnett, "You know his wife was very sick with consumption, and the Sunday the hostiles came in, I was sent for to come to the camp and give her medicine which was the first time I met Crazy Horse, and thus we became good friends" (Clark, p. 116). McGillycuddy's opinion of Crazy Horse is in Hinman, p. 43. Crazy Horse's refusal of the doctor's request for a photograph is in Brininstool A, p. 42. The failure of D. F. Barry to bribe Crazy Horse is in Brininstool B, p. 11. D. F. Barry later took perhaps the best-known photo of Sitting Bull. Red Feather's statement comes from Hinman, p. 25. Baptiste Pourier, who was an interpreter at Fort Robinson, told Judge Ricker that Lieutenant Clark was behind Crazy Horse's marriage to Nellie Larrabee (Ricker Collection, series 2, tablet 13, p. 24).

[pp. 102–3] The Sun Dance of '77 is mentioned in *Spotted Tail's Folk*, p. 250. Irwin's report to his superiors about the ration situation, and a discussion of the Indians' unwillingness to move to the Missouri, are in Kadlecek, pp. 45–46. The hunger of the Indians in the summer of '77 is in Sandoz, p. 373. Accounts of the council in August where General Crook renewed the promise of the buffalo hunt are in Kadlecek, p. 46, and Brininstool A, p. 9. The warning which followers of Red Cloud gave to Agent Irwin about Crazy Horse is in Kadlecek, p. 47.

[pp. 103–4] For more on the Nez Perce war, see *The Flight of the Nez Perce*, by Mark H. Brown (New York, 1967). In Brininstool A, pp. 9–11, Agent Lee talks about his strenuous efforts to get the Indians to give up the buffalo hunt. Irwin's cancellation of the ammunition issue for the hunt is in Clark, p. 28. Lieutenant Clark's idea of taking Crazy Horse north to fight the Nez Percé is in Garnett, pp. 1–2. The speech of Touch the Clouds is in Brininstool A, p. 15. The speech made by Crazy Horse is recounted by Dr. McGillycuddy in Brininstool A, p. 38.

[pp. 104–5] Grouard made his autobiographical claims in *The Life of Frank Grouard*, by Joe De Barthes. Excerpts from that work appear in Brininstool A, pp. 62 et seq. In 1907, Mrs. Nettie Elizabeth Goings, of Pine Ridge, South Dakota, told Judge Ricker that she and Frank Grouard were children of the same father by different mothers (Ricker Collection, series 2, tablet 13, p. 107). Much evidence points to the conclusion that Frank Grouard was indeed the son of John Brazo or Brazeau—see Sandoz, p. 426. McGillycuddy's opinion of Grouard is in Clark, p. 119. "Gruard" is not a misspelling; for years Grouard himself spelled it without an "*o*." Apparently, he was unsure how to spell his own alias.

Grouard's mistranslation appears in many sources; e.g., Clark, p. 29. Mari Sandoz makes him the villain of the piece, which interpretation others have followed, despite the fact that dozens of people from General Sherman on down wished for and assisted at Crazy Horse's destruction.

The disdain of Crazy Horse for councils is in Hinman, p. 13. In Brininstool A, pp. 15–16, Agent Lee describes his efforts to clear up the confusion.

[pp. 105–6] The anxious telegrams which brought General Crook to Fort Robinson are mentioned in Clark, p. 31.

Crook's plan for a big council, Crazy Horse's fears about it, and the speech Crazy Horse made to He Dog are all in He Dog's account in Hinman, pp. 21–23. He Dog died in 1936 at the age of a hundred; see Clark, pp. 44, 69.

[p. 106] The account of Woman Dress's warning to Crook, the plot in General Bradley's quarters against Crazy Horse, and the discovery of the plot by General Bradley are all in Garnett, pp. 2–4. I find Garnett a credible witness because of his flair for dialogue: "When I got in the room, Bradley says, 'What is that council that was held today in my room?' . . . I says, General, that is supposed to be a private council and not to be given out . . . I told him the plan was made, and about this $300.00 and horse racket, that ammunition was drawn and the Indians were to be prepared for it. He says, 'You go back where the orderly found you, and stay there.' . . . So I went to Lieutenant Clark's quarters and went in the room, and he was walking up and down in there, and when I went in he said, 'These Indians can hold nothing.' "

A sidelight: Hyde, in *Red Cloud's Folk* (note, p. 296), says that Woman Dress was a grandson of the Oglala chief Old Smoke. When Francis Parkman lived among the Sioux in 1846, he lived in Old Smoke's tipi. Assuming that Woman Dress was in his mid-thirties in 1877, it is therefore possible that he was one of the children whose heads Francis Parkman punched "with a short stick" when they climbed on him in his sleep.

[p. 107] I cannot determine exactly when Crook gave Bradley orders to capture Crazy Horse and jail him. Probably, it was sometime on September 3. General Bradley says that Crook left Fort Robinson on the morning of the fourth (Brininstool A, p. 50). McGillycuddy says that the soldiers and scouts left the fort to arrest Crazy Horse before sunup (Clark, p. 123). Mrs. Lucy W. Lee, wife of Agent Jesse Lee, gives the number of men in the party as 850 (Brininstool B, p. 63). Clark's reward for Crazy Horse's capture is in Brininstool A, p. 22, as is "I am Crazy Horse! . . ."

[pp. 107–8] The account of Crazy Horse at Spotted Tail comes from Agent Lee, in Brininstool A, pp. 16 et seq. Buffalo Chips's speech is recounted by interpreter Louis Bordeaux, who was present, in the Ricker Collection, series 2, tablet 11, p. 69. Bordeaux also states that Crazy Horse was put in the custody of Touch the Clouds for the night (Ricker Collection, series 2, tablet 11, p. 80).

[pp. 108–9] Red Feather, Black Shawl's brother, said that she was sick and that Crazy Horse left her with her mother (Hinman, p. 27). Agent Lee describes getting Crazy Horse to return with him, in Brininstool A, pp. 23 et seq. Mrs. Lucy W. Lee said that Crazy Horse said that riding in the ambulance made him sick (Brininstool B, p. 65).

[pp. 109–10] According to Dr. McGillycuddy, it was Lee's interpreter, Louis Bordeaux, who whispered to Lee that they might be killed for bringing Crazy Horse to Fort Robinson (Clark, p. 124). "I'm not going to be made a goat of . . ." is mentioned by McGillycuddy's wife (J. McGillycuddy, p. 83). The quotation from the *Times* is in the September 19, 1877, issue (5:4); that the Tortugas were Crazy Horse's destination is mentioned in many other sources. The Army prison at Fort Jefferson in the Tortugas was for the most loathed of prisoners; it was where the government sent Dr. Samuel Mudd, the man who set John Wilkes Booth's leg.

[p. 110] Mrs. Lee says that her husband told Crazy Horse he would have a chance to talk to General Bradley on the following day (Brininstool B, pp. 65–66). Agent Lee's account of what he said to Crazy Horse is in Brininstool A, p. 26. The fact that Little Big Man and Captain Kennington walked on either side of Crazy Horse is in Garnett, p. 6. Interpreter Louis Bordeaux said that Lee warned him "not to get into any trouble over Crazy Horse" and then went toward the officers' quarters (Ricker Collection, series 2, tablet 11, p. 89). Mrs. Lee says that she was at Fort Robinson staying with their "good friends, Major B. and wife," and that immediately after Crazy Horse was stabbed she saw Crazy Horse's uncle threaten to shoot Agent Lee as she watched from in front of her friends' quarters (Brininstool B, pp. 66–67). It seems clear that Agent Lee, his job done for the day, headed to where he knew his wife was staying.

[pp. 110–11] Frank Grouard's cold observation of Crazy Horse walking unknowing into the guardhouse is in Brininstool A, p. 66. Dr. McGillycuddy says that Crazy Horse half nodded at him (Clark, p. 124). Garnett (p. 6) says that a sentry was marching in front of the guardhouse. Garnett says that a moment after Crazy Horse went in there was a sound of confusion, and then "I saw a Roman-nosed Indian come out. He had a very thin face. He was a Rosebud Indian. He says, 'This is a guard house.' " Descriptions of Crazy Horse's attempt at escape are in Hinman, pp. 27, 20; Garnett, p. 7; Brininstool A, p. 38; among other places. Lee says that Crazy Horse tried to stab Kennington (Brininstool A, p. 27). Little Big Man's howling is described by interpreter Baptiste Pourier (Ricker Collection, series 2, tablet 13, p. 22). Garnett is the source for the prisoners' leg irons clattering (p. 7). "Stab the son of a bitch!" is from the account of Louis Bordeaux (Ricker Collection, series 1, tablet 11, p. 90). Information about Private William Gentles is in Clark, p. 143. Many sources say Crazy Horse was stabbed only once; He Dog (Hinman, p. 20) says, "He was gasping hard for breath. 'See where I am hurt,' he gasped. 'I can feel the blood flowing.' I pulled back his shirt and looked at the wound. He was thrust nearly through twice." Grouard describes Crazy Horse falling, in Brininstool A, p. 66. "He has killed me now" is in Garnett, p. 7.

[pp. 111–12] Dr. McGillycuddy describes the guard of twenty soldiers ringing Crazy Horse. The private who felt sorry for Crazy Horse's father was named George W. McAnulty (Brininstool B, p. 87). The Indians "bending and swaying like tigers" are in Kadlecek, p. 53, who is quoting William Garnett in the Ricker interviews. It was Grouard who heard the hammers being cocked and the shells being chambered (Brininstool A, p. 66). The member of the guard who said they were lucky no shot was fired was named Edwin D. Wood; he made that observation in a letter to his father which appeared in the Schoharie, N.Y., *Republican* (reprinted in the *Times*, September 28, 1877, 3:2). Dr. McGillycuddy's description of Crazy Horse's condition is in Clark, p. 125.

[p. 112] The request of Touch the Clouds that Crazy Horse be allowed to die in an Indian lodge is in Brininstool B, p. 33. Dr. McGillycuddy says, "I suggested [to General Bradley] that we effect a compromise and put Crazy Horse in the adjutant's office, where I could care for him until he died" (Brininstool A, p. 39). Bradley's reply is on the same page. Julia McGillycuddy says that American Horse told her husband that Crazy Horse was a chief and must not be put in prison (J. McGillycuddy, p. 84). McGillycuddy's further negotiations with Bradley are in Clark, p. 126. A description of the adjutant's office is in J. McGillycuddy, p. 85, among other places. "[American Horse] said to put him in a blanket and take him to the adjutant's office, which they did. Red Shirt and Two Dogs helped carry Crazy Horse into the office" (Garnett, p. 7).

Crazy Horse's refusal to lie on the cot comes from two sources. One is the account of Agent Lee, who says that when he went to the adjutant's office Crazy Horse was "lying on the floor as he desired" (Brininstool A, p. 29). Another is a two-page typed manuscript, "The Saga of Fort Robinson, 'Outpost on the Plains,'" by Richard L. McGhee, former curator of the Fort Robinson Museum, in the Crazy Horse file in the museum library. This says explicitly that Crazy Horse refused to lie on the cot.

[pp. 112–13] Dr. McGillycuddy's accounts of Crazy Horse's last hours are in Brininstool A, p. 40, and B, p. 46. Julia McGillycuddy says that all other Indians were ordered to leave the fort by sunset (J. McGillycuddy, p. 85). Agent Lee describes his last visit to Crazy Horse in Brininstool A, p. 29; his wife's version is on p. 34. Crazy Horse's speech about how his people preferred hunting buffalo was recounted by Captain H. R. Lemly, who was present ("The Passing of Crazy Horse," by Captain H. R. Lemly, in *Journal of the Military Service Institution of the United States*, Vols. 54–55, [1914], pp. 321–22).

The death-scene dialogue between Crazy Horse and his father is a good example of the way writers change things. Mari Sandoz, in *Crazy Horse*, pp. 412–13, says:

And when Worm [Crazy Horse's father] was brought to the bare, dusky room where Touch the Clouds was watching, he stooped over the wounded man, saying, "Son, I am here—"

But there was only the slow, heavy breathing of the medicine sleep and the feet of the soldier guard outside, walking up and down on the gravel . . .

"I am here," Worm said.

Now the son saw him. "Ahh-h, my father," he whispered. "I am bad hurt. Tell the people it is no use to depend upon me any more now—"

For a while it seemed he would say more, then slowly his head seemed to settle back . . .

Interpreter Louis Bordeaux, from whose account in the Ricker Collection this scene certainly comes, actually says, "Crazy Horse, Sr., said, speaking to his son: 'Son, I am here.' Crazy Horse, Jr., said, 'Father, it is no use to depend upon me; I am going to die.' The old father and Touch the Clouds both cried" (series 2, tablet 11, p. 92).

In my version of events, have I changed or left out anything? Well, a *New-York Times* account (May 27, 1877, 1:6) of Crazy Horse at Fort Robinson after the surrender says that Crazy Horse "knelt on the ground" and took General Crook's hand when the two first met. I left that out because (1) I don't completely believe it and (2) I don't like it.

[pp. 113–14] The time of Crazy Horse's death is in Brininstool B, p. 46. Touch the Clouds's last words over Crazy Horse are in ibid., and in Brininstool A, p. 40.

The death wail rising at the news of Crazy Horse's death is in J. McGillycuddy, pp. 85 et seq. William Garnett said he went to wake Lieutenant Clark with Frank Grouard, Louis Bordeaux, and Baptiste Pourier (Garnett, p. 8); Pourier claims not to have been there (Ricker Collection, series 2, tablet 13, p. 25). Agent Lee recalls his misery on the following day, in Brininstool B, p. 38. Parts of Lieutenant Clark's official report are quoted in Kadlecek, p. 54. The fact that General Bradley filed a similar report is in *Red Cloud and the Sioux Problem*, by James C. Olson, pp. 244–45, and Brininstool A, p. 51. The fact that no one ever collected the reward is in Kadlecek, p. 57.

[p. 114] The travels of the Sioux after Crazy Horse's death are recounted in Kadlecek, pp. 65 et seq., among other places. William Gentles died May 20, 1878; see Clark, p. 144. Dr. McGillycuddy's later career is told in J. McGillycuddy. Crow Dog served so little time in jail for the murder of Spotted Tail because at the time there was no law against an Indian killing an Indian (Kadlecek, quoting Carl Iron Shell, Jr., p. 115). Nellie Larrabee's remarriage is in "The Oglala Lakota Crazy Horse," by Richard G. Hardorff. In 1930, Black Shawl's brother told Eleanor Hinman, "[Black Shawl] died near here only a few years ago in the year when so many Indians had influenza. She must have been about 84 years old." Lieutenant Clark's death is in Clark, p. 137.

[p. 115] William Garnett is the source for his later encounters with Woman Dress and with Crook (Garnett, p. 8).

[p. 115] The journey of Crazy Horse's parents back to Spotted Tail is told by Agent Lee in Brininstool A, p. 30. The description of the parents' vigil is in ibid., pp. 32–34. Speculation on Crazy Horse's burial site is in Kadlecek, p. 61.

[p. 117] George Hyde's remarks about Crazy Horse and his admirers (". . . One is inclined to ask, what is it all about?") are in *Spotted Tail's Folk*, p. 253. These lines are also quoted in the excellent *Son of the Morning Star*, by Evan S. Connell (San Francisco, 1984).

My thanks to Tom Buecker, Curator of the Fort Robinson Museum, and his staff for their kind assistance in my research.

Chapter 7

[p. 122] The fact that Wibaux, Montana, was once the greatest primary shipping point for livestock in the West is from Howard, *Montana: High, Wide, and Handsome*, p. 140.

[pp. 129, 131] Prices of wheat and cattle have gone up since this was written.

[p. 138] Francis Parkman's description of the buffalo being chased by Indians is in *The Oregon Trail*, p. 251.

The per-mile death toll on the Oregon Trail is in *The Great Plains*, by Walter Prescott Webb, p. 149.

The study which tracks storms on the Great Plains in 1849 is "Towards a Geosophic Climate of the Great American Desert: The Plains Climate of the Forty-Niners," by Merlin P. Lawson, in *Images of the Plains: The Role of Human Nature in Settlement*, edited by Brian W. Blouet and Merlin P. Lawson (Lincoln, Neb., 1979).

[p. 139] The difference in the rate of evaporation between Texas and Canada is in *Prehistoric Man on the Great Plains*, by Waldo R. Wedel, p. 33.

Facts about mesquite trees come from *From the High Plains*, by John Fischer, p. 8, and *Killing the Hidden Waters*, by Charles Bowden (Austin, Tex., 1977), p. 19.

That you can trace old cattle trails from the air by following the mesquite I learned from Lester Galbreath, superintendant of Fort Griffin State Historical Park, near Albany, Texas.

Chapter 8

[p. 140] Information about Billy the Kid's name and family comes from "Dim Trails: The Pursuit of the McCarty Family," by Philip J. Rasch and R. N. Mullin, in *The New Mexico Folklore Record*, Vol. XIII (1953–54), pp. 6–11. Charles A. Siringo, in *A Texas Cowboy; or, Fifteen Years on the Hurricane Deck of a Spanish Pony* (Lincoln, Neb., 1979), pp. 168–69, says that Billy the Kid's mother and stepfather ran a restaurant in Santa Fe.

Biographical details about Wyatt Earp and Bat Masterson come from *Great Gunfighters of the Kansas Cowtowns*, by Miller and Snell, pp. 78–85 and 193 et seq.

[pp. 141–42] Information about the Lincoln County War comes from *The Negro Cowboys*, by Philip Durham and Everett L. Jones (New York, 1965). Charles Siringo is the source for Billy the Kid's piano playing during the siege (p. 170). The further exploits of Billy the Kid in Lincoln are also described in Siringo, pp. 172–75.

[p. 143] Santa Fe was founded in 1610. Many other New Mexico towns—Taos, Santa Cruz, etc.—date from the seventeenth century. For more on the early history of the Spanish in the Southwest, see *Storms Brewed in Other Men's*

Worlds: The Confrontation of Indians, Spanish and French in the Southwest, 1540–1795, by Elizabeth A. John (College Station, Tex., 1975).

[p. 143] Information about the Arkansas River and Bent's Fort comes from *The Reader's Encyclopedia of the American West,* pp. 46, 48, 87, 90. *Life in the Far West,* by George Frederick Ruxton, describes cactus "of all the varieties common on the plains" growing on the coping of the walls (p. 189).

[p. 144] I learned that "crystallized essence" existed in 1840 from Bill Gwaltney. Mosquito netting is mentioned in *Up the Missouri with Audubon,* by Edward Harris (Norman, Okla., 1951), p. 136. The quotation about the air mattresses is on pp. 73–74.

[p. 147] I read that Billy Dixon's hair was "something less than nine feet long" in *Dodge City,* by Fred Young.

[p. 150] "Deacon" Cox is mentioned in *The Longhorns,* by J. Frank Dobie.

Some of the information about Dodge City comes from *The Reader's Encyclopedia of the American West,* p. 185. Buffalo products shipped from Dodge City in its early years are mentioned in Fehrenbach, *Comanches: The Destruction of a People,* pp. 522 et seq.

Doc Holliday's career in Dodge City is discussed in *Doc Holliday,* by John Myers Myers (Chap. V).

[pp. 150–51] Accounts of violence in Dodge City are from *Great Gunfighters of the Kansas Cowtowns,* by Miller and Snell.

Lizzie Palmer is mentioned in *Queen of Cowtowns: Dodge City*, by Stanley Vestal (p. 19).

A table in *The Cattle Towns*, by Robert R. Dykstra (p. 144), shows a total of fifteen homicides in Dodge City during the years of the cattle boom; about five people a day died of violence in New York City in 1987.

[p. 157] A map in a published account of the 1819 Stephen Long expedition had the words "Great Desert" covering an area which is today western Oklahoma and northern Texas. A version of this map included in a popular atlas in 1822 extended the label over more territory, and another version published the following year changed it to "Great American Desert." Long went west through the Nebraska sandhills, "the deserts of the Platte," which helped convince him that the plains were a desert. See James, *Account of an Expedition*; see also G. Malcolm Lewis, "The Cognition and Communication of Former Ideas about the Great Plains." (See also note, p. 221.)

[p. 158] Old photos of Fort Robinson (in the Fort Robinson Museum) show the buildings sitting on a treeless plain like Monopoly houses on a card table.

[p. 161] I learned that names on Register Cliffs were written in hog fat and tar from a guide at the Fort Laramie National Historic Site near Fort Laramie, Wyoming.

References to Parkman, *The Oregon Trail*, are from pp. 75 and 88.

[pp. 163–64] Some information about Fort Benton comes from the entry for "Missouri River" in the *New Columbia Encyclopedia* (New York, 1975). Other facts are from *Whoop-*

Up Country, by Paul F. Sharp (Minneapolis, 1955), and from the Fort Benton Museum. Joseph Kinsey Howard was the historian who said that you couldn't see the sidewalks for the playing cards (*Montana: High, Wide, and Handsome*, p. 143).

The suspicion of Army officers about Fort Benton's illegal Indian trade is mentioned in *The Plainsmen of the Yellowstone*, by Mark H. Brown, p. 238.

The six dams between Fort Benton and St. Louis are Fort Peck, Garrison, Oahe, Big Bend, Fort Randall, and Gavin's Point. One dam, Canyon Ferry, is upstream from Fort Benton.

[p. 164] I saw a map of a block plan of Fort Benton in the office of Joel Overholser, publisher of the River Press in Fort Benton. Mr. Overholser showed me the list of the businesses (including Madame Moustache's Cosmopolitan) which had occupied each lot over the years.

Chapter 9

Information about the history of Nicodemus and the Black Exodus comes from Everett Dick, *The Sod-House Frontier, 1854–1890* (New York, 1937); Philip Durham and Everett L. Jones, *The Negro Cowboys*; David Emmons, *Garden in the Grasslands*; Walter L. Fleming, " 'Pap' Singleton, the Moses of the Colored Exodus," in *The American Journal of Sociology*, Vol. XV, no. 1 (July 1909), p. 61; Roy Garvin, "Benjamin, or 'Pap,' Singleton and His Followers," in *The Journal of Negro History*, Vol. XXXIII, no. 1 (Jan. 1948), p. 17; John G. Van Deusen, "The Exodus of 1879," in *The Journal of Negro History*, Vol. XXI, No. 2 (1936), p. 111.

Other sources include the historic marker on Highway

24 at Nicodemus, and *The Reader's Encyclopedia of the American West.*

[p. 168] The efforts made by Governor St. John and the Kansas Pacific Railroad to discourage black emigration are discussed in Emmons, pp. 88–90.

[p. 168] Verses to "The Land That Gives Birth to Freedom" appear in Fleming, p. 67. He also says that the town of Nicodemus had its own song, called "Nicodemus":

> Nicodemus was a slave of African birth,
> And was bought for a bag full of gold.
> He was reckoned a part of the salt of the earth,
> But he died years ago, very old.
> *Chorus* Good time coming, good time coming,
> Long, long time on the way;
> Run and tell Elijah to hurry up Pomp
> To meet us under the cottonwood tree,
> In the Great Solomon Valley,
> At the first break of day.

According to one source, Nicodemus was named after a slave who came in the second slave ship to America and later bought his freedom (Dick, p. 197).

[p. 171] A colorful account of Jim Beckwourth's life is *The Life and Adventures of James P. Beckwourth, Mountaineer, Scout, and Pioneer, and Chief of the Crow Nation of Indians . . . written from his own dictation, by T. D. Bonner* (Minneapolis, 1965). In it, Beckwourth prevails against overwhelming odds of Blackfeet rather more often than is credible. He had a reputation for exaggeration; one of the stock stories of the West is about the trapper who, upon hearing the Book of Revelations for the first time, said, "Why, I'd'a knowed that for one o' Jim Beckwourth's lies anywhere!" However, Beckwourth's claim that he was a chief among the Crow, as well as much else in the book, is very likely true.

Desirée, the Missouri River pilot, is mentioned in *Up the Missouri with Audubon*, by Edward Harris, pp. 83–84: ". . . We got under way at 12 O'Clock and crossed the river to where the Trapper lay to put on board of her our Mate Mr. Durac and our black Pilot Desirée who has undertaken to Pilot her down without an assistant, a pretty serious undertaking as he will be obliged to stick at the wheel the whole time the boat is running or from daylight to dark."

Britt Johnson's remarkable journey is recounted in *Comanches: The Destruction of a People*, by T. R. Fehrenbach, pp. 456–59.

Isaiah "Teat" Dorman is mentioned in many sources; e.g., *Sitting Bull, Champion of the Sioux*, by Stanley Vestal. A more thorough discussion of Dorman and his fate is in Connell, *Son of the Morning Star*, pp. 25–28.

The 4th Cavalry and its achievements are in Fehrenbach, pp. 517–21.

Isom Dart, also known as Ned Huddleston; his Shoshone love, Tickup; and her daughter Mincy are all mentioned in Durham and Jones, p. 184.

Bose Ikard's name appears in many books about the early days of the cattle business; e.g., *The Cattlemen*, by Mari Sandoz, p. 82.

Bill Pickett's life and his career in rodeo are the subject of *Bill Pickett, Bulldogger*, by Colonel Bailey C. Hanes (Norman, Okla., 1977). In a bullfight arena in Mexico, Bill Pickett once tried to bulldog a fighting bull. To the amazement of the audience and of the bull himself, Bill Pickett grabbed the bull by the head (with his arms, not his teeth) and tried to throw him. After a moment's reflection, the bull attempted to gore Pickett, rammed him against the arena wall, and shook him "like a sheet in the wind." Pickett clung to the blood-slick horns in a rain of bottles and knives from the angry crowd. He stayed in the ring for thirty-eight minutes and somehow did not die.

[p. 175] The words to "Home on the Range" were published originally as a poem titled "My Western Home" in the *Smith County Pioneer* in 1873. (Smith County, Kansas, is about fifty miles northeast of Nicodemus.) The author was Dr. Brewster Higley, of Pleasant Township, in Smith County. The music was written by a carpenter named Dan Kelly. The song was popular locally in Kansas, and by the early 1900s was a widely known folk song. In 1908, musicologist John Lomax recorded a black saloonkeeper's version of it in San Antonio, and later published the words and music in a book called *Cowboy Songs and Other Frontier Ballads*. In the 1930s, "Home on the Range" became a hit on the radio after President Franklin Roosevelt said it was his favorite song.

The history of the song, and all its lyrics, are in *True Tales of the Old-Time Plains*, by David Dary (New York, 1979), pp. 236 et seq. In the third line of the second verse, I have changed "On" to "Or" because I think it makes more sense.

[p. 176] For more on Kit Carson, see *Kit Carson's Autobiography*, edited by Milo Milton Quaife (Lincoln, Neb., 1966). As Quaife points out, Carson often describes journeys which would provide most writers with material for a lifetime in just a paragraph or two. He comes across as intrepid, resourceful, and mute.

Information on Jim Bridger is from *The Rocky Mountain Journals of William Marshall Anderson* (San Marino, Cal.,

1967), pp. 259–70; see also *Jim Bridger*, by J. Cecil Alter (Norman, Okla., 1962), Chap. 33.

[p. 176] The Gomorrah of the Cattle Trail is mentioned in *The Log of a Cowboy*, p. 259; Hell on Wheels is in *Empty Saddles, Forgotten Names*, by Doug Engerbretson (Aberdeen, S.D., 1982), p. 83 and note 13, p. 91; the Holy City of the Cow is in Sandoz, *The Cattlemen*, p. 338.

The Cottage Saloon in Miles City and Connie the Cowboy Queen are mentioned in Abbott, *We Pointed Them North*, pp. 102, 107.

[p. 177] Books which discuss the life and career of General George A. Custer make up a measurable percentage of all books about the West. I have referred to these few:

Stephen E. Ambrose's *Crazy Horse and Custer: The Parallel Lives of Two American Warriors*;

Elizabeth Bacon Custer's *"Boots and Saddles"; or Life in Dakota with General Custer* (Norman, Okla., 1961); *Following the Guidon* (Norman, Okla., 1966); and *Tenting on the Plains; or, General Custer in Kansas and Texas* (New York, 1889);

George Armstrong Custer's *My Life on the Plains* (edited by Milo Milton Quaife [Lincoln, Neb., 1966]);

Marguerite Merington, editor, *The Custer Story: The Life and Intimate Letters of General George A. Custer and His Wife Elizabeth* (New York, 1950);

Jay Monaghan's *Custer* (Boston, 1959);

Frederick Whittaker's *A Complete Life of Gen. George A. Custer* (New York, 1876).

Elizabeth Custer's assertion that her husband was the happiest man on earth is in *"Boots and Saddles,"* p. 193. Mrs. Custer lived until 1933. One of her addresses was 148 East Eighteenth Street, New York City.

[p. 177] Custer graduated thirty-fourth out of a class of thirty-four. See the Folio Society edition of *My Life on the Plains* (London, 1963), p. 7.

Custer's hell-bent marches across the Kansas and Nebraska plains in 1867 are detailed in Ambrose, Chap. 15.

One of Custer's fights with Indians was the Battle of the Washita River, on November 27, 1868, in which the Cheyenne later said they lost thirteen men, sixteen women, and nine children when Custer attacked their camp (Grinnell, *The Fighting Cheyennes*, p. 300). Among the dead was the chief, Black Kettle, who wanted peace with the whites and who had just returned from a council with General Hazen the day before. Custer's force of seven hundred lost two officers and nineteen enlisted men killed. The Indians also killed Custer's staghound, Blücher.

[p. 178] Sitting Bull's account of Custer's death is quoted in Tillett, *The Wind on the Buffalo Grass*, p. 71.

[p. 178] Merington (p. 8) describes Custer at West Point:

> Of deviltry, the young Custer had full measure. He and a comrade one day swam the Hudson, clothes tied to head. A banquet was being held in the James home on the opposite shore. The swimmers did not sit with the guests, but they did full justice to the delectable courses, served to them in the stable by a conniving butler.
>
> In French class Custer was bidden to translate at sight *Léopold, duc d'Autriche, se mettit sur les plaines*. His too-free rendering began, "Leopard, duck and ostrich . . ." [This is misquoted in Ambrose, p. 108.]

One of the pantomimes with which Custer entertained his classmates in chapel involved pretending that the red hair of a boy seated in front of him was fire. Custer mimed heating his fingers in the hair and then pounding them on an anvil (Monaghan, p. 19).

[pp. 178–79] "Do you think I am a confirmed monk?" is quoted in *"Boots and Saddles,"* p. 118.

For Custer to own a dog named Lucy Stone is rather like Oliver North owning a dog named Betty Friedan or Germaine Greer. In fairness to Mrs. Custer, she was embarrassed by the name; she says in *"Boots and Saddles"* (p. 41) that the dog had been named by a previous owner and would not respond to any other name.

Custer's accidental shooting of his horse is recounted in *My Life on the Plains*, Chap. 3.

[p. 179] "How painfully, almost despairingly exciting . . ." is in *My Life on the Plains*, p. 196.

[p. 179] The Honorable John A. Bingham, congressman from Michigan, who appointed Custer to West Point, said that he was "beautiful as Absalom with his yellow curls" when he called on Bingham shortly after the First Battle of Bull Run (Merington, p. 13).

[pp. 180–81] Accounts of Indians who were at Little Bighorn are possibly even more numerous than books about Custer. Again, I have drawn on just a few sources.

That the Indians knew the soldiers were coming after them is mentioned in many accounts; e.g., *Warpath: The True Story of the Fighting Sioux, Told in a Biography of Chief White Bull*, by Stanley Vestal, p. 185; and *Cheyenne Mem-*

ories, by John Stands In Timber and Margot Liberty, p. 191.

Sitting Bull's prophetic vision was recounted by Henry Oscar One Bull, Sitting Bull's nephew, in *Echoes of the Little Big Horn* (reprinted in Tillett, *The Wind on the Buffalo Grass*, p. 60).

The Cheyenne Chief Two Moon described Custer's advance: "While I was sitting on my horse I saw flags come up over the hill to the east like that [he raised his fingertips]." From Hamlin Garland, "General Custer's Last Fight as Seen by Two Moon," *McClure's Magazine*, Vol. XI (September 1898), p. 446.

Short Buffalo's account of Crazy Horse at the Little Bighorn is in Hinman, p. 35:

> In this Custer fight I was helping fight Reno and never noticed Custer coming. We had Reno's men on the run across the creek when Crazy Horse rode up with his men.
>
> "Too late! You've missed the fight!" we called out to him.
>
> "Sorry to miss this fight!" he laughed. "But there's a good fight coming over the hill."
>
> I looked where he pointed and saw Custer and his blue coats pouring over the hill. I thought there were a million of them.
>
> "That's where the big fight is going to be," said Crazy Horse. "We'll not miss that one."
>
> He was not a bit excited; he made a joke of it. He wheeled and rode down the river, and a little while later I saw him on his pinto pony leading his men across the ford. He was the first man to cross the river. I saw he had the business well in hand. They rode up the draw and then there was too much dust—I could not see any more.

The orderly retreat of the soldiers up the rise is mentioned by Sitting Bull in Tillett, p. 70. The formidable Chief Gall of the Hunkpapa Sioux described the attempts to kill the horse-holders in ibid., p. 75. (Gall's interviewer, from the St. Paul *Pioneer Press*, noted, "The chief's mind seemed to dwell particularly upon the number of horses they captured rather than the terrible slaughter which took place.")

The warriors flying through the dust like shadows, the eagle-bone whistles screaming, the Indians shooting each other by accident are all mentioned in *Black Elk Speaks: Being the Life Story of a Holy Man of the Oglala Sioux*, as told through* John G. Neihardt (New York, 1972). Standing Bear describes, on pp. 97–98, how a Cheyenne was mistakenly scalped.

It was the Cheyenne chief Wooden Leg who said that the battle looked like "thousands of dogs . . ." *Wooden Leg, a Warrior Who Fought Custer*, by Thomas B. Marquis, p. 237.

Standing Bear said that the Indians could have killed the soldiers with their horses' hoofs (*Black Elk Speaks*, p. 97).

Gall said, "I killed a great many. I killed them all with the hatchet. I did not use a gun" (Tillett, p. 75).

Two Moon said that the soldiers were covered with white dust; *McClure's Magazine*, Vol. XI (September 1898), p. 448.

That the fight lasted "about as long as it takes for a hungry man to eat his dinner" was mentioned during a tour of the Custer Battlefield National Monument by the guide, Ranger Clifford Nelson, who said he heard it from somebody who had heard it from somebody who had heard it from Two Moon. Accounts of the length of the battle vary. Many Little Bighorn buffs think it probably lasted about an hour.

* That's what it says on the title page.

[p. 181] The reluctance of veterans of the Custer fight to admit Indians returning from World War I to their warrior societies is in *Sitting Bull, Champion of the Sioux*, by Stanley Vestal, pp. 59–60.

In *Black Elk Speaks*, p. 101, Iron Hawk recalled how nervous he was before going to fight. Black Elk's description of his feelings after the battle is on p. 106. White Bull's "It was a glorious battle, I enjoyed it," is in *Warpath*, by Stanley Vestal, p. 199.

[p. 182] Black Elk talks about touring with the Wild West Show in *Black Elk Speaks*, pp. 182 et seq.

For more on Buffalo Bill's Wild West Show, see *The Lives and Legends of Buffalo Bill*, by Don Russell (Norman, Okla., 1960). A reenactment of Custer's Last Stand was usually the show's finale.

[pp. 182–83] The fact that there were thirty Western series on prime-time TV in the late 1950s comes from the "Inner Tube" TV column in the New York *Daily News*, March 19, 1986, p. 64.

The four "development guidelines" for screenplays at Walt Disney Studios are listed in "Touchstone's Magic Touch," by Joy Horowitz, in *Premiere* magazine, October 1987, p. 34.

Chapter 10

[p. 184] In a sense, Lewis and Clark wrote the West as they went along. They named the Clark's Fork of the Columbia River, and Lewis's River, after themselves; the Judith River after Julia Hancock, of Fincastle, Virginia, who later became Clark's wife; the Marias for Lewis's cousin Maria Wood ("It is true that the hue of the waters of this turbulent and troubled stream but illy comport with the pure celestial virtues and amiable qualifications of that lovely fair one," Lewis wrote); the Shields River, Pryor Creek, Ordway's Creek, and other pieces of geography after enlisted men with the expedition; York's Dry River after Clark's slave, York; the Jefferson River after the President; Pompey's Pillar, a rock formation in the Yellowstone Valley, after Sacajawea's infant son Baptiste "Pomp" Charbonneau; the Dearborn River after Secretary of War Henry Dearborn; the Gallatin River after Secretary of the Treasury Albert Gallatin; and the Smith River after Secretary of the Navy Robert Smith.

[p. 185] Jefferson's unsuccessful attempt to send André Michaux to explore the West is discussed in the introduction to the *Original Journals of Lewis and Clark* (edited by Reuben Gold Thwaites), Vol. I, pp. xxi, xxii.

Jefferson described John Ledyard, his journey, and his eventual fate in a preface to the 1814 edition of the *History of the Expedition under the Command of Captains Lewis and Clark*, p. ix.

[pp. 185–87] Other information about John Ledyard comes from Stephen D. Watrous, editor, *John Ledyard's Journey through Russia and Siberia 1787–1788: The Journal and Selected Letters* (Madison, Wis., 1966); Jared Sparks, *Life of John Ledyard* (Cambridge, Eng., 1828); and Kenneth Munford, *John Ledyard: American Marco Polo* (Portland, Oreg., 1939).

[p. 188] Mark Alfred Carleton lists the many similarities between the North American plains and the Russian steppes in "Hard Wheats Winning Their Way," in the *U.S. Agriculture Department Yearbook, 1914*, pp. 398 et seq., and in

"Russian Cereals Adapted for Cultivation in the United States," in the *U.S. Botany Division Bulletin, 1891–1901*, pp. 8–9.

[pp. 188–90] I read about weeds that came from Russia in *Weeds*, by Walter C. Muenscher (New York, 1935); *A Manual of Weeds*, by Ada E. Georgia (New York, 1914); *Migration of Weeds* (a pamphlet) by Lyster H. Dewey; *The Prairie World*, by David Costello (Minneapolis, 1969); and *The Conservationist* magazine, August 1969.

Anselm Hollo's description of a tumbleweed is in his volume of poetry, *Tumbleweed* (Toronto, 1968).

Information on Russian thistles in Russia comes from Russian émigré Alex Melamid.

[pp. 190–93] Almost all the information about the Mennonites is from *The Coming of the Russian Mennonites*, by Charles H. Smith (Berne, Ind., 1927).

[p. 193] Mark Alfred Carleton explains the Mennonites' farming techniques in "Hard Wheats Winning Their Way," p. 400.

[pp. 193–94] The saga of Mark Alfred Carleton, who almost by himself made the Great Plains the leading wheat-growing region of the world, then fell into debt to pay for the medical bills of a sick daughter, was suspended by the Department of Agriculture for financial misdealing, and eventually died broke in South America, is told in *Hunger Fighters*, by Paul de Kruif, Chap. 1.

Carleton describes finding the Russian wheats in his writings listed above.

[pp. 194–95] The problems of the Mennonites during World War I are detailed in Smith, *The Coming of the Russian Mennonites*, pp. 271 et seq. Because the Mennonite and Hutterite war resisters refused to put on uniforms, many served time in military prison in their underwear. A Hutterite named Joseph Hofer caught pneumonia while chained to a wall in Alcatraz prison and later died in Fort Leavenworth prison. His jailers dressed him in a military uniform and buried him. His brother, Michael Hofer, died a few days later.

[p. 195] Wheat-export figures at the beginning of the war are listed in *The War and the World's Wheat*, by Alfred Akers, a pamphlet published in 1914.

The effect of the German blockade upon international wheat markets, along with many other facts about the Dust Bowl and the events surrounding it, are in *Heaven's Tableland*, by Vance Johnson.

Howard, in *Montana: High, Wide, and Handsome*, says the price of wheat doubled between 1914 and 1918 (p. 183); Johnson says wheat was 99¢ a bushel in 1914 and $2.10 in 1917 (p. 210).

[p. 196] Speculative part-time farming of the plains is described in "Losing Ground," by Erik Eckholm, in *Environment* magazine, April 1976, p. 6; also in *Heaven's Tableland*, p. 143.

[pp. 196–97] Accounts of the big dust storms of '34 are found in the sources named above; in *Land of the Underground Rain*, by Donald E. Green (Austin, Tex., 1973); and in newspaper reports of the time.

The storm of May 10, 1934, which blew all the way to

the Eastern Seaboard, was important because it drew national attention to the problem. Shortly after that storm, Roosevelt proposed a drought-relief program to Congress. In August, he took a tour of dust-stricken counties. His idea to plant a twenty-million-acre windbreak was announced in July.

After the storms in April of '35, people started leaving the plains in large numbers. It was an appropriate time for Woody Guthrie to write "So Long, It's Been Good to Know You." Woody Guthrie told Alan Lomax that he wrote the song on April 14, 1935 (see *Land of the Underground Rain*, p. 124).

[p. 197] "Snirt" storms were mentioned during congressional hearings on the Great Plains Conservation Program before the House Committee on Agriculture, April 17 and 18, 1969.

One side benefit of the dust storms of the thirties was that they unburied signs of prehistoric human habitation, particularly in Washington and Yuma Counties in eastern Colorado (*Prehistoric Man on the Great Plains*, p. 70).

[p. 198] The Great Plains have never returned to the population levels of the late 1920s. U.S. Census Bureau figures show losses of over fifty percent in some counties.

"The people who moved away then . . ." comes from the Williston, North Dakota, *Herald*, May 15, 1983.

[p. 198] That Baca County was advertised as part of the "Rain Belt" is mentioned in Emmons, *Garden in the Grasslands*, p. 159.

According to the 1940 U.S. Census, Baca County had 10,570 people in 1930 and 6,207 in 1940. The 1980 census showed a population of 5,419.

[p. 199] A good discussion of the Ogallala Aquifer and its depletion can be found in *Cadillac Desert: The American West and Its Disappearing Water*, by Marc Reisner, Chap. 12.

Donald E. Green, in *Land of the Underground Rain* (1973), says the aquifer may run dry in twenty to forty years (p. 219).

[pp. 199 et. seq.] Facts about nuclear missiles I learned from *The Illustrated Encyclopedia of the World's Rockets and Missiles*, by Bill Gunston (New York, 1979); from a visit to Malmstrom Air Force Base in Montana in 1985; and from conversations with Thomas K. Longstreth, Associate Director for Strategic Weapons Policy at the Federation of American Scientists, Washington, D.C.

[p. 200] The six Minuteman bases are Malmstrom Air Force Base in Montana, Ellsworth AFB in South Dakota, Minot AFB in North Dakota, Whiteman AFB in Missouri, F. E. Warren AFB in Wyoming, and Grand Forks AFB in North Dakota. Grand Forks and Whiteman are not on the Great Plains. Malmstrom has 150 Minuteman IIs, which carry one warhead apiece, and 50 Minuteman IIIs, which can carry three warheads apiece. Ellsworth has 150 Minuteman IIs. Minot has 150 Minuteman IIIs. F. E. Warren has 150 Minuteman IIIs, and 50 MX missiles, which can carry up to ten warheads apiece. The total at the Great Plains bases is 300 Minuteman IIs, 350 Minuteman IIIs, and 50 MXs, or about 1,850 warheads.

[p. 200] Some of the information about missile installations comes from "This Is an Atomic Missile Base," by Winthrop Griffith, in *The New York Times Magazine*, May 4, 1969, p. 29.

The sign posted on the fence around the missile silo says:

WARNING
RESTRICTED AREA
IT IS UNLAWFUL TO ENTER THIS
AREA WITHOUT PERMISSION OF THE
INSTALLATION COMMANDER [Section
21, Internal Security Act of 1950; 50 U.S.C. 797].
WHILE ON THIS INSTALLATION
ALL PERSONNEL AND THE PROPERTY
UNDER THEIR CONTROL ARE SUBJECT
TO SEARCH.
USE OF DEADLY FORCE AUTHORIZED.

The details of what happens when you rattle the fence come from Sam Day, of the nuclear-weapons protest group Nukewatch, of Madison, Wisconsin.

[p. 201] Information about the missiles and their guidance systems comes from a tour of the missile silo at Malmstrom AFB.

[p. 203] The names of three of the Soviet ICBM bases are Uzhur, Aleysk, and Kartaly. They are located along the Siberian Railroad or its spurs in western Siberia.

Kartaly is less than three hundred miles (no great distance, in this part of the world) from the place on the Khirgis Steppe where Mark Alfred Carleton found the Kubanka wheat.

[p. 205] The fact that all the Minuteman II missiles at Malmstrom changed to remote targeting in the late summer of '85 is mentioned in an article about the Strategic Air Command in *Air Force* magazine, May 1987, p. 181.

[p. 207] Information about missile-launch procedures comes from the tour I took of the Minuteman silo. Additional details come from conversations with former SAC launch officer Bruce Blair, a research associate at the Brookings Institution.

[pp. 208–9] I got an idea of the amounts spent on the Minuteman system by reading newspaper accounts of weapons funding back through the years. When the Air Force first announced the "Minute Man" system in 1958, it tried to convince Congress of the system's low cost, and said that for $300 million it could have 1,600 missiles ready to fire (*The New York Times*, February 28, 1958, 1:2). In the following year, it awarded contracts for nearly that much just for research and development (*Times*, March 10, 1959, 8:6; December 24, 1959, 38:3). In 1962, President Kennedy presented a budget with $2.1 billion set aside for Minuteman (*Times*, January 1, 1962, 1:6). The Air Force probably continued to spend in the $2 billion range for Minuteman until it was in place in 1965; total expenditures for missile procurement in '64 and '65 were $3.57 billion and $2.63 billion (*Times*, September 21, 1965, 2:3), of which at least half went for Minuteman. In '65, the Air Force announced that replacing all the Minuteman Is with the more advanced Minuteman IIs would cost $1 billion (*Times*, May 20, 1965, 36:8). In '69, an Assistant Secretary of Defense said that the Minuteman II would actually cost about $7 billion before it was done (*Times*, June 12, 1969, 26:1). Minuteman III was a more advanced system than its forerunners, and did not cost less; according to the *Nuclear Weapons Databook* (p. 119), $12.8 billion was spent on the Minuteman III before 1981. The operating costs of the Minuteman system—the military personnel, vehicles, etc.—are over a third of a billion a year (ibid.). None of the Minuteman estimates includes the costs of developing, building, and testing the warheads, because those figures are classified. $150 billion is just a guess at the amount spent on Minuteman; if anything, it is too low. So much has gone into building, revising, and maintaining the Minuteman missile over the past thirty years that its costs are difficult to overestimate.

Costs having to do with the Peacekeeper, or MX missile, come from the testimony of Under Secretary of Defense Donald A. Hicks before the Strategic and Theater Nuclear Forces Subcommittee of the Senate Armed Services Committee on March 14, 1986. Costs of the Safeguard Anti-Ballistic Missile system come from an article in the *Times*, November 25, 1975 (1:1), announcing the plans of the Defense Department to abandon the system. (My thanks to Thomas Longstreth for his help on this subject; any errors are mine.)

Figures on the agricultural production of Pondera County, Laramie County, and the other counties on the Great Plains come from the U.S. Census Department's *County and City Data Book, 1983*. To determine which counties are on the Great Plains, I referred to a map published in 1969 by the Great Plains Conservation Program of the U.S. Department of Agriculture.

Index

THE AUTHOR GRATEFULLY ACKNOWLEDGES PERMISSION TO
REPRODUCE THE FOLLOWING PHOTOGRAPHS:

William Clark, Independence Historical National Park. *Meriwether Lewis*, Mississippi Historical Society. *Four Bears*, New York Public Library. *Kenneth McKenzie*, Montana Historical Society. *J. J. Audubon*, Library of Congress. *John Jacob Astor*, Private Collection. *Charles Larpenteur*, New York Public Library. *Rudolph Friedrich Kurz*, Gilcrease Institute of Art. *Francis Parkman*, Metropolitan Museum of Art. *James Beckwourth*, State Historical Society, Colorado. *Kit Carson*, Library of Congress. *James Bridger*, Kansas State Historical Society. *Wovoka*, New York Public Library. *Sitting Bull*, Library of Congress. *Buffalo Bill Cody*, Bill Cody Historical Society. *Sioux Police*, Clark Historical Society. *Teddy Blue Abbott*, Montana Historical Society. *Granville Stuart*, New York Public Library. *The Marquis de Mores*, North Dakota Institute for Regional Studies. *James McLaughlin*, New York Public Library. *Teddy Roosevelt*, American Museum of Natural History. *Cheyenne Dance Hall*, Culver Pictures. *Norwegian immigrants, 1886*, Nebraska State Historical Society. *Lawrence Welk*, Culver Pictures. *Bonnie Parker/Clyde Barrow*, Wide World. *Frank Hamer*, Wide World. *Doc Holliday*, Kansas State Historical Society. *Wyatt Earp*, Rose Collection, University of Oklahoma. *Bat Masterson*, National Archives. *Billy the Kid*, National Archives. *Little Big Man*, State Historical Society of Wisconsin. *Dr. V. T. McGillycuddy*, New York Public Library. *Jesse M. Lee*, New York Public Library. *W. P. Clark*, Smithsonian Institution. *General George Crook*, National Archives. *William T. Sherman*, Library of Congress. *P. H. Sheridan*, Library of Congress. *Spotted Tail*, Union Pacific Railroad. *"Big Bat" Pourier and William Garnett*, New York Public Library. *Woman Dress*, New York Public Library. *Frank Grouard*, New York Public Library. *Helen Larive*, National Anthropological Society. *He Dog*, Bureau of American Ethnology. *Korczak Ziolkowksi*, Crazy Horse Monument. *Red Cloud and American Horse*, Library of Congress. *John St. John*, Kansas State Historical Society. *Benjamin "Pap" Singleton*, Kansas State Historical Society. *George Custer*, National Archives. *Elizabeth Custer*, Granger Collection. *Thomas Jefferson*, Newsweek Books. *Two Moon*, National Archives. *John Ledyard*, Dartmouth College. *Empress Catherine II*, Newsweek Books.

Photo research by Laurie Platt Winfrey, Carousel Research

Also by Ian Frazier and available from Granta Books
www.granta.com

GONE TO NEW YORK
Adventures in the City
With an introduction by Jamaica Kincaid

In the early 1970s, writer Ian Frazier moved from a small town in Ohio to New York City. *Gone to New York* is his account of his life there over the subsequent thirty years, a book as full of vitality and charm as the city it describes. It features street scenes and oddball portraits from every corner of the metropolis – meet the man who climbed the World Trade Center and the last typewriter repairman in Manhattan, and follow Frazier down Canal Street and along Route 3 to New Jersey. Frazier makes us fall in love with America's greatest city all over again – just the way he did.

'Opening a book by Frazier is like pulling up a stool at a bar and falling into conversation' Robert Macfarlane